# HENRY JAMES AND THE COMIC FORM

# Henry James
# and the Comic Form

RONALD WALLACE

Ann Arbor    The University of Michigan Press

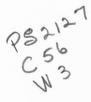
*Copyright © by The University of Michigan 1975*
*All rights reserved*
*ISBN 0-472-08954-4*
*Library of Congress Catalog Card No. 74-78990*
*Published in the United States of America by*
*The University of Michigan Press and simultaneously*
*in Don Mills, Canada, by Longman Canada Limited*
*Manufactured in the United States of America*

*Grateful acknowledgment is made to the following publishers*
*for permission to reprint materials:*

University of California Press for an essay by the author entitled
"Gabriel Nash: Henry James's Comic Spirit," © 1973 by The
Regents of the University of California. Reprinted from
*Nineteenth-Century Fiction*, vol. 28, no. 2, September, 1973, pp.
220-24, by permission of The Regents.

*Genre* for two essays by the author which originally appeared
therein:

> "Comic Form in *The Ambassadors*," 5 (March, 1972), pp.
> 31-50.
> "Maggie Verver: Comic Heroine," 6 (December, 1973) pp.
> 404-15.

Oxford University Press for passages from *The Notebooks of
Henry James*, edited by F. O. Matthiessen and Kenneth B. Murdock.

Charles Scribner's Sons for passages from The New York Edition of *The Novels and Tales of Henry James*, and from *The Art
of the Novel*, edited by R. P. Blackmur.

FOR MARGARET AND MOLLY,
AND FOR MY MOTHER AND FATHER

" 'You have found the figure, . . .' she told me one afternoon,
'but have you found the carpet?' "
—James Thurber

## ACKNOWLEDGMENTS

I would like to thank the following people for helping me with this book: Augusta Gottlieb, Robert F. Haugh, Leon Edel, C. Paul Christianson, H. V. S. Ogden, Floyd Lawrence, and Diane Boland.

# Contents

# I

# Introduction

1.

Criticism of Henry James, wrote Leon Edel in 1963, has grown obese.[1] And, indeed, faced with the vast mass of commentary and exegesis, one feels a certain hesitancy at fattening the beleaguered canon any more. But the confusing and contradictory layers which are added yearly seem to do little toward clarifying some very basic questions about the novels. Does Strether learn everything or nothing or both? Is Maggie Verver a buffoon or an artist, and do the marriages which close the *The Golden Bowl* represent anything more than a prolongation of silent pain? Are the novels primarily tragic, comic, or ironic in form, or are they some peculiar hybrid?

R. P. Blackmur offers a summary view of the perspective from which most of these questions are often answered:

> They say Swift hated the human race, but he never repudiated, as James does, the movement and the intermittences of the heart. Both writers dealt with what was intolerable: the swindle in human relations. Swift, with a lacerated heart and furious indignation, cried out, in the epitaph he wrote for himself, for human liberty; James, at the ends of his novels, for the repudiation of human behaviour.[2]

Mr. Blackmur's statement, if extreme, represents the general tenor of much James criticism. Many critics, with Blackmur, choose to emphasize renunciation and repudiation, the "tragedy of manners" and the "imagination of disaster." Indeed, one recent study of form in the novels insists that we must view James's vision as "'negative' rather than 'tragic'" in part because James could not assert positive values with any degree of success of conviction."[3]

Such assumptions, based on a misapprehension of the form and spirit of the novels, are largely, if not totally, incorrect.

At the turn of the century, as James was completing his last great works, the somewhat hypocritical Victorian belief in progress and optimism was deteriorating. What was replacing it in both criticism and fiction, as well as in the popular mind, seemed to be a new awareness of man's essential isolation and alienation, his inability to conform happily with or function creatively in established society. Modern criticism of James has emphasized this reawakened sense of despair, disaster, and man's inhumanity to man in a world where transcendental ideals are no longer viable.

Several of James's own letters seem to justify this critical perspective. Writing at the outset of World War I, James passionately cried:

> the plunge of civilization into this abyss of blood and dark-
> ness ... is a thing that so gives away the whole long age
> during which we have supposed the world to be, with
> whatever abatement, gradually bettering, that to have to take
> it all now for what the treacherous years were all the while
> making for and *meaning* is too tragic for words.[4]

But James wrote this letter years after the completion of his major novels, and whatever his feelings were at the moment, the letter does not document an essentially tragic outlook. Instead, it seems to affirm that during most of his long creative life James had believed the world to be "gradually bettering."

Years earlier, of course, James had written to Howells, "I suspect it is the tragedies in life that arrest my attention more than the other things and say more to my imagination."[5] But as Leon Edel points out, "for one who felt himself to have this penchant for the tragedies of life, Henry managed to write an amazing number of successful high comedies during the next few years: upon them, indeed, he built his greatest fame."[6] Edel's statement must come as something of a shock to a majority of James critics who have failed to find any abundance of comedy in the novels. Dismissing James's comedy as peculiar to a few early novels where it serves mainly as "comic relief," most critics have emphasized tragedy.

Our understanding of comedy has perhaps become debased today because we tend to think of it as the stuff of stand-up comedians and television shows. Some readers, lacking any clear perception of the seriousness of high comedy, seem to believe that the greatest art is necessarily tragic art, and that since James is one of our greatest novelists he must therefore write tragedies. The term "tragedy" is thus a positive value judgment of James's novels rather than a generic description of their form. To call James a writer of comedies, some critics seem to feel, is to demean his achievement.

Lionel Trilling notes this modern critical limitation in his study of E. M. Forster. Forster's comic manner, he states, "owes much to Fielding, Dickens, Meredith and James. . . . And nowadays even the literate reader is likely to be unschooled in the comic tradition and unaware of the comic seriousness." [7] Trilling goes on to point out the difference between "serious" and "solemn." It is obvious from James's own prefaces that he took his art quite seriously, but never solemnly. The lack of any extended critical discussion of James's comic manner and affinities with a comic tradition arises from a misunderstanding of the comic seriousness.

To describe James's novels rigidly as "tragic" and to insist on a spirit of renunciation or "repudiation of human behaviour" is to ignore what James termed the "many copious springs of our never-to-be-slighted 'fun' for the reader and critic susceptible of contagion."[8] His prefaces, notebooks, and letters pulse with the personal thrill of creation, celebrating the sense of life in the novels. And one of James's foremost concerns was the "anxiety of my provision for the reader's amusement."[9]

If many critics have been unsusceptible of "contagion," James himself cultivated the "fun." Although he never specifically defined comedy, it is obvious that he was aware of its high seriousness. Characteristically coupling tragedy and comedy in his preface to *The Princess Casamassima* James writes:

The tragedy and comedy of life, are things of which the common air . . . seems pungently to taste . . . .

If persons either tragically or comically embroiled
with life allow us the comic or tragic value of their
embroilment . . . .[10]

James never completely isolates these generic terms in his own
criticism, but his feelings about comedy are evident in the words
he uses to describe the form in his notebooks. He writes of "the
mystification, sadness, comedy,"[11] "the ironic, . . .the order of
fine comedy, satiric observation,"[12] and "the whole frank, bright,
manly, human little comedy."[13] At another point in the notebooks
James describes plans for "a great comedy action":

If this action is a strong one, a right one, a real one, the
elements of success ought to be there in force. But, ah, how
*charming,* how interesting, how noble, as it were, the subject
ought to be . . . . fresh, charming, superior, with a distinct
elevation, a great comedy-'lift' in it.[14]

In a sense, these observations define James's understanding of
comedy, associating the form with irony, satire, charm, elevation,
sadness, brightness, and humanity.

Commenting on Edmond Got's portrayal of some Molière
characters, James further refines these impressions in terms
which could well apply to his own art. James finds that the
"comicality is of the exuberant and tremendous order, and yet
in spite of its richness and flexibility it suggests little connection
with high animal spirits. It seems a matter of invention, of
reflection and irony."[15]

The catalogue of James's comments on comedy could easily
be extended, but these few examples will suffice to demonstrate
his assumptions about the form. Although James's own novels
are a curious mixture of elements, comedy informs the structure,
character, and vision of many of his major works. And it is a
comedy of "the exuberant and tremendous order," a serious high
comedy "of reflection and irony."

As long ago as 1931, Constance Rourke insisted that James's
form was essentially comic, and even questioned the correctness
of terming *The Wings of the Dove* tragedy. It is strange that no
published study has examined the implications of her excellent
introductory chapter. Some critics have accepted her argument
that *The American* reflects "American humor" and some critics

have seen comic overtones in other of the early novels. But Rourke's bold claim was that the whole James canon reflects the "balance of mind and feeling from which an enduring philosophical comedy may spring."[16]

The one full length study of comedy in James is Richard Poirier's collection of essays on several early novels. While some of Poirier's individual insights are enlightening, the study as a whole is disappointingly narrow. In a review of Poirier's book, Leon Edel provides suggestions for a more significant study of James's comedy. Edel complains of Poirier's "limiting his subject in . . . [such a] stringent fashion" to the early novels. According to Edel, Poirier "rambles" away from examination of the comedy, seeking "nuance and detail, rather than essence . . . . Perhaps the most serious defect in this study—at best tentative in its approach to James's comedy—is its failure to give us a working definition of the comic sense or to attach James's comedy to a tradition."[17]

When James complained of Emerson's insensibility to Aristophanes, Cervantes, Jane Austen, and Dickens he was revealing his own debt to those comic writers.[18] This study attempts to provide a broad description of Jamesian comedy and to indicate James's affinities with such a comic tradition.

In his prefaces James himself suggests the critical method best applicable to his novels. In the new critical scramble after "nuance and detail," scholars have sometimes slighted a fundamental aspect of criticism: form or genre. But James laid great stress on "kinds."

> Everything, for that matter, becomes interesting from the moment it has closely to consider, for full effect positively to bestride, the law of its kind. "Kinds" are the very life of literature, and truth and strength come from the complete recognition of them.[19]

And in another preface James complains of a penchant in criticism "to stand off from the intended sense of things, from such finely-attested matters, on the artist's part, as a spirit and a form."[20] James's comments seem to indicate that the "kinds," the "spirit" and "form" of his novels, should be a critic's primary consideration.

In his *Anatomy of Criticism,* Northrop Frye submits that

while "historical criticism" deals only with influences, and "new criticism" ignores genre, treating novels as if they were narrative poems, archetypal criticism can deal effectively with form or genre.[21] Since the new critical approach of minute analysis has rendered criticism "obese," I have chosen to employ a fresh method by examining the formal elements of comedy in James's novels. An archetypal analysis of plot and character in James reveals the generic, recurring, conventional aspects of comedy which inform the novels. James, like Shakespeare, used the same devices over and over, and it is the business of the literary critic to compare these devices with those of other dramatists and novelists in a morphological study of comic form.

E.D. Hirsch's *Validity in Interpretation* represents the most recent extension of Frye's methodology. Hirsch insists that meaning is not arbitrary or relative to each individual reader. Rather, there exists in each work of art a discoverable and sharable core of meaning. The most valid method of recovering this core of meaning is the study of genre. As Hirsch notes, "an interpreter's preliminary generic conception of a text is constitutive of everything that he subsequently understands, and . . . this remains the case unless and until that generic conception is altered."[22]

One of the major causes of disagreement and confusion over James's presentation of character and theme is a failure to examine the intrinsic genre of the novels. Thus various readers can "demonstrate" mutually exclusive interpretations of nearly all the novels, offering unqualified praise of Maggie Verver, Lambert Strether, Fleda Vetch, and Christopher Newman on the one hand, and unqualified condemnation of those characters on the other. Hirsch points out that if one rightly grasps the intrinsic genre of a work, the basis of such disagreement vanishes. The problem, of course, is that "we can never be absolutely certain that we have premised the right type."[23]

A further problem in James, of course, is that his novels are not properly either tragedies or comedies. James was one of those great writers who create new genres from existing conventions. But a new genre cannot be explained adequately until the older conventions underlying it have been isolated and described, and since the study of James's tragic sense has been critically exhausted, this study is devoted to a description of his comic sense. Perhaps such description will be a step toward a more accurate understanding of the evolution of a peculiarly Jamesian genre.

Comedy may be the elusive element in James's novels which will answer some of the perplexing critical questions. Perhaps it is Henry James talking when Hugh Vereker of "The Figure in the Carpet" says there is a secret in his works, yet not really a secret at all, just something everyone had overlooked, a "general intention" which resides in "the order, the form, the texture" of his novels.[24]

## 2.

Before discussing the generic form of James's novels it will be well to describe briefly James's comic spirit and its relation to the tragic sense. In his excellent book on Restoration drama Bonamy Dobree insists that "Great Comedy" is often "perilously near tragedy."[25] Dobree elaborates:

> The greatest comedy seems inevitably to deal with the disillusion of mankind, the bitterness of a Troilus or an Alceste, the failure of men to realize their most passionate desires. . . . It comes when the positive attitude has failed, when doubt is creeping in to undermine values.[26]

And yet, in the face of such disillusion, comedy provides man with a means for creatively controlling chaos and absurdity with both detachment and sympathy.

Criticism has made us too well aware that James's fictional world is one of hostility, perversity, and decay. But it is the spirit with which James confronts that situation which determines the basis of his literary form. While tragedy emphasizes the isolation of man from society, comedy insists on the integration of man into society. The tragic fact embodies death and destruction; the comic fact embodies continuity of life and creation. The two attitudes are not always mutually exclusive. Susanne Langer notes that "society is continuous through its members . . . and even while each individual fulfills the tragic pattern it participates also in the çomic continuity."[27] Langer echoes Ralph Touchett in James's *The Portrait of a Lady*. On his deathbed Ralph affirms:

> There's nothing makes us feel so much alive as to see others die. That's the sensation of life—the sense that we remain. I've had it—even I. But now I'm of no use but to give it to others."[28]

Even in death, Ralph and James can affirm the comic continuity. If Ralph were the protagonist, the novel would be predominantly tragic. But the story is Isabel's. Broken and disillusioned, she is yet young and has a long life ahead of her.

Both tragedy and comedy can be affirmative, but they affirm different attitudes toward man. Whereas tragedy affirms man's ability to maintain an ideal even when it means his own destruction, comedy affirms man's ability to maintain an ideal while adjusting his vision to permit a continued social existence and a knowledge of inherent human limitation at the same time.

In his classic essay on comedy George Meredith insists that all comedy is inseparable from society and the comic spirit is essentially a social spirit. The characters of comedy do not exist in isolation, but in reference to the social world which operates on them. In exposing the tragic possibilities everywhere present in the life and society of the comic form, the comic poet makes the ugliness and imperfection acceptable. L. J. Potts concludes:

> Tragedy is a bulwark of human self-respect against the superhuman or inhuman forces pressing upon us from all sides. Comedy is our corresponding weapon against the forces of disintegration within human society, and against the germs of anarchy and defeatism in our own minds.[29]

The fine line between tragedy and comedy reduces to absurdity any view of the comic which emphasizes happy endings or merely pleasurable laughter. Meredith describes the quality of laughter which comedy evokes as "thoughtful laughter," for comedy is the "fountain of sound sense."[30] And Bergson echoes Meredith when he affirms that the appeal "is to intelligence, pure and simple."[31] The "laughter of the mind" is often painful laughter because it is "capped by the grotesque, irony tips the wit, and satire is a naked sword."[32] Meredith believed that were the comic to appear again in a modern author, perhaps the change "from good-natured old obtuseness to keen-edged intelligence, which is by nature merciless, would be more than we could bear."[33]

Henry James was familiar with Meredith's essay and may even have heard it delivered in 1877. Reviewing it years later for *Harper's Weekly,* James called it "dazzling."[34] With his intellectual wit and exuberant emphasis on social forms and manners, James found himself engaged in the writing of a comedy which reflected a good deal of Meredith's essay. Meredith's description of the spirit which sees life as teetering on the brink of disaster yet recognizes and celebrates the possibility of creating and maintaining a successful, if precarious, balance, is just the spirit of much of Henry James's art. As a cerebral comedian James insists on charm, manners, wit, and an appreciation of all in life that is exquisite. The initial perception of the tragic is what enabled James to go on to affirm the comic possibilities of individual life in society.

3.

The comic spirit, then, is an attitude toward life revealed by the tone of a work of art. The preceding discussion has emphasized the comic spirit as man's weapon against chaos and absurdity and as an attitude which borders on tragedy. If the comic spirit is sometimes companionable and sympathetic, it is also "humanly malign" in Meredith's terms, a corrective of "pretentiousness, of inflation, of dullness, and of the vestiges of rawness and grossness to be found among us."[35] But the spirit of James's novels is never so theoretic and abstract. In several of the major novels James provides characters who seem to reflect his own views and attitudes toward life. The most obvious example is Gabriel Nash in *The Tragic Muse.*

A number of critics have analyzed the charming and often exasperating Nash, but most of the critical discussions have aimed at discovering a source for the character rather than revealing his function in the novel. He has been seen as Herbert Pratt, Oscar Wilde, and Henry James himself, and he has been called the symbol of the aesthetic life and of artistic inspiration.[36]

Regardless of Nash's antecedents, his function in the novel seems curiously like that which Meredith attributes to the comic spirit. Although James probably did not have Meredith's essay specifically in mind when creating his character, Nash is practically a fictional representation of Meredith's comic spirit. Meredith explains:

> The Comic Spirit conceives a definite situation for a number of characters and rejects all accessories in the pursuit of them and their speech. For, being a spirit, he hunts the spirit in men; vision and ardour constitute his merit; he has not a thought of persuading you to believe in him. Follow and you will see.[37]

Like the comic spirit, Nash conceives the situation of the characters in *The Tragic Muse* and sets the entire action in motion. He is, in a sense, the prime mover in a massive comedy of manners who creates relationships between characters and provides the complications which make for the plot. He introduces Peter Sherringham to Miriam Rooth, thereby initiating a comic love affair and launching Miriam on her career as an actress. He entices Nick to give up Julia Dallow's political aspirations and turn to a happy life painting portraits. Of Miriam, Nash boasts to Nick, "I invented her."[38] It is Nash who brings "the political case" and "the theatrical case" in the novel together. Without him there could be no unity; without him there would be no novel. Like Shakespeare's Puck, he arranges the plot and disrupts the preconceived categories of all the characters.

Nash is the wise, alert, ironical demon of the upper air who hunts the comic spirit in other men. Foremost among his targets is Nick Dormer. As Meredith continues, whenever men

> offend sound reason, fair justice; are false in humility or mined with conceit, individually, or in the bulk; the Spirit overhead will look humanly malign, and cast an oblique light on them, followed by volleys of silvery laughter. That is the Comic Spirit.[39]

When Nash meets his old friend Nick in the garden of the *Palais de l'industrie* he quickly realizes that Nick is about to offend sound reason by entering political life. "Ah it was high time I should meet you," says Nash. "I've an idea you need me." (VII, 25) Nash learns that Nick's fianceé, Julia Dallow, expects Nick to "stand" for Harsh, replacing Mr. Pinks. The absurdity is amusing to Nash who bubbles "Mr. Pinks, the member for Harsh? What names, to be sure!" (VII, 51) And when Nash discovers the economic arrangements involved, volleys of silvery laughter echo in his incredulity. "Do you mean to say you've to pay money to get into that awful place—that it's not *you* who are paid?" (VII, 54) Peter Sherringham, not yet a victim of Nash's humor, asks Nick, "Who in the world's your comic friend?" (VII, 77)

But if in his role as comic spirit Nash laughs at the absurdity of Nick's position, he also seeks to make Nick laugh at himself. When Julia bids Nick to be "a little serious" about his political career he retorts under the good influence of Nash, "My dear Julia, it seems to me I'm serious enough. Surely it isn't an occasion to be so very solemn." (VII, 102) The ultimate effect of Nick's new appreciation of the "serious" comedy of his life is renewed amusement and dedication to art. "It was a long time since he had felt so gay." (VIII, 24)

Within the novel, then, Gabriel Nash is the voice of life and moral responsibility challenging Nick to observe thoughtfully his own human comedy. Nash insists that Nick become a man and not a Parliamentary automaton led by a strong, domineering wife. And Nick is not the only victim of Nash's comic spirit.

The absurdity of Nick's "political case" is rivaled by Peter Sherringham's misplaced devotion to Miriam Rooth. Although Peter should marry the faithful Biddy, he pursues Miriam with a comically passionate impotence, hoping to persuade her to leave the stage and become his wife. Perceiving the potentially ridiculous situation, Nash constantly taunts Peter about Nick's relationship with Miriam, who is his model. While Nash jibes Peter about Nick's "intimate" association with the actress, Peter wonders "if this insistence were not a subtle perversity, a devilish little invention to torment a man whose jealousy was presumable." (VIII, 147) Acting in his character of comic spirit flashing "sunny malice"[40] Nash finally succeeds in penetrating Peter's

illusions. At the close, Peter and Biddy are happily and sensibly
united.

If Nash resembles Meredith's comic spirit he also recalls
Bergson's classic essay on laughter. Bergson writes that the comic
"demands something like a momentary anesthesia of the heart.
Its appeal is to intelligence, pure and simple."[41] When Nick
suggests that most people think Nash impudent, Nash responds
characteristically, "I've literally seen mere quickness of intelligence or of perception, the jump of a step or two, a little whirr
of the wings of talk, mistaken for it." (VII, 171)

Further, Bergson's very definition of the comic describes
Nash's typical response to life. Analyzing the situation which
gives rise to laughter, Bergson claims:

> Now, such a notion is formed when we perceive anything
> inert or stereotyped, or simply ready-made, on the surface of
> living society. There we have rigidity over again, clashing
> with the inner suppleness of life. The ceremonial side of
> life must, therefore, always include a latent comic element.[42]

Besides perceiving the comic element in Harsh and Mr. Pinks
and the whole political way of life, Nash constantly derides
categories. When Biddy asks him if he is an aesthete, he merely
wails, "Ah there's one of the formulas!" (VII, 33) Nash constantly
ridicules the inert and stereotyped, the categories and formulas
by which men mistakenly live. Nash himself is a free spirit, living
by no set or fixed categories. When Nick asks him about his "little
system," Nash "hesitated, tolerantly, gaily, as he often did, with
an air of being embarrassed to choose between several answers,
any one of which would be so right." (VII, 178) Sworn enemy to
dullness and fixity, Nash retains a gay and tolerant open mind.

Gabriel Nash is practically a fictional embodiment of the
comic spirit. Conceiving the social situation for the novel, he
molds the plot in such a way that the characters must learn to
laugh at themselves and cultivate sound sense. Further, Leon
Edel is probably right when he proposes that Nash is "the
spokesman for James's views . . . . Gabriel Nash talks undiluted
Henry James."[43] And Nick Dormer attributes to Nash "the dignity of judgment, the authority of knowledge. Nash was an
ambiguous character but an excellent touchstone." (VIII, 24)

If Nash is a close fictional embodiment of the comic spirit and speaks "undiluted Henry James," we can use him as a "touchstone" for the spirit of the James canon. Indeed, although Nash is James's most literal comic spokesman, his character appears in several other novels, in figures like Felix Young of *The Europeans,* Valentin de Bellegarde of *The American,* and Ralph Touchett of *The Portrait of a Lady.* His spirit is also evident in the whole line of Jamesian artists of life who progress toward an expanded consciousness and learn the value of personal relationship and social creativity. Nash is the affirmative force who has known the "wrongs in the world," the "abuses and sufferings," but chooses to "encourage the beautiful." (VII, 32) He espouses the wit, creativity, and consciousness in the fiction of Henry James which keep human society and individual men sane and healthy. And as Nash himself concludes, "I dare say I'm indestructible, immortal." (VIII, 411)

It is the immortal and indestructible spirit of comedy which Henry James, like Nash, plies against the tragedies of life. By exposing the evil, ugliness, and chaos everywhere evident in his comic forms, James seeks to give his characters power over possible despair. In facing evil with moral freedom and intellectual independence, the characters strive to lead lives which provide personal as well as social success. The tone of a Henry James novel is the tone of Gabriel Nash, insisting on a high comic affirmation of life.

Through a discussion of the traditional elements of comic form which recur throughout the novels I have tried to describe the peculiar success which James affirmed. Rather than presenting extended analyses of single works I have grouped related novels under the headings of character, plot, and style. This organization reveals the essential unity of the James canon which T. S. Eliot recognized in 1924:

> One thing is certain, that the books of Henry James form a complete whole. One must read all of them, for one must grasp, if anything, both the unity and the progression. The gradual development, and the fundamental identity of spirit, are both important, and their lesson is one lesson.[44]

The "fundamental identity of spirit," as I have suggested, is a comic spirit. Wylie Sypher, one of the few critics who perceives Henry James's relation to the comic tradition, concludes:

> At the radiant peak of "high" comedy—a peak we can easily sight from Meredith's essay—laughter is qualified by tolerance, and criticism is modulated by a sympathy that comes only from wisdom. Just a few writers of comedy have gained this unflinching but generous perspective on life, which is a victory over our absurdities but a victory won at a cost of humility, and won in a spirit of charity and enlightenment. Besides Shakespeare in, perhaps, *The Tempest,* one might name Cervantes and Henry James.[45]

# II

# The Jamesian Character

*"bedimmed and befooled and bewildered"*

Aristotle posits that tragedy is structured primarily on plot, and comedy primarily on character. Bergson rephrases this idea when he suggests that comedy "does not exist outside the pale of what is strictly human."[1] And L. J. Potts adds that the "strictly human" has to be envisioned as "one unit in a society composed of other similar units."[2] The comic hero is usually in pursuit of happiness, often symbolized by an attempt to integrate himself into an existent society or into a new society of his own creation. Several types of character can fill the role, ranging from buffoon or gull to wit or creator. When a character remains blissfully unaware of his victimization, like Bottom in *A Midsummer Night's Dream*, he represents the buffoon figure, while Dicaepolis in Aristophanes' *The Acharnians*, who successfully builds a society of peace around himself, represents the wit or creator. Often the hero is some combination of both buffoon and wit like Jane Austen's Emma, who is intelligent, honest, and lively, but at the same time conceited and foolish.

The comic structure, then, is based on a conception of character. And in the preface to *The Portrait of a Lady* Henry James confides that he began writing "almost always with the vision of some person or persons, who hovered before him."[3] Indeed, he rather deprecates the need for a plot at all when he writes:

> The germ of my idea ... must have consisted not at all in any conceit of a "plot, " nefarious name .. but altogether in the sense of a single character, ... to which all the usual elements of a "subject," certainly of a setting, were to need to be super-added.[4]

15

James began with a vision of character, and the plot followed from the logical playing out of the character's psychology.

As Bergson comments, "comedy depicts characters we have already come across and shall meet with again. It takes note of similarities. It aims at placing types before our eyes. It even creates new types, if necessary."[5] That James, too, was committed to creating successful "type" characters is evidenced in his complaint that Dickens's characters were "individuals without being types," that they had no "continuity with the rest of humanity."[6]

The characters of comedy, James realized, cannot exist apart from other men. James insists in his preface to *Roderick Hudson*:

> It had, naturally, Rowland's consciousness, not to be *too* acute—which would have disconnected it and made it superhuman; the beautiful little problem was to keep it connected, connected intimately, with the general human exposure, and thereby bedimmed and befooled and bewildered, anxious, restless, fallible.[7]

And in the preface to *The Princess Casamassima* James reiterates his theory. Characters "may be shown as knowing too much and feeling too much—not certainly for their remaining remarkable, but for their remaining 'natural' and typical, for their having the needful communities with our own precious liability to fall into traps and be bewildered."[8] James's comments really amount to a distinction between the tragic and comic character. As Louis Kronenberger suggests, "a great tragic hero—an Oedipus or Lear—strikes us as tremendously far removed from common humanity. But comedy . . . shows how very like at bottom the hero is to everybody else."[9] All convincing characters in literature are, of course, types. But this important distinction between the tragic and comic type suggests that James's conception of character was primarily that of comedy. The prefaces to *Roderick Hudson* and *The Princess Casamassima* define this basic difference between the tragic character, a superhuman special case who remains isolated from common society, and James's own comic heroes. James's characters, like all comic characters, are social types who reflect a natural tendency to be "bedimmed and befooled and bewildered."

## Major Characters

James desired to create types, and Christopher Newman of *The American* was indeed so successful an American type that he was radically misread by a number of American readers. Elizabeth Luther Cary, for example, in her pioneer study, concluded that Newman was "uncontentious, delicate, generous in his relation towards others, frankly without superficial taste, but with endless inner refinements."[10] Richard Poirier perpetuates this one-sided reading when he assumes that Newman is not satirized, but realizes the comedy himself. According to Poirier the comedy in the novel is "always used to enhance the hero's character or to abuse those who fail to recognize his value."[11]

But if these laudations of Newman are partially correct, it is only because in Newman James revealed his own capacity for sympathetic comic perception which Meredith described as the ability "to detect the ridicule of them you love without loving them less."[12] If James loved Newman he recognized his boastful and bathetic qualities as well and chose to emphasize and ridicule them.

Constance Rourke perceives that James's creation of Newman was the "drawing [of] the large, the generic, American character,"[13] and Leon Edel recognizes that Newman's portrait is so rich in national ambiguities that "generations of readers" have not seen that Newman "embodies also everything that Henry disliked in the United States . . . a strong and vulgar streak of materialistic self-satisfaction."[14] Edel concludes that along with Newman's "naiveté, his boastfulness . . . there is also his total failure to grasp deeper human values."[15]

That Newman embodies James's general feelings about Americans is suggested by an early letter to his mother:

> A set of people less framed to provoke national self-complacency than the latter it would be hard to imagine. There is but one word to use in regard to them—vulgar, vulgar, vulgar. Their ignorance—their stingy, defiant, grudging attitude towards everything European—their perpetual reference of all things to some American standard or precedent which exists only in their unscrupulous wind-bags . . . these things glare at you hideously.[16]

James goes on to temper his vehement criticism with the admission that Americans are a people of *"character"* who have "energy," but "what I have pointed at as our vices are the elements of the modern man with *culture* quite left out."[17]

Later in life, in the preface to *The Reverberator,* James recalled his view of the characteristic American which had appeared repeatedly in his fiction. The American is "almost incredibly *unaware of life.*"[18]

> They come back to me, in the lurid light of contrast, as irresistibly (sic) destitute of those elements of preparedness that my pages show even the most limited European adventure to call into play. This at least was, by my retrospect, the inveterate case for the men.[19]

James sees American characters as objects of "beauty and comedy and pathos"[20] and notes that their "disposition . . . had perhaps even most a comic side."[21]

From comments in his letters and prefaces it would seem that the American type represented possibilities of satire and witty comedy to James. And the text of *The American* itself amply reveals James's light satire of his hero. The opening paragraph of the novel, depicting Newman relaxing in the Louvre, establishes the general tone for the entire book. Newman sits with his "head thrown back and his legs outstretched," (a position assumed frequently by Waymarsh in *The Ambassadors*) with his "guide book" and "opera glasses" "flung" down beside him. The picture is that of a typical American tourist in Paris, "aesthetic headache" and all. James emphasizes the fact that Newman has looked "not only at all the pictures, but at all the copies that were going forward around them."[22]

If the impossible lightning tour of the massive Louvre were not in itself enough to tip off the reader, James intrudes to comment upon Newman's taste. "If the truth must be told, he had often admired the copy much more than the original." (5) "An observer with anything of an eye for national types . . . might have felt a certain humorous relish of the almost ideal completeness with which he filled out the national mould." (6) The description is capped with a delightfully exaggerated picture of Newman's head. "He had a very well-formed head, with a shapely, symmetrical balance of the frontal and occipital development." (6) He is a "shrewd and capable fellow" for whom Raphael and Titian are "a new kind of arithmetic." (5)

Throughout the novel James consistently pokes fun at Newman's value system, which is based on wealth and acquisition.

> It must be admitted, rather nakedly, that Christopher Newman's sole aim in life had been to make money . . . . Upon the uses of money, upon what one might do with a life into which one had succeeded in injecting the golden stream, he had up to his thirty-fifth year very scantily reflected. (21)

With the "golden stream" coursing through his veins, Newman comes to Europe to purchase culture and a wife, insisting that "there must be a beautiful woman perched on the pile, like a statue on a monument." (35)

The single word that constitutes the strength of Newman's French vocabulary is "*combien*," accompanied by the raising of one finger, and with it he buys a ridiculously overpriced copy from a young Parisian coquette. (8) When he tells Noémie that she is "very clever," referring to her artistic ability, he fails to realize that her very cleverness has helped her to dupe him. He ends up commissioning a dozen more copies from the young girl, and, as he assures her, quality, as well as price, is no object.

At the outset Newman is almost a caricature of the American businessman in Paris for a well-deserved holiday. His imagination is limited, and the more limited in imagination the character, the more potentially comic he is. As Newman becomes more deeply involved in the complications of his initially simple scheme and loses any sense of his own comicality, the reader's sense of it grows. Valentin, Newman's friend, serves as a foil to the hero, deprecating himself while laughing at both sides in the conflict of cultures, and wryly, if compassionately, mocking Newman's ignorance. After Newman's sight-seeing tour Valentin asks:

> "Are you interested in architecture . . . ?"
> "Well, I took the trouble, this summer," said Newman, "to examine—as well as I can calculate—some four hundred and seventy churches. Do you call that interested?"
> "Perhaps you are interested in theology." (76)

Valentin's witty response goes right over the hero's well-developed head.

Later, as the Bellegardes begin to exert themselves against Newman's boastful self-assurance, Newman demands of Valentin, "Tell me something I have *not* done—something I cannot do." (101) And Valentin merely replies, "You cannot marry a woman like Madame de Cintré." (101) Newman promptly questions the statement and Valentin replies, "You are not noble," to which he indignantly reacts, "The devil I am not!" (101)

The easiest way to render a character comic is to make him unaware of what makes him ridiculous. Newman's misplaced egotistic pride becomes the target of much of James's satire as Newman reveals his obtuseness without ever suspecting it. His words and actions have simultaneously one meaning for him and another for the reader or spectator. When Mrs. Tristram, another comic reflector in the novel, tells him, "You are the great Western Barbarian, stepping forth in his innocence and might," Newman retorts, "I am a highly civilized man." (32) And to prove it he asks Mrs. Tristram to find him a "magnificent" woman.

Another Jamesian joke on Newman's lack of self-awareness is sounded midway in the book when he becomes involved with the family of his "magnificent" woman. When the Marquis remarks, "I detest you personally," Newman replies in all candor, "That's the way I feel about you, but for politeness' sake I don't say it." (261) In defending himself, Newman conveys an insult which he is not even aware of conveying.

The reader is not the only one who perceives Newman's unconscious self-exposure. As Leon Edel notes, the finest comedy in the book results from the conflicting cultures which poke fun at each other. From the Bellegardes' perspective Newman is frightfully droll, and they constantly laugh at him. Their "visitors, coming in often while Newman sat there, found a tall, lean silent man, in a half-lounging attitude, who laughed out sometimes when no one had meant to be droll, and remained grave in the presence of calculated witticisms, for the appreciation of which he had apparently not the proper culture." (150) When the Bellegardes do make fun of him, Newman remains unaware of it, and, while this reveals his good humor and kindliness, it also displays his inability to grasp subtlety or manner.

Of course, Newman's openness is a comment on the Belle-gardes, and their pretentiousness is comic from his perspective. As Edel suggests, "the Marquise de Bellegarde is simply a European Christopher Newman; she sits upon her aristocratic sanctity with the same tough possessiveness and assurance as that with which Newman sits on his pile of dollars."[23]

Throughout the greater portion of *The American* the comedy is light satire and comedy of manners, but in the concluding chapters the plot turns melodramatic and the comedy becomes almost a comedy of humors, with Newman the prime humor. When an essentially comic character tries to adopt a tragic pose, or when a comic character is imposed on a tragic situation, the outcome is generally melodrama. The closing chapters of *The American,* which reverse Newman's progress and whisk Claire away to a nunnery, serve to emphasize Newman's pride and lack of self-knowledge, more than to marshall sympathy for the "defeated" hero. As the melodrama mounts and Newman continues to confuse absurdity with solemnity, the reader grows increasingly aware of the incongruity of the hero's wound and his wail. When Newman learns that he cannot buy the beautiful Claire for his wife, he does not mourn the cruel destruction of his love. Indeed, James had never much tried to make this love, or Claire as an individual, at all credible. Rather, Newman rants about the lack of respect paid his "noble character."

> To have eaten humble pie, to have been snubbed and patronised and satirised, and have consented to take it as one of the conditions of the bargain—to have done this, and done it all for nothing, surely gave one a right to protest. And to be turned off because one was a commercial person! (254)

Newman is less upset over the loss of a true love than he is over the loss of a prized possession. And the loss in itself is only insufferable because the defeat reflects on his own self-image. The emotions Newman displays are at best curious for a man so "in love," and James intrudes to remark that Newman becomes "lugubriously comical." (255)

Newman's emotion at the loss of Claire swiftly gives way to the elation of possible revenge. His sense of being "a good fellow wronged" (255) easily prevails over any other feeling, and he plots to use Mrs. Bread's secret to unmask and humiliate the Bellegardes. His desire for revenge becomes such an obsession that it renders the kindly Newman almost demonic. As he confides to Mrs. Bread:

> "I want to bring them down—down, down, down! I want to turn the tables upon them—I want to mortify them as they mortified me. They took me up into a high place and made me stand there for all the world to see me, and then they stole behind me and pushed me into this bottomless pit, where I lie howling and gnashing my teeth!" (267)

Newman conceives his position in exactly the exaggerated terms characteristic of the comic gull or fool. When Mrs. Bread replies, "I suppose you have a right to your anger, sir; but think of the dishonor you will draw down on Madame de Cintré," Newman murmurs, "She has moved off, like her brother Valentin, to give me room to work." (267)

The melodrama, though perhaps not in complete harmony with the expectations raised by the traditional comic plot of the novel, is not as inappropriate as some critics have suggested. For it does reveal, beyond a doubt, the negative aspects of Newman's character, aspects which are more easily dismissed in earlier sections of the novel. It has been argued, of course, that Newman is good to the end, a protagonist who gains an awareness of himself and transcends the petty machinations of a proud and narrow Parisian family. But to read the novel in that way is to miss the comedy which infuses Newman's portrait. From the beginning he is a recognizable type, and he changes little in the course of the action. Toward the close, as he ponders his revenge on the Bellegardes,

> a singular feeling came over him—a sudden sense of the folly of his errand. What under the sun had he to say to the duchess, after all? Wherein would it profit him to tell her that the Bellegardes were traitors and that the old lady, into the bargain, was a murderess? He seemed morally to have turned a sort of somersault. (305)

The hero appears at this point to have attained some vision and perspective on himself. But this is not the first "moral somer-sault" that Newman has turned, and it will not be the last. In a novel filled with reversals on the hero's part, this reversal promises to be no more permanent than the others. Early in the novel, for instance, after burning to get even with a fellow businessman who had wronged him, Newman decides heroically against revenge, recognizing its folly. He relates to Mrs. Tristram:

> "This other party had once played me a very mean trick. I owed him a grudge, I felt awfully savage at the time, and I vowed that, when I got a chance, I would figuratively speaking, put his nose out of joint." (23)

Yet, as he jumps into a taxi, a "curious thing" happens. Newman "woke up suddenly, from a sleep or from a kind of a reverie" and he rejects his plan for revenge. He "seemed to feel a new man inside my old skin." (24) The situation which Newman remembers with such clarity is suspiciously similar to the situa-tion which confronts him at the end of the novel. Again he plans revenge and gives it up. But his final action suggests that he has learned as little from this incident as he learned from the earlier one. Newman returns to visit the Tristrams, still in pos-session of the scrap of evidence which proves to himself that he is a "good fellow wronged." He self-confidently announces to Mrs. Tristram that he has "had all the vengeance I want," (324) and to prove his confidence he dramatically thrusts the paper into the fire. But James's final sentence is a minor master-piece of ironic commentary on his static, but sympathetic hero. Mrs. Tristram provokes Newman by demeaning his evidence:

> Newman instinctively turned to see if the little paper was in fact consumed; but there was nothing left of it. (325)

Newman's final "instinct" is that of the proud and self-deceived hero he has been all along.

To the end Newman remains finely unaware of his own comicality. For all his simplicity, naiveté, and lovableness, Newman is blundering, loud, and conceited as well. His boast-fulness results in unconscious self-exposure, and his regression into melodramatic deviltry at the close reveals the real danger of such ignorance.

Newman, then, is a Jamesian approximation of the gulled fool or buffoon of traditional comedy. A sympathetic figure, he is nonetheless ridiculous in the context in which he finds himself. From Newman's type James created a whole range of egoists, including Isabel Archer and Basil Ransom, and culminating in the narrator of *The Sacred Fount.*

When Frederick Crews calls Isabel Archer an "unimpeachable heroine," we must suspect that he has missed the essentially comic tradition to which she, as heroine, belongs.[24] As admirable and perceptive as Isabel Archer may at times be in *The Portrait of a Lady,* she is dogmatic, her ideals are inflated, and her self-knowledge is meager throughout. As Leon Edel suggests, she is, in fact, a female Christopher Newman, and like Newman, for all her delicacy of feeling, she is presumptuous and egotistical.[25] Although Isabel has a larger fund of self-awareness than Newman, her awareness reverses repeatedly in the novel. "She had an unquenchable desire to think well of herself," James tells us. (III, 68) She believes that "one should try to be one's own best friend and to give one's self, in this manner, distinguished company." (III, 68) "Sometimes she went so far as to wish that she might find herself some day in a difficult position, so that she could have the pleasure of being as heroic as the occasion demanded." (III, 69)

Northrop Frye observes that "comedy is designed not to condemn evil, but to ridicule a lack of self-knowledge."[26] Isabel Archer belongs to a long tradition of characters whose self-knowledge exposes them to ridicule. Oscar Cargill refers to the tradition as that of the "limited heroine,"[27] but a more precise term, perhaps, is "self-deceived protagonist." James, himself, in the preface to *The Portrait* refers to several other female characters in this tradition; George Eliot's Hetty Sorrel and Rosamond Vincy are both rank egotists.[28] Other heroines in this tradition, more closely related to Isabel than the extreme Hetty and Rosamond, are Jane Austen's Emma Woodhouse, and George Eliot's Dorothea Brooke. To see Isabel's place in this tradition, as Cargill points out, is to correct the wrong assumption that she is the ideal type of James's cousin Minny Temple.

Like Emma, Isabel is obviously misguided, selfish, egotistical, and stupidly naive, yet at the same time sympathetic and potentially intelligent. And, like Dorothea, she is the victim of her own headlong enthusiasms, her ignorance of the world and of herself, and her misplaced devotion. But Isabel is left much more alone in her self-delusion than either Emma or Dorothea. Jane Austen provides her heroine with a clear representative of right action in Knightly. Both he and the pastoral world of Highbury itself guide Emma toward a wisdom and self-knowledge symbolized by her final union with Knightly, the moral norm and emblem of an ideal society.

Dorothea's standard of conduct is much less clear to the reader or to herself. But if Dorothea lacks the objective correlative of the moral norm which Knightly provides, she is saved by the *deus ex machina* of death, and in the end marries happily; for love. Both Dorothea and Isabel, however, have principles which are inadequate for confronting the complexities of life. Dogmatism and egotism are their main obstacles to moral enlargement. And the irony which overtakes them both is that in seeking escape from narrowing influences (Dorothea wants to escape her provincial town and Isabel rejects the confinement of Warburton or Goodwood) they submit themselves to a marital narrowness far more malevolent. But whereas Casaubon dies, Osmond lives, and Isabel must accept responsibility for her own actions. She cannot marry Ralph as Emma marries Knightly and Dorothea marries Will Ladislaw.

If Emma's situation is rendered less difficult because Knightly represents the moral norm which she must merely perceive, and if Dorothea's final creation of moral value requires a *deus ex machina,* Isabel's circumstances emphasize her inability or unwillingness to rely on external help. She, like Emma, is provided a version of the ideal in Ralph. But Ralph is sick, Isabel cannot take his joking seriously, and she remains unable to adopt his perspective on life. In the end, Isabel is perhaps morally stronger than either of her predecessors when she rejects her own *deus ex machina,* Caspar Goodwood, and affirms her decision to create her own moral norm.

But despite Isabel's strength, James emphasizes her weaknesses. He intrudes to inform the reader that "the love of knowledge coexisted in her mind with the finest capacity for ignorance." (III, 284) And even when he warns the reader not to be too harsh with Isabel he comically undercuts her in the manner of George Eliot:

> Smile not, however, I venture to repeat, at this simple young woman from Albany who debated whether she should accept an English peer before he had offered himself and who was disposed to believe that on the whole she could do better. She was a person of great good faith, and if there was a great deal of folly in her wisdom those who judge her severely may have the satisfaction of finding that, later, she became consistently wise only at the cost of an amount of folly. (III, 145)

James earlier insists that despite her "meager knowledge, her inflated ideals," and her "dogmatic" confidence, she is "intended to awaken on the reader's part an impulse more tender and more purely expectant." (III, 69) George Eliot uses a similar technique to expose the pedantic Casaubon, repeatedly intruding in *Middlemarch* to protest that Casaubon isn't really as bad as he seems. But in protesting, she lists all of Casaubon's faults, making doubly sure that the reader has not missed them. James uses the same method when he lists Isabel's defects and then insists that they are not so bad.

Isabel's approach to life, like that of Emma and Dorothea, is romantic, idealistic, and theoretic. Henrietta Stackpole correctly analyzes Isabel's main fault when she tells her friend that she lives "too much in the world of your own dreams. You're not enough in contact with reality." Isabel smugly replies, "What are my illusions? . . . I try so hard not to have any." (III, 310) But Isabel's retort is comic to the reader who has seen her obviously romantic naiveté. Isabel defines "happiness" as "a swift carriage of a dark night, rattling with four horses over roads that one can't see." (III, 235) She sees Lord Warburton as the hero of a romance and exclaims, "Oh, I do hope they'll make a revolution! . . . I should delight in seeing a revolution." (III, 100) Isabel's naiveté and innocence, juxtaposed with her almost arrogant self-assurance and assumed worldly wisdom, must draw sympathetic smiles from the reader. But Isabel, like Christopher Newman, is herself rather humorless. James describes Isabel gazing "with that solemn stare which sometimes seemed to proclaim her deficient in the sense of comedy." (III, 353)

Isabel thus belongs to the tradition of Emma Woodhouse and Dorothea Brooke. But that tradition appeared long before the nineteenth century. The type of the self-deceived protagonist is perhaps most obvious in the plays of Molière, and Isabel shares many traits with the Molière comic hero.

Molière's Arnolphe and Sganarelle are type comic characters who flout established society and, as Lionel Gossman suggests:

> The rejection of society is not, clearly, confined to articles of clothing. . . . Everybody wants an entertaining, witty and sociable wife? Arnolphe and Sganarelle will choose a " bête ," and they will value precisely that in her which nobody else seems to admire.[29]

Characters like Harpagon, Alceste, Don Juan, Madame Pernelle, and Orgon refuse to admit that they are members of human society like everybody else, and possess no special sensibility which raises them to the superhuman level. Instead they pretend to themselves that they are special cases, and they use other people as instruments for asserting their "superiority" to the world around them.

> What these characters want above all is *to be distinguished,* but they refuse to adopt the usual method of social advancement and privilege, since this method offers only a *relative* superiority to others, whereas the superiority they desire is *absolute.* . . . They are comic not only because there is a constant contradiction between what they are and what they affect to be, but because their attempt to transcend all social superiorities and to reach an absolute superiority misfires.[30]

The description fits Isabel rather closely. In an early discussion with Madame Merle these comic character traits are evident immediately. Isabel tells Madame Merle that she defines success as "some dream of one's youth come true." (III, 286) And when Madame Merle insists that it never happens, Isabel replies that it has already happened to her. Madame Merle remarks:

> "Ah, if you mean the aspirations of your childhood—that of having a pink sash and a doll that could close her eyes."
> "No, I don't mean that."

"Or a young man with a fine moustache going down
on his knees to you."

"No, nor that either," Isabel declared with still more
emphasis.

Madame Merle appeared to note this eagerness. "I suspect that's what you do mean. We've all had the young man
with the moustache. He's the inevitable young man; he
doesn't count. . . ."

"Why shouldn't he count? There are young men and
young men." (III, 286–87)

Isabel, like the Molière characters, will not admit to being at
all like anyone else. *Her* affairs are special. Yet her eagerness
to contradict Madame Merle reveals to the reader an aspect of
her character of which she, herself, is quite unaware. In the same
conversation Madame Merle again undercuts Isabel's pretensions. She suggests that clothes express the person, and Isabel
disagrees:

"To begin with it's not my own choice that I wear them;
they're imposed upon me by society."

"Should you prefer to go without them?" Madame Merle
enquired in a tone which virtually terminated the discussion.
(III, 288)

Isabel bridles at any suggestion that she is a part of society to
which other people belong.

Further, like Arnolphe and Sganarelle who flout society by
rejecting women who are socially desirable and courting those
who are not, Isabel thrills to the joy of refusing two socially
respectable and desirable suitors. After sending Caspar away she
"yielded to the satisfaction of having refused two ardent suitors
in a fortnight." (III, 233) Isabel claims publicly that she wishes
no one would propose to her, but she secretly revels in the
attention and would be most disappointed if left to herself. And,
like the Molière characters, one of the reasons she finally chooses
Gilbert Osmond is just the fact that no one else appreciates him.
Ralph perceives this when he comments, "It was wonderfully
characteristic of her that, having invented a fine theory about

Gilbert Osmond, she loved him not for what he really possessed, but for his very poverties dressed out as honours." (IV, 75)

Isabel exerts much energy in avoiding any commitment which would result in "limitation." She rejects the physical coercion of Goodwood and the social restrictiveness of Warburton. She does not want this kind of relative superiority. Marrying Osmond in the face of widespread opposition, she feels, will assure absolute superiority. Isabel's bad marriage and subsequent suffering, then, are largely the result of her own comic egotism.

Like Christopher Newman, Isabel, in her pride and ignorance, becomes almost demonic toward the end of the book. She constantly assures herself that she is an unimpeachable wife to her malevolent husband, and yet James exposes a satanic streak in her. When she asks Osmond if he would like Warburton to marry Pansy, "she knew exactly the effect on his mind of her question: it would operate as an humiliation. Never mind; he was terribly capable of humiliating *her*." (IV, 182) And later she rationalizes to herself that it is her duty to keep her marital unhappiness a secret from Ralph. She calls it a "kindness" to him. But both Ralph and the reader see that Isabel's deception is just a further example of her desire to think well of herself at other people's expense. Ralph, with characteristic selfless good humor, observes:

> As it was, the kindness consisted mainly in trying to make him believe that he had once wounded her greatly and that the event had put him to shame, but that, as she was very generous and he was so ill, she bore him no grudge and even considerately forbore to flaunt her happiness in his face. Ralph smiled to himself, as he lay on his sofa, at this extraordinary form of consideration. (IV, 204)

I have, of course, emphasized Isabel's negative qualities at the expense of her more admirable traits. And it must be admitted that she does attain a kind of self-knowledge at the close when she perceives her responsibility for her bad marriage.

The character of Isabel, however, derives in part from the tradition of the self-deceived protagonist and the Molière egotist.

If the plot of *The Portrait* were a tragic plot, the flaws in Isabel's character would render her tragic. But the plot of the novel is that of tragicomedy.[31] And Isabel, in her self-exposure and resilient optimism, is a tragicomic heroine.

If Christopher Newman and Isabel Archer remain "befooled" in many ways and take their places among other comic characters in the tradition of the self-deceived protagonist, the narrator of *The Sacred Fount* remains completely "befooled." To appreciate this fact is to understand better James's intentions in writing the novel, and to see the narrator in terms of analogous characters in comic fiction is to perceive more clearly his function and nature.

James's first novel written in the twentieth century has probably caused more critical befuddlement and anxiety than any other of James's works. Although James himself referred to the book as "a small fantasticality . . . a consistent joke," and a "jeu d'esprit,"[32] critics have seen in it the most elevated themes and have compared the tone and structure to parable, autobiography, and even Greek tragedy.

The critics fall basically into three groups—those who admire the narrator, those who think James's "experiment" was a resounding failure, and those who perceive the satiric comedy of the tone and the unreliability of the obsessed protagonist. Whereas Dorothea Krook and Cynthia Ozick, for instance, praise the novel as an "exhaustive study of the creative imagination, and of the moral and philosophical difficulties inherent in its characteristic operation,"[33] and as "*the* type of the Jamesian vision: all the other novels . . . summarized,"[34] Joseph Warren Beach, F. W. Dupee, and Edmund Wilson condemn it. Beach calls the novel a "technical exercise,"[35] Dupee argues that it is "evidently a self-satire that misfired,"[36] and Wilson goes so far as to claim that "the truth is, I believe, that Henry James was not clear about the book in his own mind."[37]

Oscar Cargill, Wilson Follett, and Walter F. Wright, however, suggest a more reasonable approach. Cargill exclaims, "it is the most extraordinary misinterpretation which associates his [the narrator's] morbid constructions with the creations of artistic fancy."[38] Follett insists that the novel is a "witty extravaganza and one of the most stupendous parodies ever concocted."[39] And Walter F. Wright perceives that "to turn to *The Sacred Fount*

is to . . . enter the realm of ingenious and deeply serious comedy."[40]

To apprehend the focus of *The Sacred Fount* it is necessary
to perceive the kind of comedy which informs it, and the best
approach to the comedy is through the character of the narrator.
The narrator is a recognizable comic type—the impostor or fraud,
the gulled fool, who claims to know much more than he really
does. Society is indifferent to him and he labels Gilbert Long
"stupid" mainly because Long has never made an effort to talk
to him. Long had once met the narrator and "he had always,
in the interval, so failed to know me that I could only hold him
as stupid."[41]

In his boastful egotism, James's narrator resembles both
Christopher Newman and Isabel Archer. But the extreme nature
of his characteristics makes him more closely resemble two other
narrators in earlier fiction—Swift's mad narrator in "A Tale of
a Tub" and Hawthorne's Miles Coverdale in *The Blithedale
Romance.*

In an unsigned review of J. W. De Forest's *Honest John Vane,*
James writes:

> The author's touch, in this and similar cases, has more energy
> than delicacy, and even the energy aims rather wildly. Did
> Mr. De Forest refresh his memory of Swift before writing
> the adventures of John Vane? He would have been reminded
> that though the great master of political satire is often coarse
> and ferocious, he is still oftener keenly ingenious.[42]

James's description of Swift seems a good description of his own
method in *The Sacred Fount,* and we must wonder if James
refreshed *his* memory of Swift before writing this novel. Some
of the minor parallels are so close that they might have been
lifted straight out of "A Tale of a Tub." The narrator of that
fiction observes that "the Philosopher's Way in all Ages has been
by erecting certain *Edifaces in the Air*"[43] in order to enter the
"Palace of Learning."[44] James's narrator, of course, also reflects
on his "perfect palace of thought," (311) his "kingdom of
thought." (255) Swift's mad narrator praises the state in which
"when a Man's Fancy gets astride on his Reason, when Imagination is at Cuffs with the Senses, and common Understanding, as

well as common sense, is Kickt out of Doors; the first Proselyte
he makes, is himself."[45] Similarly, Mrs. Briss criticizes the narrator of *The Sacred Fount* for being "carried away—you're
abused by a fine fancy," (262) and he himself admits to Mrs. Briss
that "Light or darkness, my imagination rides me." (276)

The fancy that gets astride of James's narrator's reason is
his "palace of thought," his theory of sacred founts. The narrator
observes Mrs. Briss's youth and Guy's age, and posits the idea
that in a relationship one member serves as a fountain of youth
for the other. Mrs. Briss sucks youth away from her husband
and thus becomes younger herself. When the narrator sees great
intellectual improvement in Gilbert Long, he assumes on the
basis of his theory that Long, analogously, must have a fount.
He finally decides that May Server is intellectually depleted and
must therefore be Long's fount.

The narrator's whole elaborate palace in the air, his theory
of founts, which operates on a fantastical analogy, is a kind of
"tale of a tub" to divert the reader from the important problem
of the narrator's own inhumanity. There is virtually no proof
of the narrator's theory in the novel. It is formed on a single
case and never documented by any other character. "I don't
myself, you see, perceive it," (62) says Ford Obert, the real and
practicing artist in the novel. And at the close Obert affirms that
May Server "isn't changed." May Server herself repudiates any
relationship with poor Briss, thus refuting a portion of the theory
upon which the narrator notes "its solidity had depended." (144)
And Mrs. Briss, the only character in whom the narrator halfway
confides, finally condemns him as "crazy."

At the close of the novel as his palace of thought crumbles
to the ground like the airy ediface it is, he remarks on his

> frail, but, as I maintain, quite sublime structure, . . . I seem
> myself to see it again, perfect in every part . . . and to feel
> afresh that, weren't the wretched accident of its weak foun-
> dation, it wouldn't have the shadow of a flaw. (311)

This admission certainly reveals far more than the narrator
knows. If only the basic premise weren't all wrong, he seems
to be saying, the theory would be all right. James's comic strategy
here is remarkably similar to Swift's in "A Tale of a Tub" and

"A Modest Proposal." The mad narrator of each posits an absurd theory (men are suits of clothes, let us eat babies, people are vampires). If we admit these absurd postulates, if we accept the faulty premises, then we must accept the conclusions, and with an intrepid logic that obeys probability and necessity, the conclusions can be infinitely extended. But the reader is expected to bring a set of assumptions and values to bear on the stories which reject the initial postulates. It is wrong to eat babies; people are neither clothes nor vampires.

James's narrator, then, is a self-deluded egotist like Swift's mad narrators, and James's method in *The Sacred Fount* approximates Swift's. But James probably owes more to Hawthorne than to Swift for his obsessed protagonist, and *The Blithedale Romance* may be a possible source for the "germ" of *The Sacred Fount*. Both novels are told in the first person, an uncommon practice for both authors. Both heroes are analytic voyeurs searching out the secrets and facts of mysterious relationships. Both narrators are chastised by powerful women, and both are obliquely in love with the pale heroines of the tales. Virtual equations could be drawn between James's narrator and Coverdale, Mrs. Briss and Zenobia, and May Server and Priscilla. Old Moodie's depleted condition in *The Blithedale Romance* resembles Guy Brissenden's, and Zenobia lives on Moodie as Mrs. Briss supposedly lives on Guy. The most important parallel, however, is that of the two narrators.

Late in *The Sacred Fount* the narrator admits "I wasn't there to save *them*. I was there to save my priceless pearl of an inquiry and to harden, to that end, my heart." (296) Coverdale admits the same thing in *The Blithedale Romance,* and in doing so reveals one of Hawthorne's and James's methods of undercutting their fallible protagonists. Coverdale speculates:

> That cold tendency, between instinct and intellect which made me pry with a speculative interest into people's passions and impulses, appeared to have gone far towards unhumanizing my heart. . . .
>
> . . . . . . . . . . . . . . . . . . . . . . . . . . . . . . . . . . . . . . . . . . . . . . . . . . . .
>
> To escape the irksomeness of these meditations, I resumed my post at the window.[46]

Having perceived his own perverse propensities toward
voyeurism, having intelligently and perceptively analyzed his
own distorted values, Coverdale immediately succumbs to them
and returns to his window.

James uses the same method to undercut his narrator. In
a moment of perceptive self-analysis the narrator remarks, "It
comes back to me that the sense thus established of my superior
vision may perfectly have gone a little to my head." (177) And,
having perceived this knowledge, he, like Coverdale, immediately dispenses with it. "*I* alone was magnificently and absurdly
aware—everyone else was benightedly out of it." (177) James's
strategy is, like Hawthorne's, first to reveal the narrator's faults
to the reader and then allow the narrator to perceive them, thus
marshalling some sympathy for him. But the narrator goes on
to justify himself or repeat the fault in such a way as to exaggerate
it.

Zenobia's final harangue at Coverdale is a good, if hyperbolic, description of James's narrator as well:

> "Bigotry; self-conceit; an insolent curiosity; a meddlesome
> temper; a cold-blooded criticism, founded on a shallow
> interpretation of half-perceptions; a monstrous skepticism in
> regard to any conscience or any wisdom, except one's own;
> a most irreverent propensity to thrust Providence aside, and
> substitute one's self in its awful place."[47]

*The Blithedale Romance* thus closes on Coverdale's "defeat";
*The Sacred Fount* closes on its narrator's "defeat" at the hands
of Mrs. Briss:

> "My poor dear, you *are* crazy, and I bid you goodnight!"
> . . . . . . . . . . . . . . . . . . . . . . . . . . . . . . . . . . . . . . . . . . . . . .
> I *should* certainly never again, on the spot, quite hang
> together, even though it wasn't really that I hadn't three
> times her method. What I too fatally lacked was her tone.
> (318, 319)

There are two conflicting "tones" in both books—the comedy
directed at the narrators' self-delusion, and the sinister possibility
of gruesome death. In *The Blithedale Romance* the plot turns
melodramatic, and Zenobia's body is hauled out of the commu-

nity pond. The early comedy directed at Coverdale sours as Hawthorne reveals the terrible circumstances of Zenobia's suicide. But in *The Sacred Fount* the tone of satiric comedy finally prevails. The founts are kept at a distance and are ultimately obscured behind the narrator's distorted personality. And, unlike *The Blithedale Romance, The Sacred Fount* ends with the suggestion of a return to normality as the narrator is routed, and May and Long seem the same as they were before the Newmarch party.

The theme of James's novel, like that of "A Tale of a Tub" and *The Blithedale Romance,* is finally the negative statement of a positive theme. By comically exposing the narrator's egotism, his scientific analysis of fellow human beings, his lovelessness and his mechanical personal relationships, James argues the necessity of their opposites.

But no labels or categories or allegories will suffice to describe the novel adequately. *The Sacred Fount* is a framework on which the reader can hang any number of correct interpretations. All that can finally be said is that the narrator is a comic gull who stands for whatever perversions of mankind—false pride, egotism, lovelessness, obsessiveness—we choose to see in him. He is Henry James's purest example of the self-deceived protagonist, and the action of the book submits him to the thrashings of the comic spirit in the hope of reestablishing right reason and love.

*The Bostonians,* a novel structured on the opposition of two kinds of egotists, offers a final example of James's use of the self-deceived protagonist as hero. Too often critics have damned Olive Chancellor and elevated Basil Ransom, thus failing to appreciate the satiric comedy that James aimed at both characters.

"There are women who are unmarried by accident, and others who are unmarried by option; but Olive Chancellor was unmarried by every implication of her being."[48] So James describes the comically obsessive female lead in *The Bostonians.* Living by a theory which inverts Pope's famous lines to "Whatever is, is wrong," (6) Olive projects a sexlessness, a hatred of men, and a zeal for unqualified reform that renders her humorously mechanical. The consequences of her theory are an annihilation of sex and ultimately of any relationship, in an insane and sterile world. Like the narrator of *The Sacred Fount,* Olive's heart is atrophied. And, like the other Bostonian reformers, she worries eternally about the "general condition" of women while remaining blissfully unaware of the deterioration and growing ugliness of her personal life.

As James informs us, "Olive, thanks to the philosophic cast of her mind, was exceedingly fond of illustrations of laws." (164) And her "laws" are that all women suffer from "the great masculine conspiracy," (173) and all men "must pay." (186) Another of her "laws" prevents her from hating anyone. James wryly reveals that she has "forbidden herself this emotion as directed to individuals." But "she hated men as a class." (10) Olive will thus hate only classes, never individuals. But she ingeniously transforms every individual she encounters into a "class" so that no individual ever exists for her. Later in the novel she tells Verena that she hates Verena's parents, and James remarks, "As we know, she had forbidden herself this emotion as regards individuals; and she flattered herself that she considered the Tarrants as a type, a deplorable one, a class that, with the public at large, discredited the cause of the new truths." (111) Similarly, when Olive meets Mrs. Burrage at an afternoon party, she "saw the type to which Mrs. Burrage belonged—a type into which nature herself had inserted a face turned in the very opposite way from all earnest and improving things." (313) Olive's feminist obsession renders her unmistakably comic as she finally hates everyone, even members of her own sex. She shares in the type of comic villainy of Faulkner's Jason Compson in *The Sound and the Fury* who claims, "I have nothing against jews as an individual . . . . It's just the race."[49]

If few critics fail to appreciate the gross humor with which James invests Olive, many fail to perceive James's similar treatment of Basil Ransom. Lionel Trilling, for example, compares Ransom to the "ideal intelligence of the group of gifted men, who half a century later, were to rise in the South and to muster in its defence all the force of intelligent romantic conservatism . . . he is akin to Yeats, Lawrence, [and] Eliot."[50] To see Ransom as romantic hero and southern gentleman confronted with a crass and hollow Bostonian reform movement is to miss much of James's comedy.

Ransom's mind, like the road behind his rooms, is filled with "immemorial accumulations of stagnant mud." (190) When he submits an article to a prominent magazine, the editor returns it with the comment that "his doctrines were about 300 years behind the age." (193) And Verena, the weak but pure heroine of the novel, tells him that he has "the superstitions of the old bookmen. You ought to have been at one of those really medieval universities." (245) James's initial description of Ransom is capped with comedy. "These things, the eyes especially, with their smouldering fire, might have indicated that he was to be a great American statesman; or, on the other hand, they might simply have proved that he came from Carolina or Alabama." (5)

Like Olive, Basil lives according to certain "laws" which, when adhered to strictly, become that element of the mechanical encrusted on the living that Bergson found to be comic. Basil's "laws" are civility, chivalry, good manners, grace, charm, and male superiority. He has no doubts that "women were essentially inferior to men." (197)

By the end of the novel he is as obsessive in his male chauvinism as Olive is in her feminism, and his goal shifts, as Newman's had before him, from consummation of his love to revenge on his adversary. Near the conclusion he wants, more than anything else, to defeat Olive; "to 'squelch' all that, at a stroke, was the dearest wish of his heart. It would represent to him his own success, it would symbolize his victory. It became a fixed idea with him." (405) With his "fixed idea," Basil manipulates Verena for his own ends, and the "union, so far from brilliant," will produce tears. (464)

Basil wins Verena and celebrates his masculine superiority not because he is the direct representative of Henry James, but because his obsessions and ignorance are not so radical as Olive's. In this clash of egos the more sympathetic character must win. Basil, while far from ideal, does affirm some of the values James held dear. Olive's shortcomings are much more fundamental.

Olive's peculiar earnestness is, according to James, "inharmonious with the scheme of the universe." (304) And like Molière's Alceste, Olive won't lie. Indeed, as Mrs. Luna tells

Ransom several times, "Nobody tells fibs in Boston." (3) Olive "never went through any forms." (8)

Ransom, however, does believe in forms and manners, seeing them as his human responsibility. At the close of the novel, in a scene which, more than any other, reveals the basic difference between the two characters, Basil chooses to protect a weak fellow human being from undue pain. Miss Birdseye is dying and Basil is at the peak of his obsessive anti-feminist feelings, but he compassionately allows Miss Birdseye to believe that he has been converted to the feminist cause. Exercising the forms and manners which enable him to respond humanly to Miss Birdseye, he preserves the necessary illusion which permits her to die happy. "You are not mistaken if you think I desire above all things that your weakness, your generosity, should be protected." Ransom's response is respectful and compassionate. "I shall remember you as an example of what women are capable of." (412) Ransom is able at the crucial moment to go beyond himself and think of others. Olive, on the other hand, thinks only of herself. "I shall see nothing but shame and ruin!" she shrieks and rushes across the room at Miss Birdseye. (412)

In *The Bostonians*, then, James juxtaposes two comic types—Ransom, who resembles Newman and Isabel, and Olive, who resembles the narrator of *The Sacred Fount.* Ransom, the more sympathetic type, is victorious.

### Fools: Villains and Confidants

Many of James's major characters are comic in their self-deception and egotism. But the minor characters are most obviously comic, representing Jamesian caricature and often serving as artistic abstractions of the central consciousness. James writes of his minor characters, "the fixed constitutents [sic] of almost any reproducible action are the fools who minister, at a particular crisis, to the intensity of the free spirit engaged with them."[51] And again, "I think no 'story' is possible without its fools—as most of the fine painters of life, Shakespeare, Cervantes and Balzac, Fielding, Scott, Thackeray, Dickens, George Meredith, George Eliot, Jane Austen, have abundantly felt."[52] James's fools have much in common with those of the comic writers in his catalogue.

One major function of the Jamesian fool is that of villain. Evil exerts a powerful force in most comedy and a writer has a number of methods for meeting it. He can treat it as impotent, as a temporary aberration which ultimately gives way to happy results. Such treatment provides typical romantic comedy like *The Europeans* or *The Reverberator.* The writer can lead his audience to ignore real suffering, averting attention to the laughable. This method characterizes the comedy of humors, and is evident in *The American* and *The Bostonians.* Or a writer can create a character who surmounts evil and suffering by rising superior to it through sheer moral excellence. This method is perhaps most characteristic of James.

Comedy, then, does treat of evil, but only that evil which is not ultimately destructive and which can be overcome by recognition, reformation, or ridicule. The blocking character or fixed constituent in James takes a number of forms in opposition to the hero's wishes. The villain is often an individual or group of individuals who exert much force but become absurd in their fixity. These villains render themselves unconsciously comic through a tenacity to absurd ideals or perversions of behavior. Often such characters become humors or churls, refusers of festivity. As blocks to the hero's happiness they are nonetheless finally unable to destroy goodness or freedom, and in the process of asserting their evil they usually become comically impotent. James undercuts their pretensions by ridiculing them.

Throughout the novels a family unit as representative of society often serves as block to the hero. The Bellegardes, the Proberts, the Farranges, and the Pococks all reflect similar functions, symbolizing a kind of evil which the hero must surmount. The family unit itself becomes a kind of humor figure.

In *The American* the Bellegardes confront Christopher Newman with an ancient and corrupt French nobility and finally succeed in disrupting his marriage. But if the Bellegardes win the plot conflict, they unquestionably lose the personality conflict. If James treats Newman as a comically self-deceived protagonist, Newman does remain sympathetic and "heroic." James's consistent satire of the Bellegardes, however, renders them comically absurd. The description of Madame de Bellegarde, for example,

immediately undercuts her. Newman contrasts the lovely Claire
to her mother:

> Her face was a larger and freer copy, and her mouth in
> especial a happy divergence from that conservative orifice,
> a little pair of lips at once plump and pinched, that looked,
> when closed, as if they could not open wider than to swallow
> a gooseberry or emit an "Oh dear, no!" (117)

Madame de Bellegarde's face is, for Newman, "a thing of parch-
ment, ink, and ruled lines." (117)

The discrepancy between the Bellegardes' superficial
haughty pride and their willingness to compromise themselves
is comic. Newman asks Madame de Bellegarde whether she will
favor his marriage to Claire:

> "Favor it? . . . No!" She said softly.
> "Will you suffer it, then? Will you let it pass?"
> "You don't know what you ask. I am a very proud and
> meddlesome old woman."
> "Well, I am very rich," said Newman.
> . . . "How rich?" (125–26)

The Bellegardes manage to obstruct Newman's marriage, but
they are finally impotent to defeat him. They remain fixed and
comic while he somewhat regains his balance.

The Proberts in *The Reverberator*, like the Bellegardes, oppose the marriage of their child to a "vulgar" American. But the
Proberts, unlike their predecessors, are Europeanized Americans,
only second generation French. Their protestations of tradition
and noble family thus ring like hollow boasts. More obviously
absurd, they are less a force in the novel than are the Bellegardes,
and Gaston marries Francie.

The Farranges of *What Maisie Knew* represent a more grotesque form of villainy. Throughout much of the novel, Ida is
a force of unrelieved monstrosity. Toward the end, at Folkestone,
Ida confronts Maisie with a suddenly sympathetic and affection-
ate tone that fills the air with pathos and possibility. But when
Maisie mentions the Captain, Ida's old lover, Ida drops her
money and her pose back into her purse, gives Maisie nothing,
and storms out, a villain to the end.

Yet if Ida is grotesque and monstrous, those very qualities render her comic. Her billiard playing and physical stature contrast humorously with her moral stature and her inability to be a mother. The Farranges "made up together for instance some twelve feet three of stature. ... The sole flaw in Ida's beauty was a length and reach of arm conducive perhaps to her having so often beaten her ex-husband at billiards."[53]

Grotesque villains that they are, the Farranges finally fail to destroy little Maisie. They are rather comical Dickensian symbols of triviality and decadence which set off Maisie's purity and innocence. In the notebook entry for 1893 James listed the pair as the "Hurters." Later he decided to change the name of "Farrange" probably because for all their "far-ranging" they are unable to hurt anybody but themselves.

All three of the families mentioned above proudly boast to the hero or heroine whom they confront that they have made great sacrifices for him. While in reality they oppose the hero's happiness, they gull themselves into believing that they are martyrs. The Bellegardes insist to Newman that they "are stretching a point; we are doing you a great favor." (146) As spokesman for the Proberts, Mme de Cliché impresses their great sacrifices upon Gaston who "must never, never, never be allowed to forget what we've done for him."[54] And nurse Moddle informs Maisie, "Your papa wishes you never to forget, you know, that he has been dreadfully put about." (XI, 11) In their mock kindness and self-delusions the family units are "humors" and comically absurd.

As the families are a kind of group humor, Mrs. Gereth of *The Spoils of Poynton* is a prime Jamesian example of the individual humor. As James tells us in the preface, she is "the very reverse of a free spirit." "She was not intelligent, was only clever."[55] Like her eighteenth-century predecessors, Mrs. Gereth has wit without judgment or sentiment, and Art without Nature. Being "clever" but not "intelligent," she swells into foppery and madness as do the hypocrites and pedants of Fielding and Pope. In Mrs. Gereth James created a complex humor who sometimes deviates into sense and true suffering. But she remains predominantly ridiculous.

Mrs. Gereth's "ruling passion" which renders her inhuman

and mechanical is her love for her "things." She thinks more of her house than of her son. Her obsession derives from a sensibility so refined that the flowers on her wallpaper can keep her awake. She suspects that "such a special sensibility as her own could have been inflicted on a woman only as a source of anguish."[56] Fleda sees the truth of Mrs. Gereth's character when she observes that Mrs. Gereth's "ruling passion had in a manner despoiled her of her humanity." (X, 37) And James ridicules her obsession fondly when he compares her to "Don Quixote tilting at a windmill." (X, 31) Fulfilling the role of a clown, Mrs. Gereth is mock-heroic, humorous, and sad, and doomed to defeat.

In several novels evil takes the form of the "churl," or refuser of festivity, and Mr. Brand in *The Europeans* and Waymarsh in *The Ambassadors* belong to this type. Mr. Brand is obviously the traditional refuser of festivity. Brand, who "walked with a joyless, meditative tread, and his eyes were bent upon the ground,"[57] is the loveless, strict, and narrow Calvinist with an overriding sense of duty, and a masochistic distrust of pleasure. He fears art and imagination, and his character reveals the dangers inherent in American innocence. When Felix comes upon the scene Mr. Brand is in the process of teaching Gertrude how to stifle her "peculiarities," that is, her joy of life, her creative sensibility, and her hatred of narrowness and solemn piety. Mr. Brand, truly believing that he is helping Gertrude by destroying her individuality, will "brand" her. Brand is a fixed character, a churl, but he is nevertheless converted by Felix who manages to redirect Brand's energy. In the end, unable to impose himself negatively, Brand imposes himself positively by marrying Felix and Gertrude.

> Charlotte thought he looked very grand; and it is incontestable that Mr. Brand felt very grand. This, in fact, was the grandest moment of his life. (266)

But James renders Brand faintly absurd even in triumph through the repetition of the word "grand" which rhymes mockingly with the "villain's" emblematic name.

Waymarsh is another example of the refuser of festivity. James's initial description of Waymarsh represents him as "joyless" and "almost wilfully uncomfortable."[58] He is the "voice of Milrose" (XXI, 28) who will "sit through the ordeal of Europe" as one would sit through a particularly unpleasant train ride. (XXI, 26) Throughout the novel Waymarsh is an anti-Strether, serving at times almost as Strether's American conscience, condemning Strether's enjoyment of the monster, Europe. "Dear dyspeptic Waymarsh" is Strether's "splendid encumbrance." (XXI, 10, 177)

Waymarsh, who has seen two plays and a circus in Europe, feels that he has seen enough. He tells Strether, "such a country as this ain't my *kind* of country anyway. There ain't a country I've seen over here that *does* seem my kind." (XXI, 29) But despite all his morbid thrashing about, and despite his moral criticism of Strether's liberality and amusement, Waymarsh finally and embarrassedly succumbs to the influence of Europe.

> Waymarsh was having a good time—this was the truth that was embarrassing for him, and he was having it then and there, he was having it in Europe, he was having it under the very protection of circumstances of which he didn't in the least approve. (XXII, 190)

Strether counsels Waymarsh, as he had Little Bilham, to "*Let* yourself, on the contrary, go—in all agreeable directions. These are precious hours—at our age they mayn't recur." (XXII, 194) Waymarsh's protest is weak. "It was the conscience of Milrose in the very voice of Milrose, but, oh it was feeble and flat! . . . it lacked its old intensity; nothing of it remained." (XXII, 194) Like Brand, Waymarsh is converted.

The families, the humors, and the churls all represent forces of a kind of evil in the novels, an evil which is ultimately impotent to destroy good. One of James's strategies, as we have seen, is to ridicule the evil character by turning him into a boastful and self-deluded egotist. James applied this technique to his most completely evil character, Gilbert Osmond.

Osmond's immediate source in literature is probably George Eliot's Henleigh Grandcourt or Casaubon. His predecessor in James's own fiction is perhaps the early and melodramatic villain of *Watch and Ward,* George Fenton. But Osmond is also the traditional type whose obsession renders him ridiculous. He is humorless, as Isabel remarks. "She even wondered if his sense of fun, or of the funny—which would be his sense of humour, wouldn't it?—were by chance defective." (IV, 138) And Leon Edel suggests that Osmond is what James "might, under some circumstances, have become. He is what Henry could be on occasion when snobbery prevailed over humanity, and arrogance and egotism over his urbanity and his benign view of the human comedy."[59]

James's strategy is to present Osmond first obliquely through Ralph and Isabel and then to force him to unmask himself. Osmond's evil is more solemnly terrifying when it is described obliquely and when, at the beginning of our acquaintance with the villain, the evil is mostly a pervasive undertone of hostility.

Ralph observes that Osmond "has a great dread of vulgarity; that's his special line; he hasn't any other." (III, 358) And Isabel sees that Os.nond had "consulted his taste in everything—his taste alone perhaps." (III, 377) Everyone in the novel but Isabel has serious reservations about his character. The stage is thus set for real and destructive evil.

As the novel proceeds, however, Osmond's malevolence becomes so exaggerated as to be grotesquely absurd and finally almost painfully humorous. He admits that he wants to be the Emperor of Russia, the Sultan of Turkey, and the Pope of Rome. And if his desires are comic, his social activity is more so. When Isabel abides by his objection to Henrietta Stackpole and refrains from inviting her to dinner, Osmond

> would have liked her to urge a little the cause of her friend, insist a little upon his receiving her, so that he might appear to suffer tor good manners' sake. . . . The right thing would have been that Miss Stackpole should come to dine at Palazzo Roccanera once or twice, so that (in spite of his superficial civility, always so great) she might judge for herself how little pleasure it gave him. (IV, 286)

And when Isabel wearies of her social Thursdays, Osmond "still held [to them] for the sake not so much of inviting people as of not inviting them." (IV, 292)

Osmond's pettiness extends to his persecution complex, and his psychotic nature becomes so exaggerated that it is simply melodramatic. Of Ralph he tells Isabel, "That's why you like

him—because he hates me." (IV, 355) And when Isabel wants
to go to England to see the dying Ralph, Osmond asserts,

> "Let it be clear. If you leave Rome today it will be a
> piece of the most deliberate, the most calculated, opposi-
> tion."
> "How can you call it calculated? I received my aunt's
> telegram but three minutes ago."
> "You calculate rapidly; it's a great accomplishment."
> (IV, 354)

We hate Osmond but laugh at him for his obsessiveness and
lapses of logic. More convincingly evil when he is quietly malevolent, Osmond loses power when he becomes absurd and
deranged. Osmond's exaggerated psychosis led Leo B. Levy to
conclude that he displays "the didactic bias of the novel's melodrama."[60] And melodrama, according to Levy, is a kind of mock
tragedy which demonstrates "the ultimate goodness of man" and
"the triumph of good over evil."[61]

As Wylie Sypher notes, "suffering in comedy takes the form
of humiliation, disappointment, or chagrin, instead of death."[62]
Christopher Newman, Fleda Vetch, Isabel Archer, and the others
are humiliated and disappointed by the villains that confront
them, but they survive. In rendering evil characters comically
absurd, James asserts the power of good over evil.

A second major function of the Jamesian fool is that of
reflector, either representing a simplified version of the major
character or contrasting comically with him. Bergson notes that
"above all, a tragic poet will never think of grouping around
the chief character in his play secondary characters to serve as
simplified copies, so to speak, of the former."[63] Thus confidantes
like Henrietta Stackpole and Fanny Assingham are inherently
comic.

The Jamesian confidant is often a rather fascinating character in his own right, but more often than not James uses the
confidant mainly as a device for clarifying the plot and revealing
the character of the protagonist. In the preface to *The Portrait
of a Lady*, James himself defines the confidant as

> but wheels to the coach; neither belongs to the body of that
> vehicle, or is for a moment accommodated with a seat in-

side. . . . Maria Gostrey and Miss Stackpole then are cases,
each, of the light *ficelle*, not of the true agent; they may run
beside the coach "for all they are worth," they may cling
to it till they are out of breath . . . but neither, all the while,
so much as gets her foot on the step.[64]

From James s comments it seems evident that the confidants
are not to be confused with the protagonists, and we should not
be surprised or disappointed when they fail to achieve personal
or social success. Instead, they exist for the reader, drawing out
or blurting out facts, serving as simplified copies of the hero
and his plight, and predicting the future, while providing a kind
of running commentary on the novel.

R. P. Blackmur perceptively defines the confidante's special
role:

> Generally speaking, the confidante is stupid, or has the kind
> of brightness that goes with gossip, cunning, and malice. . . .
> each confidante has a kind of bottom or residual stupidity
> and each is everlastingly given to gossip; but the gossip has
> a creative purpose—to add substance to the story—and the
> stupidity is there to give slowness and weight and alternative
> forms to the perceptions and responses which they create.[65]

As representatives of a general and universal human "stupidity"
or limitation, certain Jamesian confidants, like the villains already described, fall into two basic categories; the churl or
refuser of festivity is evident in Henrietta Stackpole and Caspar
Goodwood, and the buffoon or humor figure is evident in pre-
tenders to social status like Delia Dosson, Mrs. Wix, and Mrs.
Tristram. Fanny and Bob Assingham are a kind of culmination
and parody of the confidant convention.

Isabel Archer regards Henrietta Stackpole as a "model" for
herself (III, 70) and Henrietta acts in the novel as Isabel's
conscience, as a female Mr. Brand or Waymarsh. Like Waymarsh
she deprecates everything European. Henrietta argues to Ralph
that Caspar's presence will call back Isabel's thoughts. When
Ralph asks, "Call them back—from where?" Henrietta confidently replies, "From foreign parts and other unnatural places."
(III, 173) Nothing in Europe can match the splendor of America.

Henrietta "was obliged in candour to declare that Michael An-
gelo's dome suffered by comparison with that of the Capitol at
Washington." (III, 425) And yet, after all her smug and fatuous
blathering about the virtues of America, the despicable nature
of expatriates, and the horrors of Europe, Henrietta marries the
English Bantling and settles in his country. Like Waymarsh, she
is converted.

Throughout the novel Henrietta provides undiminished
comedy. At the outset James wittily relates her character to her
career. "She was as crisp and new and comprehensive as a first
issue before the folding. From top to toe she had probably no
misprint." (III, 117) And she sees *herself* as an aspect of the
mechanical encrusted upon the living. She insists, "I consider
that my conversation refers only to the moment, like the morning
papers." (IV, 285) Like Falstaff, she "prompted mirth" in Ralph,
(III, 122) and by the end of the novel he is able to claim that
"he had never doubted for a moment that she was an excellent
fellow." (IV, 295)

Henrietta aligns herself with Caspar Goodwood who represents an exaggeration of the churl elements present in Henrietta,
and who is a good deal like Mr. Brand. Like Brand, he hopes
to marry the heroine and manfully protect her from her own
individuality. Like Brand, he faces life with a "characteristic
grimness." (III, 230) He "had a habit of looking straight in front
of him, as if he proposed to take in but one object at a time."
(IV, 288) For Isabel, Goodwood represents oppression, limitation, and coercion on the plain physical level. He possesses "an
energy—and she had already felt it as a power—it was a matter
of the spirit that sat in his clear-burning eyes like some tireless
watcher at a window." (III, 162) The bathetic simile does not
obscure Isabel's sense of the danger Caspar poses to her. But
in the end the converted Henrietta attempts to convert Goodwood
as well. "Just you wait," she tells him. (IV, 437)

Henrietta Stackpole and Caspar Goodwood are the confidants who represent the churl or refuser of festivity corre-
sponding to the same type among the villains. The confidantes
who correspond to the humor villains, like the families and Mrs.
Gereth, are Delia Dosson, Mrs. Wix, and Mrs. Tristram.

Delia is the perpetual busybody who, at the outset of *The Reverberator,* "seemed to be doing nothing as hard as she could." (XIII, 4) A pretender to social status, Delia reveals her false pride and affectation. Elated at the prospect of forming a liason with the "aristocratic" Proberts through the marriage of her sister Francie to Gaston, Delia awkwardly tries to adopt a dignified manner herself. Her efforts to appear aristocratic evince only scorn from the French family, and the discrepancy between her aspirations and her capabilities is humorous. In the novel she serves as a parody of the pretensions of the more capable Proberts.

Mrs. Wix is a more fully developed comic humor, obsessed with a surface moralism and possessing faulty vision. She is obviously a "frump" and her "straighteners" are inadequate to clear up her vision or straighten Maisie's "morals." Like Delia Dosson, she is outside the social hierarchy and aspires futilely to enter it. As the meddling confidante, she wants control over a situation which she can but imperfectly understand. Her poverty, ignorance, and moral righteousness contrast comically with her strutting assurance, and she fails to appreciate her own ridiculousness. She is the minor confidante running along behind the coach and trying to play the role of rival woman to Mrs. Beale. Her best attribute, and the one which ultimately makes her a sympathetic figure and something more than a mere Dickensian caricature, is her love for Maisie. "What Maisie felt was that she had been, with passion and anguish, a mother, and that this was something Miss Overmore was not, something (strangely, confusingly) that mama was even less." (XI, 24)

Mrs. Wix's most absurd moment occurs midway in the novel when she conceives the plan to run away with the handsome Sir Claude. Like Fanny Assingham, she carefully figures out all the details.

> "You stay here with Maisie, with the carriage and the larks and the luxury; then I'll return to you and we'll go off together—we'll live together without a cloud. Take me, take me. . . . Here I am, here I am!" she spread herself into an exhibition that, combined with her intensity and her decorations, appeared to suggest her for strange offices and devo-

tions, for ridiculous replacements and substitutions. (XI, 262–63)

Mrs. Wix is certainly not the moral standard for the novel as is sometimes claimed. Her speech and action is always slightly preposterous and she is too high-pitched, narrow, and unsophisticated to embody James's sense of moral vision. She is a Mrs. Micawber, as Mrs. Beale notes, who attains a kind of blundering heroism.

Like Mrs. Wix, Mrs. Tristram of *The American* is a pretender after social success. She is a clever woman oppressed by an unhappy marriage, and she is full of frustration, zeal, and un-asked-for advice. Her obsessiveness recalls Mrs. Wix, and her plotting of Newman's marriage foreshadows Fanny Assingham's manipulations in *The Golden Bowl.* As in *The Golden Bowl*, Mrs. Tristram's pretensions are undercut by her dull cynical husband Tom, one of a long line of Jamesian husbands. Whenever Mrs. Tristram becomes too much the grande dame of affairs, Tom mediates with his simple and humorous reality to balance her.

It is probably from the example of the Tristrams that James drew his most complex set of confidants, the Assinghams. Whereas the convention is barely suggested in *The American,* Fanny and Bob Assingham become an integral part of the action of *The Golden Bowl.* And in their private "conversations" they parody the confidants who had preceded them. Like Maria Gostrey, Fanny is clairvoyant; like Mrs. Tristram, she finds a possible wife for the hero; and like Mrs. Wix, she falls absurdly in love with the leading man.

From the outset, in her desire to be a part of the action, indeed even to direct the action, Fanny is ineffective. Her common birth and involuted logic contrast comically with her vision of herself as "a creature formed by hammocks and divans, fed upon sherbets and waited upon by slaves."[66] She is the distressingly ordinary middle-aged wife trying to play the part of far eastern harem mistress. In her desire to be wise and perceptive she is more often merely blundering and confused. Her ultimate pretension is her desire to accept the credit for the unhappy marriages though the blame is not at all hers. By admitting responsibility, she seems to feel, she will be a part of the whole affair.

At the outset Fanny is seemingly the powerful confidante of the Prince, advising him and providing him with a moral sense. As the action progresses she loses her status to Charlotte and is thrown upon the expediency of confiding in her husband. When Fanny decides "heroically" to lie for the Prince and Charlotte, to preserve the marriages, she has an ulterior motive. While she convinces herself that she is acting only in good faith, the reader perceives that her lie preserves her own integrity as well.

Fanny's role in the novel is less that of a force of clarification than a force of incremental complication. Of complications she boasts, "I don't fear them—I really like them. They're quite my element." (XXIII, 43) They are indeed so much her "element" that even the simplest facts become complex for her.

Throughout the novel as Fanny struggles to complicate an already complicated situation and to foresee ends that she is incapable of understanding, Bob Assingham undercuts her with his impervious good humor and earthy reality. As James relates, Bob is "the simplest, the sanest, the most obliging of men." (XXIII, 64) He serves, in a way, as a confidant to the confidante, the doubling of confidants thus adding to the parody of the convention.

James describes the two together as "Darby and Joan," and when Fanny is "the immemorially speechless Sphinx about at last to become articulate," the Colonel is "not unlike, on his side, some old pilgrim of the desert camping at the foot of that monument." (XXIII, 364–65) Their conversation is "divergent discussion, that intercourse by misunderstanding." (XXIII, 365)

Reduced to virtual unimportance by the Prince and Charlotte, Fanny relies on her husband to give her a sense of superiority. "You think of nothing that I haven't a thousand times thought of, and . . . I think of everything that you never will." (XXIII, 73) Yet, despite all her efforts to demean Bob by scorning him and pretending that he isn't even there, Bob is often more perceptive than Fanny. "All their case wants . . . is that you should leave it well alone." (XXIII, 75)

Fanny, however, ignores Bob's suggestions, preferring to complicate the case as· much as possible.

"Of which case," she asked, "are you speaking?"

He smoked a minute: then with a groan. "Lord, are there so many?"

"There's Maggie's and the Prince's, and there's the Prince's and Charlotte's."

"Oh yes, and then," the Colonel scoffed, "there's Charlotte's and the Prince's."

"There's Maggie's and Charlotte's," she went on—"and there's Maggie's and mine. . . . In short, you see, there are plenty." (XXIII, 75)

And later in the book Fanny continues to talk as if to herself. When Bob offers another suggestion James explains:

> Her silence seemed to characterize this statement as superficial, and her thoughts, as always in her husband's company, pursued an independent course. He made her, when they were together, talk, but as if for some other person; who was in fact for the most part herself. Yet she addressed herself with him as she could never have done without him. (XXIII, 278)

While Fanny meditates, unheedful of Bob, he functions as a figure in the stage shadows directing humorous asides at the audience. When Fanny admits that she might begin to see more in Maggie than she had seen before, Bob jibes, "You certainly will if you can." (XXIII, 280)

Fanny, then, is the confidante pushed to comic extreme, and her conversation with Bob is a virtual parody of previous confidantes' exchanges with their heroes. She is a caricature of the Jamesian clairvoyant, and the absurdity of her lucidity is always pointed up by the placid common sense of her slow but realistic husband.

The Assinghams provide a running commentary on *The Golden Bowl* as Maria Gostrey and Strether do on *The Ambassadors*. But Maria's questions and suggestions serve to clarify Strether's thoughts and reveal information which could be gotten in no other way, while Fanny serves to muddle up the situation, providing misinformation that could be gotten in no other way. Fanny is Maggie's anti-self, an inverse reflection of the artist-heroine who is able in the end to direct the plot toward her own happiness.

Many of James's minor characters are clearly "bedimmed and befooled and bewildered," and although the major characters are never as flatly comic as the "fools" who surround them, Christopher Newman, Isabel Archer, Basil Ransom, Olive Chancellor, and the narrator of *The Sacred Fount* all share an egotism which relates them to the tradition of the self-deceived protagonist. Believing themselves to be superior, they are nevertheless "connected intimately" with the "general human exposure." Faulty vision is a recurring theme of Henry James's art.

# III

# The Jamesian Character

*"fine intensification and wide enlargement"*

There is, of course, a wide range of perception in James's characters. Some remain more befooled than others; some are seemingly not befooled at all. James writes, "I never see the *leading* interest of any human hazard but in a consciousness . . . subject to fine intensification and wide enlargement."[1] A number of James's major and minor characters seem to possess a special sensibility which prevents them from acting as blindly as the fools.

If the Jamesian comic hero is often a gull or partially a gull, he also has the potential to be a creator or a "wit." As F. O. Matthiessen notes, James had "the ability to endow some of his characters with such vitality that they seem to take the plot into their own hands, or rather, to continue to live beyond its exigencies."[2] In the pursuit of happiness or the integration of society, the James character employs a conscious effort to mold the plot around himself, to determine a society which is to his liking.

## Major Characters

Christopher Newman remains unsuccessful in his attempts to write his own plot; the co-hero of the sister novel, *The Europeans*, succeeds. Felix Young, unlike Newman, deprecates himself before his American cousins. He claims he is only a "good natured featherhead," "a Bohemian," "an adventurer." (106) And he confides to Gertrude that in Bohemia he would have passed for a gentleman. Felix never fools himself or fails to appreciate his own latent comicality.

In his exuberant zest for life and experience, Felix is both literally and figuratively an artist. Though he characteristically depreciates his actual art work, he molds the entire plot toward a sensible and harmonious conclusion. Seeing life with a painter's eye, he views his situation as "a large sheet of clean, fine-grained drawing-paper, all ready to be washed over with effective splashes of water-colour." (83) And he finds "the whole affair . . . very amusing. I must make a sketch of it." (84) The subtitle of *The Europeans* is *A Sketch* and we must wonder if it is not Felix's work. When Felix offers to paint morbid Mr. Wentworth's portrait, he wittily prophesies, "I won't promise . . . not to work your head into something!" (98) "I think I should make a very fine thing of it." (97) Much of the novel is concerned with just what Felix will work Mr. Wentworth's and the other characters' heads into.

Like Gabriel Nash, Felix is the prime mover of the plot. In the course of the novel he manages to pair Charlotte and Mr. Brand while curing Clifford's alcoholism by thrusting him upon Eugenia. Like Prospero, he controls the plot, and, like the handsome prince of the fairy tale, he "awakens" Gertrude to the creative possibilities of love. Early in the novel, as Felix and Eugenia gaze at their fire, Eugenia comments that it is hideous. But for Felix "the crimson embers, are extremely picturesque. They are like a fire in an alchemist's laboratory." (6) Felix is the alchemist who will transform the dross metal of the Wentworths to gold.

Throughout the novel Felix sets the tone and represents the value center of the work. Talking with Gertrude, he says:

> "I don't think it's what one does or one doesn't do that promotes enjoyment. . . . It is the general way of looking at life."
> "They look at it as a discipline. . . ."
> "Well, that's very good. But there is another way," added Felix, smiling. "To look at it as an opportunity." (105)

And, as James intrudes to point out, "Felix extracted entertainment from all things, and all his faculties— his imagination, his intelligence, his affections, his senses—had a hand in the game." (81) Like Nash, he affirms "I mean to live long."

Even Eugenia, who refuses to enjoy very much in the novel, and, like the refuser of festivity in Old Comedy must be expelled at the close, finally appreciates Felix. "Sometimes she had said to herself that his happy temper, his eternal gaiety, was an affectation, a pose; but she was vaguely conscious that during the present summer he had been a highly successful comedian." (209)

As a witty self-deprecator, Felix takes the form of an almost dionysiac figure and revels in the joy of living. His type represented for James an ideal possibility of "fine intensification and wide enlargement," and James's pervasive concern to provide realism prevented him from allowing many characters to attain the ideality of Felix. But heroines like Maisie Farrange and Nanda Brookenham, and confidants like Ralph Touchett and Maria Gostrey, all share certain qualities with Felix. Demeaning themselves before the less perceptive members of society, they subtly reveal their true nature to the more perceptive.

In *What Maisie Knew* the child-heroine is faced with a whole society of boastful antagonists and self-seekers. No one in the book (except the shadowy relative at the outset and perhaps Sir Claude at the close) sees any more in Maisie than an opportunity to further his own ends. Maisie becomes a little "shuttlecock" tossed back and forth between warring parents and serving as a kind of ammunition for them. Maisie, finding the situation to be quite natural since she has never known anything else, solemnly carries messages back and forth. "You're a nasty horrid pig!" the six-year-old girl tells Ida from Beale. (XI, 13)

If Ida and Beale use Maisie to carry on their mutual hatred, Miss Overmore (later Mrs. Beale) and Sir Claude use her to carry on their illicit relationship. For Miss Overmore, Maisie is "a little duenna." Even faithful old Mrs. Wix uses Maisie as a substitute for her poor dead little Clara Matilda and as bait to attract Sir Claude. In the course of the novel Maisie is forced into a position where everyone relies on her for something. She becomes the bond between Beale and Ida, Claude and Mrs. Beale, and Claude and Mrs. Wix.

As James affirms in his preface, Maisie is "the extraordinary 'ironic centre'" of the novel.[3] Her response to the problems thrust

upon her by self-seeking fools is the response of more sophisticated characters like Felix Young and Gabriel Nash. Early in
the novel Maisie becomes obliquely aware of danger. "A new
remedy arose to meet it, the idea of an inner self or, in other
words, of concealment." (XI, 15) Her pose is like that of the
self-deprecator who knows a great deal but claims to know
nothing. Maisie's parents accordingly proclaim her "stupid,"
"shockingly dull." (XI, 15) When Ida, in a moment of characteristic anger, shouts at Maisie, "and you had better indeed for
the future, miss, learn to keep your thoughts to yourself," James
comments, "This was exactly what Maisie had already learned."
(XI, 19)

Later Maisie practices the same method on both Sir Claude
and Mrs. Wix. Claude interrogates Maisie about the Captain and
she plays dumb. James confides, "It was of the essence of her
method not to be silly by halves." (XI, 156) "It brought again
the sweet sense of success." (XI, 157) And when Mrs. Wix
constantly questions Maisie about her "moral sense" Maisie
cleverly lies to keep Mrs. Wix happy. Mrs. Wix asks Maisie what
she would do if she knew that Mrs. Beale were unkind to Sir
Claude, and Maisie answers, "'I'd *kill* her!' That at least, she
hoped as she looked away, would guarantee her moral sense."
(XI, 288) Maisie affects a manner with Mrs. Wix, for Maisie's
intuitive moral sense has little in common with Mrs. Wix's more
conventional system of morality. The result of this pose on
Maisie's part is a multiplicity of vision unavailable to the other
more fixed characters. "Nothing was less new to Maisie than the
art of not thinkingly singly." (XI, 222-23)

The question most often raised about this novel is the one
James raised in his title: what does Maisie know? An initial
answer is that Maisie's knowledge consists first and foremost of
her ironic pose, her ability to maintain a multiple point of view.
Like Felix Young, Maisie is destined to be a kind of artist.
Despite her extreme youth, her final actions are the actions of
an artist of life, and her final "knowledge," while largely unconscious and intuitive, exceeds that of any other character in the
book.

In her movement toward a "knowledge" which will elevate
her morally above the other characters in the novel, Maisie is

exposed to more ugliness and hypocrisy than any other Jamesian character. As James comments, she was "morally at home in atmospheres it would be appalling to analyze." (XI, 205) This exposure, however, develops in Maisie a wonderful sense of analogy. After seeing Ida in the park with her Captain, Maisie is confronted by Beale and his Countess. Maisie immediately perceives that "Papa's Captain—yes—was the Countess." (XI, 193) Her innocent perception of such analogies enables her to control her experience and survive in the face of perversity. At the close James intrudes to affirm that Maisie has developed within her "something still deeper than a moral sense." And, whatever it is, Sir Claude exclaims that "it's exquisite, it's sacred." (XI, 354)

Although Maisie is too young and naive fully to understand the "exquisite" quality which runs deeper in her than a moral sense, it seems obvious that the quality is compassion. Earlier in the novel when Maisie sees the Captain and Ida, she feels a renewed love for her mother through the kindly man. "Something strange and deep and pitying surged up within her." With the strange feeling surging in her, Maisie questions the Captain about his motives with Ida. In exasperation the Captain shouts, "Of *course* I love her, damn it, you know!" (XI, 153) And Maisie confesses, "So do *I* then," and bursts into tears. Finally she encourages the Captain, "Then don't do it only for just a little. . . . Like all the others." (XI, 155)

Maisie's natural capacity for love, combined with her ability to practice a manner, enables her artfully to let her father and mother off as easily as possible. When Beale asks her to go to America with him and the Countess, Maisie's first response is to declare, "Dear papa, I'll go with you anywhere." (XI, 184) But "then she understood as well as if he had spoken it that what he wanted, hang it, was that she should let him off with all the honours—with all the appearance of virtue and sacrifice on his side." (XI, 187)

Maisie's "knowledge" involves both her compassionate nature and her ability to adopt a manner. Her affirmation is that of essential human goodness, and her cultivated stupidity is positive. With her intuitive morality of love she is nevertheless victim to the traditional fate of the comic protagonist. Northrop Frye asserts:

It is more usual, however, for the artist to present an ironic deadlock in which the hero is regarded as a fool or worse by the fictional society, and yet impresses the real audience as having something more valuable than his society has.[4]

Maisie's case is surely the most difficult that James ever solved by soliciting our credulity and compassion through comedy. The reader must smile at a tiny child acting diplomatically and artistically with love, to "square" all the older characters in her fictional world. But incredible as it may seem, Maisie remains free, and neither heredity nor environment can cripple her. It is a triumph for the comic spirit.

In her childish way Maisie manages to be an artist of life, and actually succeeds in retaining a sense of love when little exists in the society around her. Maisie's extreme youth, however, and her incredibly crass surroundings prevent her from triumphing in any way other than remaining "free." But the more mature Nanda Brookenham, faced with a similar problem in *The Awkward Age*, is more pragmatically successful.

In both novels a precocious young girl in a decadent but superficially brilliant society develops a sense of love and moral strength. But while Maisie, in her knowledge, is unable to re-create or renew the society, Nanda, in her knowledge, can ensure the continuity of the old society in new form. In one sense Nanda's problem is less complex, for she is older and has a moral norm to turn to in Longdon, whereas little Maisie has only a comic parody of a moral norm in Mrs. Wix.

Nanda, like Maisie, deprecates herself while elevating others. Throughout the novel she constantly insists that she herself is a poor, meager thing but little Aggie, the Duchess's daughter, is beautiful and "magnificent." Despite Nanda's modest protestations, the reader sees the effect of French versus English methods of child rearing in the two young women. Aggie and Nanda are examples of what James termed "fixed" and "free" characters. Aggie, raised in the French system, is shielded from knowledge and knows nothing of the salon or the world of society. Nanda, reared in the more open English system, knows "everything." Thus Aggie is a potential fool and Nanda a potential wit.

By the end of the novel, realizing that Van has no intention of marrying her, Nanda accepts her role as artist and takes control of the plot. In the concluding chapter, entitled "Nanda," the young heroine schedules meetings with the three major male characters—Van, Mitchy, and Longdon. Her composure and tact with each of these characters ensures the "happy" ending that marks many romantic comedies, while revealing at the same time the sense of loss that characterizes many comedies of manners.

Van is her first visitor. He nervously flits about the room talking voluminous trifles, commenting on the flowers and books, the furniture and the view. Recognizing his discomfort, Nanda sets Van at ease by directing the conversation away from his relationship to herself. She asks Van not to give up Mrs. Brook, and Van, relieved that he need not justify his previous inattention to Nanda, promises that "one simply *can't* if one would, give your mother up."[5] Realizing that Van's true place is with Mrs. Brook, Nanda ensures their continued relationship by giving Van the office of being loyal to her.

When Mitchy arrives after Van has left, Nanda confides to him that Van "was awfully beautiful and kind" (IX, 514) although in truth Nanda has been beautiful and kind and Van merely weak. Nanda enjoins Mitchy, too, to be faithful to Mrs. Brook.

When Nanda finally meets Longdon and agrees to accompany him into the country as his adopted daughter, she implies a conscious adoption of his values. Having successfully ensured the reestablishment of Mrs. Brook's salon, she retires with the character who represents the value center of the book. But even at the close James suggests that Nanda will not retire completely from the society herself. Rather, having created it, she will remain a positive force within it.

Because she fails to marry Van, Nanda has been called tragic by a number of critics. But a heroine who retains her freedom and moral awareness and succeeds in recreating a society can hardly be tragic. Nanda is James's vigorous affirmation of the moral superiority of the exposed innocent, a moral superiority symbolized by self-deprecation and an ability to renew society creatively.

## Wise Fools: Confidants and Bad Heroines

While few of James's protagonists approach the ideality of a
Nanda or a Felix, many of the important secondary characters
are obviously subject to "fine intensification and wide enlargement." When James casts a humorous character like Christopher
Newman in the leading role of a novel he usually casts a witty
and perceptive character in a secondary role to question the
hero's actions and values and lead him toward increased self-
knowledge. Thus Newman is paired with Valentin, Isabel with
Ralph, the narrator of *The Sacred Fount* with Mrs. Briss, and
Roderick Hudson with Rowland Mallett.

   If a number of Jamesian confidants remain "fools" in their
fixity and wrongheadedness, many of the minor characters seem
more intelligent than the protagonists. Characters like Gabriel
Nash, Maria Gostrey, Ralph Touchett, and Valentin de Bellegarde are for the most part clever, intelligent, and disengaged
from the major action, and their comments provide a perspective
on the other characters. These "wise fools" represent an ideal
standard by which the protagonists are measured, a standard of
responsible freedom and moral and aesthetic consciousness un-
dimmed by any undue solemnity. They face life with the spirit
of high comedy.

   As I noted in the introduction, Gabriel Nash is a supreme
representative of this type of character, and his type recurs
throughout the canon. In *The Awkward Age*, Mitchy fills the role,
assuming the guise almost of a clown. His clothes are a chaos
of color, a modern version of motley, and he pretends to be easily
fooled with the hope of not being fooled at all. He deprecates
his physical appearance (which is less than beautiful) but his
moral beauty shines through. And even at the end when he is
cuckolded by Petherton in true Restoration fashion, he manages
to laugh and veil his grief. Mitchy, in his role as confidant,
sets an example for Nanda while providing a running comic
commentary on the social world of Mrs. Brookenham's salon.

   Maria Gostrey is the perceptive confidante of *The Ambassadors*. At the outset, when Strether sighs to her that "Woollett
isn't sure it ought to enjoy," (XXI, 16) Maria offers to teach him
the value of amusement. "I'm a general guide—to 'Europe,' don't

you know? I wait for people—I put them through." (XXI, 18) "Europe" in quotation marks in this novel stands for growth, perception, and amusement. It is only with Maria's help that Strether grows to final self-awareness.

Maria Gostrey shares with the Assinghams a delight in gossip and complication. But unlike the Assinghams, she, in her own right, combines integrity with an appreciative sense of adventure. She, like Ralph, lives imaginatively in others and sees into the center of things to become a part of them. Her powers are ultimately opposite those of the Assinghams because her questions lead to clarity of vision and creative possibility. She is, perhaps, the most complex of James's confidants, and she really transcends the type through her incredible clairvoyance and human involvement.

Valentin de Bellegarde, in *The American*, more obviously fits the type. Like Gabriel Nash and Felix Young, Valentin deprecates himself. "I'm a good deal of a donkey," he insists. And he positively cultivates a comic attitude toward life. In the original edition of the novel "M. de Bellegarde's face, it seemed to Newman, expressed a sense of lively entertainment." (82) In the revision for the New York Edition, James clarifies that Valentin's face expressed "not less than usual a sense of the inherent comedy of things."[6] Newman is never quite able to understand this comedy, and he must continually ask himself, "What the devil is he laughing at now?" (82) Irritated that he fails to share in the jokes, Newman accuses Valentin of laughing at life. "Certainly I am a great laugher," Valentin responds, "and it is better to laugh too much than too little." (83) When Newman confronts Valentin with the idea of Newman's marrying Claire, Valentin says he is "charmed." "I can't stand on my head, but I can applaud a clever acrobat." (169) Valentin sums up his role as comic confidant in terms that could apply to Ralph Touchett, Gabriel Nash, or Felix Young. "In the good old times . . . marquises and counts used to have their appointed fools and jesters, to crack jokes for them. Nowadays we see a great strapping democrat keeping a count about him to play the fool." (139–40)

Ralph Touchett, in *The Portrait of a Lady*, is another wise fool or comic confidant. Some readers might question how a man dying slowly from tuberculosis could ultimately be a comic figure. But James counters the objection in his preface to *The Wings of the Dove*. "His deplorable state of health was not only no drawback; I had clearly been right in counting it, for any happy effect he should produce, a positive good mark, a direct aid to pleasantness and vividness."[7] Early in the novel we learn that despite Ralph's physical condition "the imagination of loving—as distinguished from that of being loved—had still a place in his reduced sketch." (III, 54) Ralph's illness makes "the simple use of his faculties . . . an exquisite pleasure." (III, 53)

Ralph is the recurring Jamesian artist figure, enjoying everything in his imagination and striving to exert an influence for happiness and good upon the society around him. If the other characters in the novel fail to understand him completely, the reader sees that he sets an example for Isabel. Isabel accuses him "of laughing at all things, beginning with himself." (III,82) Although Isabel intends her comment as negative criticism, the reader perceives that one important positive quality which Isabel lacks is just this ability to laugh at herself.

But Ralph is no mute example. He constantly verbalizes his comic philosophy for Isabel and the reader. "The great point's to be as happy as possible," (III, 65) he explains. When Mr. Touchett complains that life is getting more serious Ralph counters, "The increasing seriousness of things, then—that's the great opportunity of jokes" (III,10)

Ralph, like Gabriel Nash, seems to speak "undiluted Henry James," and he serves as a touchstone for the other characters in the novel. When he expresses his dislike for Madame Merle and Gilbert Osmond the reader is forewarned that the two are up to no good.

Even on his deathbed Ralph manages to maintain his comic perspective on the "increasing seriousness of things." Tired of the pompous doctor Sir Matthew Hope, Ralph instructs his mother "to send word he was now dead and was therefore without further need of medical advice." (IV, 410) Capable of joking at his own death, Ralph attains the serious wisdom of high comedy and imparts it to Isabel before he dies:

> "There's nothing makes us feel so much alive as to see others die. That's the sensation of life—the sense that we remain.

I've had it—even I. But now I'm of no use but to give it to others." (IV, 413)

Even death contributes to the continuity of human life.

The comic confidant or wise fool, as represented by Gabriel Nash, Valentin de Bellegarde, Maria Gostrey, and Ralph Touchett, is a standard by which the other characters can be measured. His philosophy is one of enjoyment and creativity, and he possesses a comically serious self-awareness. He is usually a self-deprecator and artist, and he belongs to a long tradition of similar figures who have reappeared in the more desperate and chaotic comedy of contemporary fiction. Isabel says to Ralph, "you live on air." (III, 75) The *luftmensche*, the man who lives on air and darts in and out of the lives of men, reappears in characters like Bernard Malamud's marriage broker in "The Magic Barrel." As Nash himself remarked, he is immortal.

I suggested earlier that Henry James often casts fools, "fixed constituents," in the role of villain. By rendering evil ridiculous James succeeds in making it impotent and laughable. For all their pretensions to power these villains are finally able to destroy only themselves while setting the hero into relief. But there is another type of Jamesian blocking figure who is no fool. This other type of character shares many of the qualities which James invested in Felix and Nanda. His characteristic description of these figures is "magnificent," and the group of women who make up this type in James have been called "bad heroines." These almost superhuman characters would be tragic if they were cast in the protagonist's role. For all their magnificence, however, they block the hero's pursuit of happiness and must ultimately be expelled from or accommodated by the society.

Perhaps the prime example of this type of character in earlier comedy is Millamant in Congreve's *The Way of the World.* Millamant has a gift for interpreting situations as a whole, and molding her caprices to suit the temper of the occasion. Mirabel likes Millamant for "her faults. Her follies are so natural, or so artful, that they become her."[8] Mirabel's description of Millamant is a good description of James's bad heroines.

These women include Eugenia of *The Europeans,* Madame Merle of *The Portrait of a Lady,* Julia Dallow of *The Tragic*

*Muse,* Mrs. Brook of *The Awkward Age,* Mrs. Beale of *What Maisie Knew,* and Charlotte Stant of *The Golden Bowl.* Although these characters are often boastful, they function as artists, displaying their superiority at all times and controlling much of the novel's plot.

Eugenia, the Baroness Münster of Silberstadt-Schreckenstein, seems to be an early Jamesian egotist, but if her name implies a comic pretentiousness, by the end of the novel she has proven herself to have dignity and intelligence. Early in the novel, depressed by the weather and the prospect of meeting her unrefined American cousins, Eugenia seems to reveal the typical traits of James's boastful fools. As she passes by a mirror, "her face forgot its melancholy." (2) The weather changes, and Felix and Eugenia delight in the "splendid sunset."

> She was perhaps the more easily pleased from the fact that while she stood there she was conscious of much admiring observation on the part of various nice-looking people who passed that way, and to whom a distinguished, strikingly dressed woman with a foreign air, exclaiming upon the beauties of nature on a Boston street corner in the French tongue, could not be an object of indifference. (19)

But if James touches Eugenia with pastel shades of egotism, the reader can never ridicule her. She is an imposing and socially artful creature, displaying a good deal of beauty of character. If she is vain and self-centered, she is also charming. And she is socially the "largest" character in the novel, remaining a mystery to everyone. James tells us early in the book that Eugenia displays "a suggestion both of maturity and flexibility" and her "eyes were charming . . . full of intelligence." (4–5) From the outset she is unusually perceptive. When Felix returns from a visit to the Wentworths he provides a *mise en scène* for Eugenia.

> "There are two, Charlotte and Gertrude."
> "Are they pretty?"
> "One of them," said Felix.
> "Which is that?"
> The young man was silent, looking at his sister. "Charlotte," he said at last.

She looked at him in return. "I see. You are in love with Gertrude." (48)

Throughout the novel Eugenia reflects the clairvoyance which is a hallmark of the Jamesian confidant discussed above. But despite her obvious value and her social magnificence, Eugenia represents a threat to the spontaneity of the young lovers and she is, at the end of the novel, expelled. No character, however, forces her withdrawal; she chooses to return to her element herself.

> The conditions of action on this provincial continent were not favorable to really superior women. The elder world was, after all, their natural field. The unembarrassed directness with which she proceeded to apply these intelligent conclusions appeared to the little circle of spectators who have figured in our narrative but the supreme exhibition of a character to which the experience of life had imparted an inimitable pliancy. (279)

Eugenia is the bad heroine who refuses to deprecate herself because she is superior and knows it. But her real superiority renders her too large for the picture, and she must remove herself from the final society of the novel.

One of James's most obvious representatives of this type of character is Mrs. Brook in *The Awkward Age.* If that novel, in which society is the actual hero, has a villain, it is Mrs. Brook. The plot of the book grows from Mrs. Brook's introduction of her daughter Nanda into a drawing room where fast and witty talk thrives and illicit relationships flourish under the brilliant camouflage of impeccable manners. It is suggested at the outset that Mrs. Brook has been lying about her daughter's age as well as her own to postpone bringing Nanda into the salon. Mrs. Brook claims that her hesitancy to bring Nanda "down" results from a fear that the "talk" will suffer in deference to the innocent girl whose virgin ears will have to be protected. As she insists to Van,

> "I spoke of the change in my life of course; I happen to be so constituted that my life has something to do with my

mind and my mind something to do with my talk. Good
talk: you know—no one, dear Van, should know better—
what part for me that plays. Therefore when one has deliberately to make one's talk bad. . . . stupid, flat, fourth-rate. . . ."
(IX, 284)

But while Mrs. Brook explains her problem in these terms, the
reader perceives that her problem is of quite another sort. For
although it is never directly stated in the novel, it is strongly
implied that Mrs. Brook and Van are engaged in some kind of
intimate affair, and Nanda, whom Van admires, therefore represents a rival to her.

Faced with a rival, Mrs. Brook seeks to manipulate people
and circumstances so that Van will remain free for herself. Her
"evil" is her willingness to sacrifice other people to her system.
Her complex plan consists basically of an attempt to marry the
affable and wealthy Mitchy to Nanda, thus keeping Van for
herself. The situation is complicated, and will be examined in
more detail later. Mrs. Brook, however, is a brilliant social artist,
almost a comic variation on the Jamesian manipulator.

Despite her magnificence James submits Mrs. Brook to light
satire. Mitchy, the Ralph Touchett of the novel, wittily undercuts
her on several occasions. When Mitchy sends Mrs. Brook some
French novels she fashionably protests and finally condemns
them. Mitchy asks, "Why, were they particularly dreadful? . . .
I rather liked the one in the pink cover—what's the confounded
thing called?—I thought it had a sort of something-or-other."
(IX, 79) When Mrs. Brook defines the quality, calling it a "morbid
modernity," an "abject horrid unredeemed vileness from beginning to end," Mitchy immediately trips her up. "So you read
to the end?" (IX, 80)

James himself directs some oblique satire at her. Forty-two
years old, she is constantly referred to in terms of her "youth,"
and her "lovely silly eyes." (IX, 42) And she cultivates woe. "She
suggested for the most part the luxury, the novelty of woe, the
excitement of strange sorrows and the cultivation of fine indif-
ferences. This was her special sign—an innocence dimly tragic."
(IX, 42) Her secret sorrows and tragic tone are initially comic
because their immediate source is light-fingered Harold's affinity
for five-pound notes.

But if Mrs. Brook is partially humorous she is continually referred to by the other characters as "magnificent," and her magnificence is thrown into relief by her dull husband who is rather ignominiously compared to a fire extinguisher. Further, she herself perceives the comic potential of her complicated machinations. "I often feel as if I were a circus-woman, in pink tights and no particular skirts, riding half a dozen horses at once." (IX, 188)

At the close of the novel, trapped in a world threatening chaos, Mrs. Brook retains a felicity and detachment which enable her to play her necessary role with great finesse. James does not fully expose her, because to do so would be to destroy much of the comedy of the novel, and because it is the very nature of her character to avoid exposure. Her genius for conversation and social form makes her a social entity of such force that she can never be completely defeated. At the end she is even sympathetic because her scheme, whatever her original motives, *has* secured the best for Nanda. Mrs. Brook's selfish maneuvers ultimately produce a heroism in Nanda and enable the innocent girl to find a kind of moral happiness as Longdon's adopted daughter.

Leon Edel offers the best summary of Mrs. Brook's attraction:

> Disillusioned, ambiguous, arbitrary, she is beset by all the troubles of her world: her vapid, ineffectual husband, her daughter who loves her lover, her light-fingered son; even her cherished salon is foundering in the crisis between mother and daughter. In the midst of her tottering empire Mrs. Brook holds her head high, looks out at us with her "lovely silly eyes" and speaks with an absurd wit that is often deadly serious, and with a wry twist in her logic that steers her through her perilous situations.[9]

A final example of the bad heroine who shares the "free spirit's" potential for artistry is Charlotte Stant in *The Golden Bowl.* Like Mrs. Brook, Charlotte is eulogized by most of the other characters in the book. At the end of the novel Charlotte asks Maggie, "Have you any ground of complaint of me? Is there any wrong you consider I've done you?" (XXIV, 247) and Maggie promptly denies any, vowing that Charlotte has been "beautiful, wonderful and good." (XXIV, 251) Maggie is, of course, lying to some extent to protect Charlotte. Maggie knows full well the extent of Charlotte's duplicity. But this is not the only time in the novel that Maggie finds Charlotte "beautiful." Earlier Maggie affirms that Charlotte is "great in nature, in character, in spirit. Great in life." (XXIII, 180) And at the close she realizes that Charlotte "wasn't to be wasted." She is "great," "beautiful." (XXIV, 366)

Like the other characters of this type, Charlotte would be a tragic heroine if she were placed in the role of leading lady. A misconception of the novel's form has indeed led several critics to suggest that since the novel is a tragedy, Charlotte is the tragic heroine.[10] But Charlotte is not the heroine, and her presence does not make the novel tragic. She is the blocking figure who must, by the conventions of comedy, be displaced or transcended or evaded.

Critics sympathetic to Charlotte resent Maggie's final "punishment" of her, whereas that punishment should bring mixed relief to the reader, as a symbol of Maggie's triumph and revenge. Although we admire Charlotte for her skillful manipulation of a decadent and fool-ridden society, we must feel some satisfaction at her final moral comeuppance. Charlotte may, of course, be ignorant of her true motives, of the way her whole life is a series of maneuvers and deceptions used to further her own ends, but the reader is not. Society, in the person of Maggie Verver, must assert itself, and Charlotte must be gently, generously, compassionately, lovingly, defeated.

The bad heroine recurs throughout James's novels as a subtle combination of villainy and magnificence. Whereas many of James's villains are comically inefficient, dull, impotent, and ultimately self-defeating, the bad heroines are fascinating, "magnificent," and intelligent, but ultimately unable or unwilling to destroy good. Both character types represent the kind of constriction that appears in comic art.

Although a majority of James's protagonists are "bedimmed and befooled and bewildered," revealing their community with the "general human exposure," characters like Felix, Maisie, and

Nanda manage to transcend their natural limitations. Deprecating themselves, they face evil but escape unscathed, eventually becoming artists of life and controlling the plots of their novels. While James's minor characters are most obviously comic types, the major characters are also typical. Yet none of the protagonists is as simple as the discussion may at times imply. Like all great comic characters, they invariably possess a marked ambivalence. In "the major phase" James returned to an examination of the possibilities of a complex combination of types in Lambert Strether and in Maggie Verver. Both characters are important enough to command extended treatment later.

# IV

# The Jamesian Plot

*"organizing an ado"*

Henry James characteristically thought of his fictions in terms of character, and the conflict of free spirit and fool is the skeleton basis of his comic plots.

Two basic plot patterns typically inform comedy. The first consists of a movement which makes all the actions of a character work against himself. Whereas the curve of the tragic action is one of self-discovery, the curve of the comic action is one of self-exposure. *The Sacred Fount, The American,* and *The Portrait of a Lady* reflect this pattern.

The second basic pattern is the integration of a character into society or the formation of a new society around the character. In the tragic plot the character is isolated from his community and remains unable to establish any new connections; the comic character is incorporated into the existent community or into one of his own making. Integration of the comic hero into society often takes the form of a marriage or surrogate marriage, and *The Europeans, The Awkward Age,* and *The Golden Bowl* reflect this pattern.

Both patterns require the opposition of characters, and on the level of plot this opposition often takes the form of a conflict of societies. In the novels of Henry James such a conflict is usually expressed in a juxtaposition of American and European societies.

The "international theme" which brought recognition to James is based on a somewhat ambiguous opposition of national types. For James, America suggests innocence, conscience, and moral spontaneity, qualities which can be cruel, dogmatic, narrow, fatuous, frigid, and haughty, as well as morally sound, beautiful, and charming. It is the negative aspects of the American character, however, that stimulated James's imagination. As he wrote in the preface to *The Reverberator*, "if I hadn't had, on behalf of the American character, the negative aspects to deal with, I should practically, and given the limits of my range, have had no aspects at all." The sense that most Americans were "incredibly *unaware of life*" is what fascinated him.[1]

The European type represents for James the antithesis of the American. Standing for experience as opposed to innocence, tradition opposed to conscience, manners opposed to social naiveté, Europe also reveals both positive and negative qualities. European manners can ensure social relationships and protect human frailty from destruction but at the same time they reflect a potential for cruelty, hypocrisy, and viciousness under the calm surface.

The juxtaposition of these two radically antithetical cultures provides the arena for James's comedy of manners. The incredibly innocent and open ingenue placed in an ancient and corrupt, if aesthetically beautiful, society, or the worldly-wise sophisticate placed in a young and morally rigid society, exposes both that society and himself and provides the situation for Jamesian drama.

James's favorite version of the "international theme" is the American type confronted by European society, a plot resembling the conventional conflict of country visitor in the big city. If James had been primarily a satirist he would have ridiculed these "type" characters and left them unchanged at the ends of his novels. Instead, he reveals what he calls their "conversion":

> Conscious of so few things in the world, these unprecedented creatures . . . were least of all conscious of deficiencies and dangers; so that, the grace of youth and innocence and freshness aiding, their negatives were converted and became in certain relations lively positives and values.[2]

James concludes that their "disposition . . . had perhaps even most a comic side."[3] James's keen perception of manners and social types enables him to see Americans through European eyes and Europeans through American eyes. Juxtaposed, both sides are charming and comic. But success is not always as easy as

James implies in the preface to *The Reverberator*. His morally scrupulous heroes, faced with a more sophisticated society, have to win their positive values and relative happiness through humiliation, ritual death, and an often painful expansion of consciousness.

The Jamesian plot, then, originates in a conception of character, and character on the level of plot is often a conflict of national types. The hero is usually in pursuit of happiness, and both the other characters and the society itself can "block" the hero from his quest. The balance and contrast of characters and society is the comic situation.

### The International Comedy of Manners

James's international comedy of manners is perhaps best approached through a brief discussion of the two early novels which are prime examples of the form, *The American* and *The Europeans*. I suggested earlier that a number of Jamesian characters resemble Christopher Newman or Felix Young. The two novels also introduce the typical plot structures that recur in later novels, *The Ambassadors* being formally related to *The American*, and *The Golden Bowl* to *The Europeans*. The dramatic comedy of these novels is created when the protagonist is placed in a situation which shows him absurd by contrast. Culturally barren Newman in the Louvre, high-toned Eugenia Baroness Münster of Silberstadt-Schreckenstein in rural America, "Ambassador" Strether and the Pococks in Paris, panic-stricken Adam Verver hiding from Mrs. Rance in his billiard room—such situations provide the tone and material for endless comic dramatic scenes. The confrontation of two opposing sensibilities, one or both of whom possess faulty vision, establishes the incongruity necessary to comedy.

In *The American* James sends his confidently gregarious and unconsciously innocent hero to Europe. As Leon Edel points out, the plot is conventional, combining two basic mythic patterns: a Columbus or a Gulliver traveling to strange countries and marvelling at curious customs and modes of behavior which seem so divergent from his own, and the humble but honorable lover wooing the lady of high estate who lives in a well-guarded castle.[4] The novel begins as a typical romantic comedy in which the hero-adventurer wants a wife and is opposed by blocking figures who are converted by some twist in the plot, enabling the happy marriage to take place. In *The American*, of course, James denies his hero the happy ending in the interests of "realism," but up to the melodramatic conclusion the novel is true to the form.

The comic romance form is summarized by Claire de Cintré herself in a short symbolic tale she tells to little Blanche and Newman:

> "But in the end the young prince married the beautiful Florabella ... and carried her off to live with him in the Land of the Pink Sky. There she was so happy that she forgot all her troubles, and went out to drive every day of her life in an ivory coach drawn by 500 white mice. Poor Florabella," she explained to Newman, "had suffered terribly."
>
> "She had had nothing to eat for six months," said little Blanche.
>
> "Yes, but when the six months were over, she had a plum-cake as big as that ottoman." (136)

Earlier in the novel Claire had told Newman not to press his suit for six months. He is both the young prince of the tale, wanting to carry his Florabella off to America, and the giant plum-cake that awaits his beloved. Claire is talking about more than her story of Florabella when she concludes, "I could never have gone through the sufferings of the beautiful Florabella ... not even for her prospective rewards." (137)

Newman is the prince, the Gulliver, the American, confronting the wicked witch, the Lilliputians, the Europeans. The plot, based on the opposing sensibilities of Newman and the Bellegardes, is thus a framework for creating scenes which reflect on both the American and the Europeans. From Newman's perspective the Bellegardes are curious; from the Bellegardes' perspective Newman is the curiosity.

It is Newman's lack of understanding of his situation that produces the finest comedy in the book. Although several characters try to explain the plot to him he never quite perceives his true position. Mrs. Tristram in her role as confidante relates, "In

France you may never say Nay to your mother, whatever she requires of you. She may be the most abominable old woman in the world, and make your life a purgatory; but after all she's *ma mère*." (72) Newman responds jovially that it is "like something in a play." (73)

Later Valentin in his role as confidant warns Newman, "Old trees have crooked branches, old houses have queer cracks, old races have odd secrets. Remember that we are eight hundred years old." (105) And in his unquenchable buoyancy of confidence and naiveté Newman smiles, "Very good . . . that's the sort of thing I came to Europe for. You come into my programme." (105) Newman's misunderstanding of the whole affair is wittily emphasized when he mistakes the Marquis for the butler and sees the Duchess as the fat lady at a fair. (42, 192)

One of Newman's first conversations with the Bellegardes provides a scene of fine high comedy of manners, and lightly satirizes Newman's droll inability to adjust to his sophisticated antagonists. Urbain asks Newman,

> "You are in—a—as we say, *dans les affaires?*"
>
> "In business, you mean? Oh no, I have thrown business overboard for the present. I am 'loafing,' as *we* say. . . ."
>
> "Ah, you are taking a holiday," rejoined M. de Bellegarde. "'Loafing.' Yes, I have heard that expression."
>
> "Mr. Newman is American," said Madame de Bellegarde.
>
> "My brother is a great ethnologist," said Valentin.
>
> "An ethnologist?" said Newman. "Ah, you collect negroes' skulls and that sort of thing."
>
> The marquis looked hard at his brother, and began to caress his other whisker. Then, turning to Newman, with sustained urbanity: "You are traveling for your pleasure?" he asked.
>
> "Oh, I am knocking about to pick up one thing and another." (121)

Madame de Bellegarde's dry explanation, "Mr. Newman is American," sums up the short scene. Newman's exaggerated vernacular juxtaposed with the ultra-polite society conversation of the Bellegardes causes us to laugh at the situation itself as much as at both participating types. In groping toward some medium of meaningful communication both sides seem perversely to prevent understanding by the other. The frontier humor and the formal wit clash, creating a muddle of misunderstanding.

If Newman misses most of the jokes and dry irony directed at him by the Bellegardes, the Parisian family misses the jokes which reflect back upon them. When old Madame de Bellegarde haughtily insists that her family pride and aristocratic heritage absolutely preclude the possibility of any marriage between Claire and Newman, Newman merely mentions his wealth and Madame de Bellegarde quickly and conveniently forgets her proud heritage.

Despite the numerous comic scenes engendered by the comedy of manners form, the novel degenerates toward the close into melodrama complete with strange and grotesque mysteries, tearful departures to the convent, a fiendish murder, and a talking corpse. But while feeling the elation of possible revenge course through him, and indignantly proclaiming himself a "good fellow wronged," Newman undergoes the "ritual death" which Northrop Frye suggests is a typical convention of ironic comedy.[5] After insisting that he has been thrown into "this bottomless pit, where I lie howling and gnashing my teeth," (267) Newman departs for America. When he returns to Mrs. Bread who is "removing individual dust particles" (319) from his rooms in Paris, he gazes at the convent wall which separates him from Claire:

> This seemed the goal of his journey; it was what he had come for. It was a strange satisfaction, and yet it was a satisfaction; the barren stillness of the place seemed to be his own release from ineffectual longing. It told him that the woman within was lost beyond recall. . . . He turned away with a heavy heart, but with a heart lighter than the one he had brought. (321)

The subplot of the novel, which follows Valentin and Noémie, represents a kind of comment on Newman's own adventure with Claire. Valentin, like Newman, devotes himself somewhat ridiculously to a girl he cannot and should not marry. But the subplot is really a tragic counterpart of the major plot. For whereas Valentin dies for his foolishness, Newman undergoes the ritual death, release, and dedication to new life typical of comedy. As he concludes at the end, "He was glad he was rich and tolerably young . . . it was a gain to have a good slice of life left." (317)

*The Europeans*, written in the same year as *The American*, provides an interesting contrast to it. The majority of comic scenes and dialogue in *The American* result from the dramatic conflict between Newman's self-confident lack of manners and the Bellegardes' adroit and refined social behavior. Newman's spontaneity is incongruous with the practiced formality of the Parisian nobility. In *The Europeans* James inverts the situation; the Europeans descend upon the small rural community of their American relatives and the comic situation is reversed.

Eugenia and Newman both cross the ocean in search of mates, and both lose their romantic adventure because of a lack of understanding of the culture. But in *The Europeans* James focuses on no single major character as he does in *The American*; the hero is society itself. And whereas the melodramatic turn at the end of *The American* results in almost a comedy of humors, the sustained light comedy of *The Europeans* militates against melodrama and ensures a unity of tone.

The plot itself is the typical plot of the romantic comedy of manners and perhaps owes some debt to Dumas *fils*, Augier, and Sardou in its witty grace and carefully balanced construction, and to Turgenev's comedy *A Month in the Country*.[6] In its imagistic movement from the narrow graveyard and wintry weather at the outset to the marriages at the close, the novel parallels the usual movement of comedy from irrational law to freedom and celebration of a social order. And the expulsion of Eugenia is reminiscent of the expulsion of the blocking figure or refuser of festivity. The novel further reflects the typical pattern of the conversion of a traditional society by youthful intruders to a renewed expression of life, and the triumph of young lovers over paternal opposition.

The most obvious opposition upon which the plot is structured is that of the Europeans versus the Americans, as it was in *The American*, emphasizing the confrontation of urbane with rustic, sophisticate with innocent, those people who believe in manners and those who fear them, freedom and oppression, happiness and gloom. At the outset Felix notes the main difference in sensibility between his country cousins and himself. He reports to Eugenia:

> "I think there is something the matter with them; they have some melancholy memory or some depressing expectation. It's not the epicurean temperament. My uncle, Mr. Wentworth, is an extremely high-toned old fellow; he looks as if he were undergoing martyrdom, not by fire, but by freezing. But we shall cheer them up." (48)

And later when Felix meets Gertrude the two discuss their national differences. Felix begins:

> "I think the tendency—among you generally—is to be made unhappy too easily."
> . . . . . . . . . . . . . . . . . . . . . . . . . . . . . . . . . . . . . . . . . . . . . . . . . . . . . .
> "We are not fond of amusement."
> . . . . . . . . . . . . . . . . . . . . . . . . . . . . . . . . . . . . . . . . . . . . . . . . . . . . . .
> "You don't seem to me to get all the pleasure out of life that you might."
> "To 'enjoy,' . . . to take life—not painfully, must one do something wrong?" (103–4)

But James does not structure the novel on so simple a contrast as European epicureanism versus American Puritanism. Recognizable differences exist between Felix and Eugenia, and between Gertrude and the Wentworths.

In the opening scene Eugenia complains of America as "this dreadful country" while Felix celebrates "This comical country, this delightful country." (8) Eugenia more obviously represents European society than does Felix. Her name suggests her elevated social status, and her initial conversation recalls Madame de Bellegarde. Of the Wentworths she admits, "I don't count upon their being clever or friendly—at first—or elegant or interesting. But I assure you I insist upon their being rich." (14) She is, in some ways, the opportunist dedicated to exploitation. Felix, too, is after money and a wife, but his approach is lighter and more detached.

Whereas Felix is young, Eugenia is old. Eugenia says to her brother, "You will never be anything but a child." And he replies, "One would suppose that you, madam . . . were a thousand years old." (21) Further, images of winter surround Eugenia while images of spring surround Felix. Chapters 1 and 10, for instance, open on Eugenia in a cold and wintry rain, but when Felix enters the clouds dissipate and the sunset is brilliant.

If Felix and Eugenia are contrasted, so are Gertrude and Charlotte. Although the European–American confrontation seems to be one of art versus nature, and manners versus openness, Gertrude respects the importance of artful social manner as much as Eugenia does. Charlotte upbraids Gertrude:

> "I think father expected you would come to church . . . what shall I say to him?"
> "Say I have a bad headache."
> "Would that be true?" asked the elder lady. . . .
> "No Charlotte," said the younger one simply. (26)

Later, when Gertrude tries to straighten Charlotte's ribbon, Charlotte complains:

> "Indeed, I don't think it matters . . . how one looks behind."
> "I should say it mattered more. . . . Then you don't know who may be observing you. You are not on your guard. You can't try to look pretty."
> Charlotte received this declaration with extreme gravity. "I don't think one should ever try to look pretty." (27)

Charlotte's innocence and simplicity will not allow her to employ the fine art of duplicity which comes to the aid of the more complex Gertrude. Gertrude, like the Europeans and unlike the Americans, realizes that manners are at once the overt expression of man's nature and aspirations, and his capacity to falsify them. The dramatic conflict between those characters who believe in manners and those who don't produces much of the comedy in the novel.

Eugenia's belief in manners and her magnificent social presence make her final expulsion from the newly established harmonious society almost painful. But, as representative of a rigid European adherence to the old traditional society, Eugenia is inimical to the youthful renewal at the close. Her relationship with Robert Acton parallels Felix's with Gertrude much in the same way that Valentin's relationship with Noémie parallels that of Newman and Claire in *The American*. Like Valentin, Eugenia provides the tragic subplot which contrasts with the comic major plot. Felix and Gertrude are the free spirits who can successfully compromise. Felix adheres to his European manners while appreciating and absorbing Gertrude's moral spontaneity, and Gertrude maintains her naturalness but appreciates Felix's manners. But Eugenia and Acton are unable to compromise. Eugenia remains rigidly European in her duplicity, and Acton remains rigidly American in his fear of lies. "She is not honest, she is not honest," he concludes. Peter Buitenhuis correctly observes that Eugenia "is too much a creature of the old world to be able to adjust to the conditions of the new."[7]

The final scene is typical of light comedy where characters, without changing or being enlightened, stumble onto the combination of attitudes proper to a happy ending. With grand Shakespearean finality the new society is celebrated by no less than four marriages. But as Lyall Powers points out, "Most significant of all is the meaning of the union of Felix and Gertrude, a union that almost realizes James's ideal reconciliation of American and European qualities—'manners' happily wedded to 'morals.'"[8] Whereas neither extreme view, that of the American "type" nor that of the European "type," can provide the necessary freedom, a fusion of the two attitudes which realizes that freedom is concomitant with form and order, suggests an ideal possibility. Richard Poirier expresses surprise that in this novel James should exalt the very manners that he seemed to condemn in *The American*, and he concludes that the view expressed in *The Europeans* is a view exceptional to the James canon. Yet Peter Buitenhuis correctly points out that "in this nouvelle we can see James working in a lighter vein with a theme that was to become a major creative preoccupation."[9]

James was to return to the theme and structure of *The Europeans* in *The Golden Bowl*, a novel in which the American–European fusion represented by Maggie Verver's marriage to Prince Amerigo attains an almost metaphysical significance. And in *The Ambassadors* the problem of morals and manners receives its most complex treatment through the growing consciousness of Lambert Strether.

## Parodicomedy

The international comedy of manners was Henry James's favorite form and it was responsible for his popularity. But James experimented with other comic forms and even tried his hand at a curious and often imperfectly described form of parody, the purest example of which is *The Spoils of Poynton*. Critics have repeatedly misread the novel and misunderstood the heroine through a confusion over the genre of the novel.

E. D. Hirsch writes that "an interpreter's preliminary generic conception of a text is constitutive of everything that he subsequently understands, and . . . this remains the case unless and until that generic conception is altered."[10] To interpret novels like *The American* and *The Europeans* correctly a reader must perceive their relationship to the comedy of manners genre. To apprehend *The Spoils of Poynton* correctly the reader must understand its peculiar genre. But the Jamesian genre is never purely the convention which it resembles, and *The Spoils of Poynton* is almost a unique creation.

James notes in the preface to *The Portrait of a Lady*:

> Here we get exactly the high price of the novel as a literary form—its power not only, while preserving that form with closeness, to range through all the differences of the individual relation to its general subject-matter, all the varieties of outlook on life . . . but positively to appear more true to its character in proportion as it strains, or tends to burst, with a latent extravagance, its mould.[11]

James's refusal in *The American*, for instance, to provide the traditional happy ending is an effort to burst the mold of the novel's form, thus revealing a complexity of experience and multiplicity of attitude. The parodicomedy of *The Spoils of Poynton* is a successful attempt to do the same thing while avoiding the sacrifice of artistic unity.

The first chapter, perhaps the outright funniest passage in

all of James, arouses certain generic expectations. The chapter opens on Mrs. Gereth at Waterbath, the hideous house of the Brigstocks. Mrs. Gereth, who has spent a sleepless night cruelly tormented by the tasteless wallpaper in her room, meditates on her aesthetic misery. For her, ugliness and stupidity in interior decorating are practically synonymous with physical assault. The poorly decorated house exerts a perverting force on nature itself, and Mrs. Gereth speculates that the birds will sing out of tune and the flowers will go wrong in color. Surrounded by such antagonism, Mrs. Gereth suffers further from her fear that Owen, her dull son, will marry a "frump."

In the midst of her baleful meditations Mrs. Gereth meets young Fleda Vetch, and because Fleda is less than pretty Mrs. Gereth concludes curiously that Fleda is no frump. An appreciation for beautiful furniture allied with an indifferent physical countenance is Mrs. Gereth's gauge of a good person, and Fleda immediately links herself with Mrs. Gereth by commenting on "the ugliness fundamental and systematic" of Waterbath. (X, 6) As the two new friends sit discussing their aesthetic afflictions, Owen Gereth appears with his sweetheart Mona Brigstock, "the massive maiden at Waterbath." (X, 200) Mona has apparently planted her big feet squarely on Mrs. Gereth's soul by associating with Owen, and Mrs. Gereth takes immediate action. She spirits Mona away, thrusting Owen upon the sensitive Fleda. Fleda notices "Mrs. Gereth's quick management in the way the lovers, or whatever they were, found themselves separated." (X, 10) And Fleda's active imagination begins to conjure up a wonderful picture of a relationship with Owen in which she will provide all the intelligence. As the chapter closes Fleda looks toward "a future full of the things she particularly loved." (X, 11)

The opening chapter sets the tone for the novel and introduces the themes and conflict of the subsequent action. But the opening remains somewhat ambiguous. The satiric tone diminishes Mrs. Gereth's stature through hyperbole, but it also marshals sympathy for her suffering. Owen and Mona may be lovers, but Fleda is not sure, and Fleda's own relationship to the three is uncertain.

In chapter 3, however, James provides a hint which ultimately defines the novel's structure. In describing Mrs. Gereth he remarks, "Her handsome high-nosed excited face might have been that of Don Quixote tilting at a windmill." (X, 31) The simile is an apt description of Mrs. Gereth's relationship to Owen. In her obsession with the ideal beauty of her "things," she is like the knight of La Mancha, and Owen, in his gross reality, is like the earthy Sancho Panza. Further, James's reference to *Don Quixote* reveals the similar plot techniques of the two novels. Dorothy Van Ghent describes Cervantes' technique in *Don Quixote* as "parody" and her comments have an important bearing on James's technique in *The Spoils of Poynton.*

> Loosely, we tend to mean by parody a burlesque imitation of something, showing the weaknesses or falsehood of the object imitated. In this sense, the main feature of parody would be not unlike the main feature of debate, implying that one view of things was a "wrong" view and another the "right" view. . . . But it is possible for parody to be much more complex than debate. Instead of confronting two opposing views with each other, in order that a decision between them be arrived at, parody is able to intertwine many feelings and attitudes together in such a way that they do not merely grapple with each other antagonistically but act creatively on each other, establishing new syntheses of feeling and stimulating more comprehensive and more subtle perceptions. Parody . . . is a technique of presentation; it offers a field for the joyful exercise of perception.[12]

Part of the critical disagreement surrounding *The Spoils* stems from this aspect of parody which provides for a multiplicity of attitudes. Fleda, like the Don, need be neither completely heroic and admirable nor totally perverse and despicable; and she could be both.

The structure of *Don Quixote* reflects a parody of knight-errantry. The governing shape of *The Spoils of Poynton* reflects a parody with a different base. The plot of *The Spoils* resembles that of *The Europeans, The American,* and *The Reverberator* in that two lovers are blocked by antagonistic parents who object to some quality in their child's lover. Mr. Brand and the Wentworths fear Felix's joy of life, the Bellegardes dislike Newman's commercial heritage, and the Proberts bridle at Francie's incredible ignorance. In *The Spoils of Poynton* Mrs. Gereth objects to Mona's lack of aesthetic taste. But the basic structural difference between the earlier romance comedies and *The Spoils* is that the former were told conventionally from the point of view of the lovers (Felix, Newman, Francie), while *The Spoils* is told from the point of view of the blocking figures (Mrs. Gereth and Fleda). In a sense, James is parodying his own previous romance comedies but, more importantly, he is parodying the whole convention of romance comedy.

In inverting the typical plot structure of romance comedy, James creates an extremely complex movement of shifting roles on the part of the characters, and shifting sympathies on the part of the reader. Typical comedy presents two lovers who are blocked by a figure of authority, usually parental or courtly. The audience sympathizes with the lovers, and after some kind of ritual death the lovers triumph, defeating the blocking figure by expelling him from society or by converting him and thus incorporating him into a new society.

At the outset of *The Spoils of Poynton* the two lovers are Owen and Mona, and they act as normal lovers do in comedy. Their love is a healthy passion, sensuous and unintellectual. In chapter 1 we meet them "in the act of scrambling and helping each other," with Mona "laughing and romping." Fleda observes, "There had been intimacy—oh yes, intimacy as well as puerility—in the horse-play of which they had just had a glimpse." (X, 9) Later, when Mona visits Poynton, Fleda imagines a conversation between the lovers:

> "Don't you think it's rather jolly, the old shop?"
> "Oh it's all right!" Mona had graciously remarked; and then they had probably, with a slap on a back, run another race up or down a green bank. (X, 29–30)

Unapologetically physical, and sporting gaily on green banks, Owen and Mona are clearly the typical lovers of comedy. In the first chapter, Mrs. Gereth's quick and powerful separation of the lovers, which Fleda observes, establishes her as the blocking figure, and Fleda becomes her ally. But whereas audience sympathy in a typical comedy is on the side of the lovers, in *The Spoils* the reader finds himself championing Fleda and Mrs.

Gereth, and opposing the lovers, Owen and Mona.

However, James shifts the roles a second time. Toward the end of the novel Mona and Mrs. Brigstock become the new blocking figures preventing the marriage of the new pair of lovers, Owen and Fleda. At this point the reader's sympathy is that of traditional comedy, supporting the lovers against the blocks to their happiness.

But there is yet a third shift in the plot which returns the characters to their original roles, Mrs. Gereth and Fleda opposing Owen and Mona. And James provokes a subtle shift of audience sympathy, for at the close the reader actually supports Owen and Mona against Fleda and Mrs. Gereth. The action of the story has revealed to the reader, if not to Fleda, Owen's essential worthlessness and moral weakness. If Owen marries Mona, Fleda will be saved from a bad marriage despite herself. The final marriage of Owen and Mona becomes a kind of triumph for Fleda, keeping her "free."

Thus, at the beginning of the novel the reader supports the traditional blocking figures against the lovers; by the end of the novel the reader finds himself supporting the lovers as he would in conventional comedy. But his reasons are subtly different. In typical comedy the lovers' triumph results in a new society of their own creation. In James's parodicomedy the marriage of Owen and Mona results in the freedom of Fleda Vetch, the "defeated" blocking figure and heroine. Her defeat paradoxically becomes her triumph. The reader's sympathy never really deviates from Fleda. But James's reversals and inversions of typical plot structure force the reader finally to desire Fleda's "failure" and the lovers' "success" as in typical comedy because the very terms "success" and "failure" have, in the course of the action, been inverted.

The parodicomic form is further enhanced by battle imagery and religious imagery which elevates the conflict to the level of mock epic. James ridicules the whole basis of the struggle by describing the fight for Poynton in Homeric terms, presenting silly and trifling events with heroic pomp in the manner of Pope and Fielding. Fleda, for instance, thinks of her plight in terms of "indignity and misery, of wounds inflicted and received." (X, 56) The exaggerated nomenclature of war—seiges, surrenders, campaigns, enemies, and myrmidons—juxtaposed with Mrs. Gereth's religious devotion to her furniture make the novel resemble an account of a comical holy war. Mrs. Gereth calls her "things" "our religion," (X, 30) and Fleda talks of going "to the stake. Oh, he may burn me alive!" (X, 114) The structure of the novel, then, is best described as a parody of romantic comedy enhanced by mock epic allusions.

Within the peculiar structure of the novel Fleda Vetch gains her significance. She, like Don Quixote, is a parody figure, but whereas the Don is a parody of knight-errantry, Fleda is a parody of the idealistic and virginal romance heroine. And, like the Don, her intensity is both comical and beautiful.

A number of critics have complained of Fleda's exaggerated scruples, but few have interpreted them correctly in terms of the kind of novel *The Spoils* is and the kind of heroine Fleda is. Yvor Winters accuses Fleda of "moral hysteria,"[13] J. A. Ward suggests that Fleda "imposes on her circumstances an archaic conception of honor that strikes . . . the reader as an irrelevance,"[14] and Lyall Powers dubs her reticence to pursue Owen a "hyperscrupulosity, a kind of elephantiasis of the moral sense. It offers another example of the evil effects of an excess of virtue."[15] Mrs. Gereth herself calls Fleda's scruples "the inanity of a passion that bewilders a young blockhead with bugaboo barriers, with hideous and monstrous sacrifices. . . . Your perversity's a thing to howl over." (X, 225) All these descriptions reflect a general truth about Fleda, but none of them explain James's purpose in attributing such qualities to his heroine.

Yet James himself tells us early in the first chapter that Fleda "was in her small way a spirit of the same family as Mrs. Gereth." (X, 11) Like Mrs. Gereth, therefore, Fleda resembles Don Quixote. Like Quixote, she reads her own exaggerated sense of morality and delicacy into situations and people. Like Quixote, she wishes to do "some high and delicate deed." (X, 106) She refuses to oppose Mona actively because Mona's vows to Owen are "sacred." "How could Fleda doubt that they had been tremendous when she knew so well what any pledge of her own would be?" (X, 106) Like the Don, Fleda imbues the most common and dull situations with her own sense of honor, beauty, and moral intensity.

In *Don Quixote*, illusion, silly and absurd as it may be, remains preferable to dull reality, for illusion seems to contain the love, beauty, goodness, devotion, and humanity that reality seems to lack. Fleda's illusions are similar. Her exaggerated moral finicalness is best seen as an imaginative ideal. Although it has, perhaps, little to do with gross reality, with Owen and Mona, it is nevertheless spiritually beautiful. Fleda tilts at moral windmills but her madness reveals essential goodness.

In her Quixote-like role, parodying the moral scrupulosity of the romance heroine, Fleda creates a beautiful illusion out of Owen. As Quixote imagines Sancho Panza, the short, pot-bellied rustic, to be his squire, Fleda imagines the impossibly dense but lovable Owen to be her paramour. After James has painstakingly impressed upon the reader Owen's lack of man-liness and moral courage, Fleda "thought of him perpetually and her eyes had come to rejoice in his manly magnificence more even than they rejoiced in the royal cabinets of the red saloon." (X, 58) And Fleda constantly feels impelled to discover depths and intentions in Owen which could never exist. "Wasn't it at all events the rule of communication with him for her to say on his behalf what he couldn't say?" (X, 91)

The danger in such active imagining is the creation of delusions which become ultimately painful. In a climactic scene near the end of the novel Fleda reads her own fondest wishes into a simple and abrupt speech of Owen's. Owen comments on Ricks:

> "I think it's awfully nice here. . . . I assure you I could do with it myself.
>
> . . . . . . . . . . . . . . . . . . . . . . . . . . . . . . . . . . . . . . . . . . . . . . . . . . .
>
> I mean I could put up with it just as it was; it had a lot of good things, don't you think? I mean if everything was back at Poynton, if everything was all right." (X, 100–101)

Owen, of course, in his own confused and awkward way, is trying to tell Fleda that he wants the "spoils" returned to Poynton so that Mona will marry him. And Ricks, he insists, with the maiden aunt's furniture, is quite adequate for the comfort of his mother. But Fleda dreams quite different, far fetched meanings into the simple speech:

> Fleda didn't understand his explanation unless it had refer-
> ence to another more wonderful exchange—the restoration
> to the great house not only of its tables and chairs but of
> its alienated mistress. . . . Once more she heard his un-
> sounded words. "With everything patched up at the other
> place I could live here with *you*." (X, 101)

In the manner of the original Don Quixote, Fleda creates the
illusion of Owen's love, an illusion so real that the weak man
eventually comes to believe it himself.

But if Fleda is self-deceived, she also gains a degree of
painful self-awareness, at last acknowledging the flimsiness of
her embroideries on the real situation. When Mrs. Gereth insists
that Owen has been in love with Fleda all along, Fleda replies,
"No—I was only in love with *him!*" (X, 211) And finally, at the
close, she manages to use her powerful imagination to create
a beautiful dream out of Owen's marriage to Mona. Observing
that the two seem happy, she reasons that Mona's nature withers
under defeat and blooms under success. Having successfully
won the "spoils" and Owen, Mona has bloomed causing Owen
to love her again. Owen requests that Fleda accept a present
from him, and Fleda hypothesizes:

> He had found in his marriage a happiness so much greater
> than, in the distress of his dilemma, he had been able to
> take heart to believe, that he now felt he owed her a token
> of gratitude for having kept him in the straight path. (X,
> 260)

To the end, Fleda creates beautiful illusions which may be
more true than any dull reality. The fire which ends the novel is
less the destruction of Fleda's illusions than the final detail in a
carefully wrought mock romance structure. Fleda's beautiful illusions remain, for they are not tied to the concrete "things" as
are Mrs. Gereth's. The fire merely represents the end of the
foolish devotion to furniture.

The parodicomic form afforded James an opportunity to
express a multiplicity of attitudes. In the late nineteenth century
neither the conventional themes nor the conventional forms of
romance comedy were harmonious with James's sense of reality

and his vision of the deterioration of old values. But with parody
he could have it both ways. Parody allowed James to affirm
conventions and traditional values while at the same time criticizing them. Comedy purges melodrama and sentimentalism on
the thematic level, and parody qualifies structural conventions
on the formal level. *The Spoils of Poynton* is based on the typical
plot structure of romance comedy, but the subtle structural shifts
serve to redefine and alter that form and its meaning. The essential values are affirmed while the pretensions are criticized.

The result is a full and flexible moral position in which
Fleda's "scrupulosity" is as insane and admirable as Don Quixote's knight-errantry. It is a morality which realizes the mixed
nature of human beings and understands that virtue does not
always triumph or even understand the nature of true triumph.
The conclusion of the novel is far from tragic. No one's life is
ruined; Owen and Mona, who have certainly deserved each other
all along, marry happily; Mrs. Gereth loses her "spoils" but
retains Ricks and Fleda; and Fleda retains her imagination and
her freedom. In part a satire on the collecting instinct, and in
part a parody of romance comedy, *The Spoils of Poynton* is one
of James's most intriguing experiments in the form of the novel.

The parody structure of *The Spoils* recurs in several later
novels including *The Ambassadors*, in which Strether is a converted blocking figure whose life in Paris is treated as a diplomatic mission, and *The Golden Bowl*, in which Maggie Verver
is her own blocking figure, ironically opposing her own marriage
by creating the situation for Prince Amerigo's adulterous relationship with Charlotte Stant.

## Social Satire

Between the early comedies of manners and the later return to
that form, James experimented with the parodicomedy of *The
Spoils of Poynton* and the tragicomedy of *The Portrait of a Lady*.
He also wrote some fine social satire in *What Maisie Knew* and
*The Awkward Age*.

In his preface to *The Tragic Muse* James suggests that satire
is the appropriate form for dealing with London social life. He

comments that "satiric treatment [was] the only adequate or effective treatment I had again and again felt, for most of the distinctively social aspects of London."[16] Thus it is reasonable to assume that a prime concern in *What Maisie Knew* and *The Awkward Age* is social criticism.

The notebook entries on *What Maisie Knew* stress the scenic method which James realized was at the base of his comedy. "I realize—none too soon— that the *scenic* method is my absolute, my imperative, my *only* salvation. The *march of an action* is the thing for me to, more and more, *attach* myself to."[17] In *What Maisie Knew* the action certainly "marches," sometimes with bewildering rapidity and reversal. According to James the action is that of an "ugly little comedy."[18]

James structures the novel on his favorite comic techniques—balance, repetition, and symmetry—techniques which embrace both the large plot movement and the organization of particular scenes and conversations. Allied to the balance and symmetry is the complexity and muddle of the social world which the technique encloses.

After being divided between her two parents "in a manner worthy of the judgment-seat of Solomon," (XI, 4) Maisie is snatched or batted from one warring parent to the other. At the outset it is a triumph for one parent to wrest Maisie from the other, but it soon becomes a triumph to thrust Maisie upon the other. The action alternates between the warring houses.

The alternating possession of Maisie becomes completely natural to her and she gains "the positive certitude . . . that the natural way for a child to have her parents was separate and successive, like her mutton and her pudding or her bath and her nap." (XI, 17) The alternation is itself somewhat comical, and soon James begins to double and triple the parties involved in the game of battledore with little Maisie as shuttlecock. Miss Overmore, Maisie's governess under Ida, follows Maisie to Beale's, ostensibly because she cannot live without her charge. Ida then hires Mrs. Wix. But two parents and two governesses are not enough. Sir Claude moves in to live with Ida, balancing Miss Overmore in her role as Beale's lover. Maisie begins to appreciate the aesthetic symmetry and explains to Miss Overmore that she has as much right to live with Beale as Sir Claude has to live with Ida. When Miss Overmore protests that *she* is a *real* governess, Maisie responds with comical innocence, "And couldn't he be a real tutor?" (XI, 40)

The problem is, however, soon resolved as Mrs. Wix haughtily announces Ida's engagement to Sir Claude. Not to be outdone, Miss Overmore counters with an announcement of her engagement to Beale, providing Maisie with two sets of parents. The doubling is not complete, however, until Miss Overmore, now Mrs. Beale, and Sir Claude have paired up, creating a third set of parents for Maisie, and until Beale and Ida have acquired several lovers each—the Captain and the Countess whom Maisie meets in parallel scenes.

The device of doubling renders a situation absurd by showing not the natural, individual one, but two of everything. Twins are amusing but Shakespeare found two sets of twins even more so. The arrangement of parents, stepparents, governesses, and lovers around Maisie is so mechanically symmetrical that it seems to militate against her spontaneity. And at the close Maisie herself tries to act on a theory of symmetry when she requires Sir Claude to give up Mrs. Beale if she will give up Mrs. Wix.

The comic devices of repetition and doubling extend to the level of dialogue, providing a number of frankly funny scenes. Toward the end of the book Sir Claude reports to Maisie:

> "I'm free—I'm free."
>
> She looked up at him; it was the very spot on which a couple of hours before she had looked up at her mother. "You're free—you're free."
>
> "Tomorrow we go to France." He spoke as if he hadn't heard her; but it didn't prevent her again concurring.
>
> "Tomorrow we go to France."
>
> Again he appeared not to have heard her. . . . "I'm free—I'm free!"
>
> She repeated her form of assent. "You're free—you're free." (XI, 229–30)

The comic repetition of the work "free" suggests that Claude is not really free at all. And his failure to hear Maisie reveals his final inability to keep from "dodging" responsibility.

Repetition, balance, and symmetry enclosing a squalid social arrangement and militating against the freedom of the characters is a criticism of the London social world. F. R. Leavis points out that *What Maisie Knew* is James's most Dickensian novel, suggesting that it resembles *David Copperfield.* But the technique, plot, and theme more strongly recall *Bleak House.* Sir Claude calls Maisie "my dear old woman" which is what Jarndyce fondly calls Esther in *Bleak House.* Esther advances from infancy to young womanhood so quickly that, like Maisie, she seems born old. Both heroines are naive, open, innocent, and trusting, though incredibly precocious, and both are shuttled between parents and guardians. The plot in *Bleak House* develops, as in *What Maisie Knew,* not so much as a result of anything the heroine does, but rather as a result of things that are done to her. Devastating things happen to each from birth, but neither environment nor heredity can destroy them and both girls gradually emerge with a moral sense and a capacity for love.

The characters surrounding Esther resemble those surrounding Maisie. In *Bleak House* Lady Dedlock has an affair with Captain Hawdon and marries Sir Leicester. In *What Maisie Knew* Ida has an affair with the Captain and marries Sir Claude. Like Ida, Lady Dedlock fails as a mother, human being, and wife by rejecting love for money and social position. Both mothers represent the hypocrisy, cant, frivolity, and ugliness of London society.

Sir Leicester resembles Sir Claude in his basic goodness stunted by a weak and injurious idleness. And Skimpole, the childish villain of *Bleak House* who lacks all principle, is a more vicious version of Beale. Of course there are major differences in the two novels—Maisie, for instance, never becomes the somewhat insipidly compliant Victorian woman that Esther does—but the similarities are instructive.

Both novels are radical criticisms of London social life, and the action of both is engendered by the force of an irrational law. The Chancery suit in *Bleak House* proceeds indefinitely, indifferent to whom it may destroy along the way. In *What Maisie Knew* the law does what Solomon in his wisdom only threatened to do, dividing Maisie up and throwing the pieces to the parents. The law in both novels seems to sanction greed and make injustice respectable.

We feel the oppressive and teeming Dickensian world of absurdity suffusing James's novel. It is a nightmare world of grotesque law and caricature people where abnormality is accepted as normal. The games Sir Claude buys for Maisie and Mrs. Wix have no rules and neither the governess nor her charge can understand or play them. The world is confusing, chaotic, and discontinuous, and fidelity, integrity, and loyalty seem impossible. At one point in the action Maisie tries to figure out the various loyalties:

> If it had become now, for that matter a question of sides, there was at least a certain amount of evidence as to where they all were. Maisie of course, in such a delicate position, was on nobody's; but Sir Claude had all the air of being on hers. If therefore Mrs. Wix was on Sir Claude's, her ladyship on Mr. Perriam's and Mr. Perriam presumably on her ladyship's, this left only Mrs. Beale and Mrs. Farrange to account for. Mrs. Beale clearly was, like Sir Claude, on Maisie's, and papa, it was to be supposed, on Mrs. Beale's. . . . It sounded . . . very much like puss-in-the-corner, and she could only wonder if the distribution of parties would lead to a rushing to and fro and a changing of places. (XI, 94–95)

Life itself becomes a childish game and the rules remain ambiguous. The incredibly balanced symmetry of the book only serves to throw the squalor of the social world into sharp relief. Innocent Maisie is surrounded by buffoonery and farce, which renders every situation a muddle. Whereas James's early novels rely on the international theme to provide muddlement through the juxtaposition of two opposing sensibilities, the novels of the middle period reveal a different conflict. Here the bewildered intelligence is pitted against the self-confident fool in his own society.

A reversal of usual roles further adds to the confusion. Older and more mature persons should lead the young and innocent, but in this London society Maisie becomes the judge and guide of those who should judge and guide her. Maisie in her innocence becomes the wisest and most mature character, and when Sir Claude calls her "old fellow" he has reason. If wisdom and age are concomitant, Maisie is the oldest character in the book.

But despite James's criticism of the squalor produced by ritualized social behavior, and the absurdity of the world's infringement on the fresh and innocent, his tone prevents the novel from being a bleak picture of despair. Comic irony prevents Maisie's experience from being too pathetic and keeps the environmental squalor at a distance. The discrepancy between Maisie's innocent apprehension of "normality" and what the reader sees to be an abnormal situation provides the comic incongruity which distances the ugliness. And, at the close, Maisie manages to remain unimpaired, retaining her freedom as does Fleda Vetch in *The Spoils of Poynton.*

*What Maisie Knew* looks forward to James's next attempt at social satire in *The Awkward Age.* The social world of *What Maisie Knew* is condemned outright; that of *The Awkward Age* is both beautiful and ugly. And whereas Maisie, the child, in her knowledge is powerless to effect any social change, Nanda, the young woman, in her knowledge is able to recreate a society around her mother and provide for the other characters in her world. Mrs. Wix's comic standard of morality becomes a serious standard of value in the person of Mr. Longdon.

A number of critics have insisted that although *The Awkward Age* seems superficially a comedy it is actually a tragedy. Yvor Winters calls it a "tragedy of manners,"[19] F. R. Leavis agrees that the novel, "though it exhibits James's genius for social comedy at its most brilliant, is a tragedy,"[20] and Dorothea Krook affirms that it is more than a "brilliant comedy of manners. For it is essentially not a comedy at all, but a tragedy."[21] Such critical misreadings are the more incredible when we remember that James himself protested just the opposite.

In a letter to Miss Henrietta Reubell James expressed his distress at the poor reception of the novel and the unfavorable reviews. He writes Miss Reubell that

I had in view a certain special social (highly"modern" and actual) London group and type and tone, which seemed to me to *se prêter à merveille* to an ironic—lightly and simply ironic!—treatment, and that clever people at least would know who, in general, and what, one meant. But here, at least, it appears there are very few clever people!"[22]

And later, in the preface to the New York Edition, James clarifies more precisely that he "invoked, for my protection, the spirit of the lightest comedy" for "brevity, for levity, for simplicity, for jocosity, in fine, and for an accommodating irony."[23] Comedy, irony, levity, and jocosity are adjectives seldom applied to tragedy.

James suspected that the general confusion over his intention resulted from his experimental form. As he explains in the preface, he modeled the form of *The Awkward Age* on the fiction of Gyp. Gyp was the pen name of Sibylle Gabrielle Marie Antoinette de Riquetti de Mirabeau, Countess de Martel de Janville, a French social satirist who parodied French manners in witty dialogues which were printed like plays and called "romans dialogués." In *The Awkward Age* James emulates Gyp in his attempt to write social satire in the form of drama, with no "going behind."[24] James insists, "I did, positively and seriously—ah so seriously!—emulate the levity of Gyp."[25] It is probably the seriousness of James's high comedy that has misled critics into seeing tragedy.

The plot itself follows the title, Nanda being at the "awkward age" when her presence in the drawing room will cause the "talk" to suffer in deference to her innocence. It is the situation caused by her exposure that James focuses on rather than her individual plight. Her exposure is the occasion for a juxtaposition of values inherent in an old traditional and stable society with those of a modern and changing one. The conventions have survived in the salon, but the integrity that gives them substance is now in question.

Longdon's introduction into the London salon parallels Nanda's. He, too, is an innocent exposed to a sophisticated society which he cannot understand, though he is, ironically, the oldest figure in that society. He is strangely the ingenue in the experienced society, and the comedy of the juxtaposition is that of James's earlier international novels. As James observes, Longdon "might have been a stranger at an Eastern court—comically helpless without his interpreter." (IX, 198) And to Van it is "tremendously interesting to hear how the sort of thing we've fallen into ... strikes your fresh, uncorrupted ear." (IX, 12) If the youthful Maisie is the oldest character in her society, Longdon is in some ways the youngest character in his. And he is ultimately the standard of value in the novel, representing honor, integrity, friendship, and understanding.

The presence of Nanda and Longdon complicates the lives of the members of Mrs. Brook's salon, and the action of the novel is largely the struggle between various characters for control of the plot. Mrs. Brook is the major focus, and her plot consists of an attempt to obtain Van for herself by marrying Nanda to Mitchy. Mrs. Brook perceives the danger Nanda represents to herself, and she fears the loss of her somewhat ambiguous relationship with Van. If her primary plan fails Mrs. Brook can rely on a secondary option which she has skillfully prepared by hinting to Longdon that the lecherous Mr. Cashmore might take Nanda as his mistress. Mrs. Brook knows that Longdon, who feels a close attachment to Nanda through his earlier love for her grandmother, will do everything possible to protect Nanda from such corruption. If necessary he will perhaps even remove Nanda from the salon, thus leaving Van to Mrs. Brook.

The Duchess has her own plan for marrying her daughter Aggie to Mitchy, and she perceives the consequent animosity of Mrs. Brook. In order to further her plan the Duchess suggests to Longdon that he provide Nanda with a dowry so that Van will marry her. Mitchy himself is rich, and with Nanda out of the way the Duchess will be able to procure Mitchy for Aggie.

Longdon responds to the Duchess' suggestion and settles a dowry on Nanda, confiding his action only to Van in the hopes that Van will marry Nanda and thus rescue her from the decadent salon. Seeing that Van will never marry her, Nanda takes the plot into her own hands and recreates the society which has by the end of the novel all but crumbled. The plot of the novel, then, consists of a clash of characters fighting for control of the comic society.

The plot and characters of the novel thus resemble those of the comedies of Molière and Restoration drama in which characters seek a way to live in an amoral society. The two young marriageable girls with their two duennas, the two eligible but difficult young men, and the strange assortment of social entities who hover about the protagonists are all typical of Molière. The drawing room setting, the juxtaposition of personages from high

society with those from the country, the graceful rake, the faith-
less housewife with her dull and deceived husband, the charming
young heroine and the false ingenue, and the repartee for its
own sake are all typical of Congreve and Restoration drama. *The
Awkward Age*, like the plays of Molière and Congreve, is both
a satire of current society and a romantic vision of an aesthetic
ideal. The main satire of the novel is directed not against the
characters but against the traits of society which they embody.
The society itself is both hero and villain.

The role of society as hero is best seen in the quality of
the "talk" which Mrs. Brook fears that Nanda's presence will
damage. Dorothea Krook describes it precisely when she writes,
"It is the speech of a homogeneous, closely-knit social group,
sharing common standards, attitudes, forms of behaviour; and
precisely because so much is shared, no part of what is shared
need ever be explicitly referred to."[26] The society places prime
value on wit, the free play of intelligence, and the disinterested
cultivation of awareness. It insists that each member of the group
should be able to discuss the most personal and even painful
questions with the others.

James himself describes the particular kind of "talk" which
the characters of the novel thrive on in an essay on Molière.
Referring to the scene in *The Misanthrope* in which "the circle
at Célimène's house hit off the portraits of their absent friends"
James concludes that "it is good society still, even though it be
good society in a heartless mood."[27] Mitchy describes the similar
circle of Mrs. Brook. "We're simply a collection of natural affinities ... meeting perhaps principally in Mrs. Brook's drawing-
room ... and governed at any rate everywhere by Mrs. Brook,
in our mysterious ebbs and flows, very much as the tides are
governed by the moon." (IX, 124) And Mitchy affirms that the
circle is "one beautiful intelligence." (IX, 297) The following
passage is perhaps the best example of the beauty of the "talk"
in the book. Marvelling at the solidarity of the circle, Mitchy,
Van, and Mrs. Brook discuss Mr. Longdon's offer to Van and
his settlement on Nanda. Van begins:

> "What *is* splendid, as we call it, is this extraordinary
> freedom and good humor of our intercourse and the fact that

we do care—so independently of our personal interests, with so little selfishness or other vulgarity—to get at the idea of things."

. . . . . . . . . . . . . . . . . . . . . . . . . . . . . . . . . . . . . . . . . . . . . . . . . . .

"But we *are* sincere."

"Yes, we *are* sincere." Vanderbank presently said. "It's a great chance not to fall below ourselves: no doubt therefore we shall continue to soar and sing. We pay for it, people who don't like us say, in our self-consciousness—"

"But people who don't like us," Mitchy broke in, "don't matter. Besides, how can we be properly conscious of each other—?"

"That's it!"—Vanderbank completed his idea: "without my finding myself for instance in you and Mrs. Brook? We see ourselves reflected—we're conscious of the charming whole. I thank you," he pursued after an instant to Mrs. Brook—"I thank you for your sincerity."

. . . . . . . . . . . . . . . . . . . . . . . . . . . . . . . . . . . . . . . . . . . . . . . . . . .

"The thing is don't you think?"—She appealed to Mitchy—"for us not to be so awfully clever as to make it believed that we can never be simple. We mustn't see *too* tremendous things—even in each other." (IX, 301-3)

The conversation with its constant reference to the three as "we," the sociable style which allows one individual to finish another's thought, the constant effort of each character to complete and balance the others, reveals the "talk" at its best. And even at the close of the novel when Mrs. Brook mourns the "smash" of her salon, the reader sees that the "smash" itself will afford years of witty commentary.

But if the "talk" represents ideal possibilities of relationship inherent in the society, it also reveals inherent dangers. If the society is hero it is also villain. Longdon perceives that "anxiety itself may sometimes tend to wit," (IX, 249) and when characters must constantly insist on their own beauty and happiness we begin to suspect a lack of such qualities.

The salon has elements of what Edmund Wilson, in an influential essay, calls the "whole host of creepy creatures," the "gibbering disemboweled crew."[28] Van himself perceives this

when he refers to the London world as "a huge 'squash,' . . . an
elbowing pushing perspiring chattering mob." (IX, 20)

And if the talk is beautiful it also fails to discriminate
between significant and trivial topics, thus destroying any real
appreciation of beauty. In a long *tête-a-tête* with Mitchy in
which Mrs. Brook discusses love, suffering, and happiness she
concludes:

> "I've been trying for months and months to remember
> to find out from you—"
>
> "Well, what?" he enquired, as she looked odd.
>
> "Why if Harold ever gave back to you, as he swore to
> me on his honour he would, that five pound note—!" (IX,
> 474)

When there is no discrimination between the relative importance
of topics for discussion there is most likely no discrimination
between morality and immorality, or significance and triviality.

Further, James never allows us to forget that much of the
elegant "talk" is a blind for illicit affairs. From the beginning
the Duchess is having an affair with Petherton, and later Petherton has an affair with Aggie. Cashmore presses an unwelcome
affair on Nanda, having become tired of his wife Lady Fanny.
And Fanny in turn flirts with Captain Dent-Douglas. Mrs. Brook
and Van have an ambiguous arrangement, but it is important
enough for Mrs. Brook to sacrifice her daughter to preserve it.

At the end of the novel the society itself is responsible for
Van's inability to marry Nanda. He, like Longdon, wants Nanda
to be pure if she is to be his wife, and yet, to keep her pure
he would have to remove himself from the corrupting society
as well. But Van cannot exist apart from it. The very society
that nurtures him blocks his marriage and thus that society is
a kind of villain.

And yet, despite its corruption and deception, the society
is a purely human medium, containing the possibility for human
relationship. In *The Misanthrope* Alceste retires to the desert
because he feels that truth is only possible in a social void. *The
Awkward Age* is more optimistic, for Nanda, through a private
adherence to principle, manages to reconstruct the society in a
new and more human configuration. In cultivating her individual

consciousness she is able to transform her society. The surrogate union of Nanda and Longdon represents a fusion of old and new values, and the two together, while retaining their individuality, become the moral standard for the new society. The ability to retain individuality and develop consciousness through an employment of social manner, the ability to have illusions while remembering paradoxically that they are illusions, was to become the central theme of James's novels in his major phase.

## The Comic Ending

Those critics who describe James's novel form as essentially tragic usually argue from the conclusions of the novels. The novels often begin with a predominantly comic tone but they seem to end with a somewhat tragic one. Yet to argue from the endings is to risk misconstruing their true form. If there is one thing upon which all theorists of comedy agree it is the independence of the comic form from a "happy ending." L. J. Potts emphasizes, "it is not the happy ending that makes a comedy."[29]

Certain types of plot and character determine the comic form, not any criteria of "happiness." When Prospero and Miranda return to the very society that originally exiled them we cannot conclude that the ending is "happy." When Dionysus of Aristophanes' *The Frogs* returns from Hades with Aeschylus to the rapidly decaying Athenian society that will reject him we can but painfully smile. When Mirabel marries Millamant and prepares to live in a chattering, hypocritical society we perceive that the end is likewise far from "happy." The greatest comedies, as evidenced by Shakespeare, Aristophanes, and Molière, characteristically reveal sobering endings.

Comedies do, however, usually move toward some affirmation which skirts or transcends death and destruction. If the Jamesian novel were tragic in form, one would logically expect an emphasis on death. But James himself insists that "the poet essentially *can't* be concerned with the act of dying. Let him deal with the sickest of the sick, it is still by the act of living that they appeal to him."[30] In only three of James's twenty novels does the protagonist die: Roderick Hudson in *Roderick Hudson,* Hyacinth Robinson in *The Princess Casamassima,* and Milly

Theale in *The Wings of the Dove.* The deaths to which the other
heroes of the novels are submitted are the ritual deaths typical
of comedy in which "suffering . . . takes the form of humiliation,
disappointment, or chagrin"[31] and all that is finally destroyed
is narrowness, fixity, and self-deception.

Comic resolutions emphasize continuity of life, and the
continuity is often symbolized by marriages celebrated at the
close. Many of James's novels end with marriages or surrogate
marriages representing the triumph of both society and individual. *The Europeans, The Tragic Muse,* and *The Golden Bowl*
end with multiple marriages; *The Reverberator* and *The Bostonians* end with single marriages; and *What Maisie Knew* and *The
Awkward Age* end with symbolic unions which approximate
marriage.

But James realizes that marriage, an affirmation of the social
order, can also represent a new restriction, a new fixity, and that
the heroes and heroines who do not marry often attain a freedom
which enables them to create a new society around themselves.
Thus James really provides a redefinition of the concept of
"happy ending." But, as in most comedy, triumph is implied
in James's endings. As Constance Rourke recognizes, "the sphere
had altered from outer circumstances to the realm of the mind
and spirit; and triumph was no longer blind and heedless, but
achieved by difficult and even desperate effort."[32] James's plots
characteristically move toward this individual freedom and away
from formulation. James affirms:

> The free spirit, always much tormented, and by no means
> always triumphant, is heroic, ironic, pathetic or whatever,
> and, as exemplified in the record of Fleda Vetch, for instance,
> "successful" only through having remained free.[33]

The all important values of moral consciousness, freedom, and
affirmation of life are never destroyed at the ends of his novels.
The protagonists nearly always remain "free."

Their freedom is, however, never an irresponsible freedom.
If James's protagonists sometimes assert total freedom at the
outsets of the novels, James himself never does. He clearly
perceives human limitation and the necessity of compromise.
Tragic heroes do not compromise. Jamesian heroes do, learning

that form without freedom produces fixity while freedom without form yields irresponsibility. The conclusions of the novels typically celebrate the fusion of freedom and form, the absolute necessity of "living" and "seeing" while maintaining a consciousness of human limitation.

The endings of nearly all of James's novels, then, reflect a pattern which is typical of the comic form. If the humorous society sometimes triumphs or remains undefeated, the protagonist either remains free or manages to escape that society. And in some cases the protagonist is able to create a new society around himself.[34]

The ending of *The Portrait of a Lady* has occasioned the critical interest that James predicted in his notebooks:

> The obvious criticism of course will be that it is not finished—that I have not seen the heroine to the end of her situation—that I have left her *en l'air.*—This is both true and false. The *whole* of anything is never told; you can only take what groups together.[35]

*The Portrait* does what all good novels, according to E. M. Forster, should do: it "opens out."

If James retains certain ambiguities in the end, he nevertheless provides an ending which is true to the comic form of the novel. Ralph twice predicts Isabel's future. When his father questions the wisdom of leaving Isabel a fortune Ralph foresees that "at first . . . she'd plunge into that pretty freely. . . . But after that she'd come to her senses, remember she has still a lifetime before her, and live within her means." (III, 263) Later, when Ralph is dying he assures Isabel, "You're very young." She replies in her world-weariness, "I feel very old," and Ralph insists, "You'll grow young again." (IV, 416)

Isabel herself recognizes the truth of Ralph's comments. When she meets Madame Merle at the convent and learns that Madame Merle is fleeing to America, Isabel feels that "This in itself was a revenge, this in itself was almost the promise of a brighter day." (IV, 379) And later James explains:

> She saw herself, in the distant years, still in the attitude of a woman who had her life to live, and these intimations

contradicted the spirit of the present hour. . . . Deep in her soul—deeper than any appetite for renunciation—was the sense that life would be her business for a long time to come. . . . It was a proof of strength—it was a proof she should someday be happy again. (IV, 392)

At the close, when Caspar Goodwood with *deus ex machina* precision comes to Isabel in Gardencourt, she has good reason to reject him once again. As she revealed early in the novel, "she was not in love with him." (III, 165) More importantly, Caspar's proposal of flight represents for Isabel a peace like unto death. "She believed just then that to let him take her in his arms would be the next best thing to her dying." (IV, 435) But when Caspar aggressively wrests a kiss from Isabel she experiences the ritual death which confirms her in her purpose to continue living. Her future, of course, will be painful, but the entire novel has been a catalogue of people living full lives in the face of adversity, and if Isabel learns anything she learns this possibility. Mr. Touchett has a bad marriage and poor health but lives happily. Ralph is tubercular but finds great amusement in everything. At the close Isabel refuses to trade life and a sense of freedom for the peaceful possessive death of Caspar Goodwood.

Paradoxically, flight with Caspar would be a denial of freedom, while a return to Osmond is an affirmation of freedom. Flight with Caspar would be a recognition of Osmond's successful manipulation of Isabel into a false position. By returning to Osmond, ostensibly to help Pansy, Isabel asserts her moral strength and will. She insists "I am not at all helpless, there are many things I mean to do." (IV, 303)

In *The Portrait of a Lady* James takes the action beyond the normal final curtain of comedy and reveals the truth of Charles Lamb's statement that the end of a comedy may be the beginning of a tragedy. The comedy blurs and "tragedy" threatens with Isabel's marriage to Osmond. But James does not finally end the novel as tragedy. Isabel experiences her ritual death, suffers vicariously with Ralph, and ends up on the other side of tragedy, affirming her youth and freedom once again. If Isabel is not fully self-aware at the close, she has regained her balance. And if the humorous society remains undefeated, it has failed to destroy her.

In *The Bostonians* the humorous society also remains undefeated; it is merely replaced by another humorous society. The women's liberation movement which controls Verena remains grotesquely powerful to the end. This sexless, distorted world view, represented by Olive Chancellor, affords James some of his most pointed satire, and Olive's fall in front of the Bostonian audience at the close is the typical comic fall of the fixed humor figure. At the end of the novel, expecting and even hoping to be martyred for the cause she has lost, Olive rushes out onto the concert hall stage only to be greeted by a polite Boston audience.

As Ransom spirits Verena away to the altar James concludes: "It is to be feared that with the union, so far from brilliant, into which she was about to enter, these were not the last [tears] she was destined to shed." (464) James realizes that Basil is also a kind of humor figure, a man obsessed with his masculinity, and almost more interested in defeating Olive than in winning Verena. But whereas Olive's humorous society represents for James a sterile termination of normal social relations, Basil's humorous society represents the triumph of a fertile social relationship, even if it is limiting and chauvinistic. Basil's society retains the values of life and continuity which Olive rejects.

The endings of *The Portrait* and *The Bostonians*, then, reflect what Northrop Frye has called "the most ironic phase of comedy" in which "a humorous society triumphs or remains undefeated" and "the demonic world is never very far away."[36] Frye goes on to suggest, however, that James's favorite form is

a comedy in which the hero does not transform a humorous society but simply escapes or runs away from it, leaving its structure as it was before. A more complex irony in this phase is achieved when a society is constructed by or around a hero, but proves not sufficiently real or strong to impose itself. . . . Because of its unrivaled opportunities for double-edged irony, this phase is a favorite of Henry James: perhaps his most searching study of it is *The Sacred Fount*, where the hero is an ironic parody of a Prospero figure creating another society out of the one in front of him.[37]

*What Maisie Knew, The Tragic Muse, The American,* and *The*

*Ambassadors* are other Jamesian examples of this comic pattern. The protagonist remains free by escaping the humorous society without being able to transform it.

As Frye notes, *The Sacred Fount* is an extreme example of this type of comedy. The narrator withers before Mrs. Briss at the end but manages to escape Newmarch on the morning train. Maisie Farrange, like the narrator of *The Sacred Fount,* also escapes her humorous society; her plan to transform it by establishing a surrogate marriage with Sir Claude is likewise too weak to succeed finally. But Maisie's escape, like that of Nick Dormer, Christopher Newman, and Lambert Strether, is much more positive than that of the narrator of *The Sacred Fount,* James insists that "the very principle of Maisie's appeal [is] her undestroyed freshness, in other words [her] vivacity of intelligence."[38]

The ending of *The Tragic Muse* is reminiscent of the typical romance comedy in which young lovers overcome some blocking figure and establish a new society represented by marriage. In *The Tragic Muse* Peter Sherringham marries Biddy, and Basil Dashwood marries Miriam Rooth. But James leaves the conclusion ambiguous as Nick and Julia remain unmarried at the end. While the union of Nick and Julia is implied, Nick's "law" of portraits provides the ambiguity. When Nick paints a portrait of Gabriel Nash the comical fellow literally disappears from Nick's life while his very image fades from the canvas, and when Nick paints Miriam Rooth she disappears figuratively from Nick's life by marrying Dashwood. Thus Nick reasons that by the "law" of his portraits Julia will never marry him if he paints her.

At the end, however, although Nick has painted Julia she has not disappeared, and the final sentence implies that she has undergone a change which will make the union possible and happy.

> I must not omit to add, this lady has not, at the latest accounts, married Mr. MacGeorge. It is very true there has been a rumour that Mr. MacGeorge is worried about her— has even ceased at all fondly to believe in her. (VIII, 441)

Mr. MacGeorge is the symbol of the political life that Nick has rejected, and the rumor that MacGeorge no longer believes in

Julia suggests that she has given up her obsession with politics. Previously Julia didn't "believe" in Nick because he wasn't serious about public life, now MacGeorge doesn't "believe" in Julia. Perhaps the "law" of Nick's portraits has caused the old Julia to disappear and a new one, created by Nick's imagination, to grow.

In any case, Nick does escape the humorous society represented by the old Julia and his mother Lady Agnes. Lady Agnes' advice to Nick reads like a parody of Strether's advice to Little Bilham in Gloriani's garden. Lady Agnes exhorts Nick to "Be great—be great. I'm old, I've lived, I've seen. Go in for a great material position. That will simplify everything else." (VII, 252–53) Nick escapes the advice of this humor figure and devotes himself to art.

Christopher Newman, like Nick Dormer, fails to marry at the end of the novel but does succeed in remaining free. Up to the close, *The American,* like *The Tragic Muse,* seems to reflect the movement of typical romance comedy, and James himself admitted in the preface to *The American* that he "had been plotting arch-romance without knowing it."[39] The Bellegardes "would positively have jumped then, . . . at my rich and easy American."[40] And James gave the play version of the novel the "happy" ending that the original lacked. What James realized in retrospect was that the form of his novel was actually that of romance comedy, but he had written an ending for an ironic comedy. The mixture yields melodrama.

But the ending is nonetheless comic. While the humorous society remains undefeated, Newman escapes with his freedom and with a personal triumph that exceeds that of the Bellegardes. He forgoes his revenge and remembers that he is "rich and tolerably young." (317) Like Isabel Archer, he has a long life ahead of him.

James's favorite form of comedy, then, is that in which "a society is constructed by or around a hero, but proves not sufficiently real or strong to impose itself." *The Sacred Fount, What Maisie Knew, The Tragic Muse,* and *The American* are representative. In *The Ambassadors* James realizes the "unrivaled opportunities for double-edged irony"[41] of this form as Strether escapes two humorous societies, Woollett and Paris, and creates a new moral vision within his own consciousness.

Several of James's novels more closely reflect the normal pattern of romance comedy in which young love opposed by blocking figures finally triumphs.[42] *The Reverberator* and *The Awkward Age* are examples, and *The Spoils of Poynton* is a parody of the normal pattern. In these novels the protagonist surmounts the obstacles of his humorous society to create a new society or transform the old one.

The plot of *The Reverberator*, while reversing the sex of the protagonist and revising the ending, almost exactly parallels that of *The American*. It is as if James, realizing the faulty ending of the earlier novel, decided to rewrite it with a "happy ending." Both novels begin with an American in Paris (Francie, Newman) who is introduced to a French character of the opposite sex (Gaston, Claire) by a fellow American (Flack, Mrs. Tristram) and immediately falls in love. Then one of the lovers leaves on a previously planned trip (Gaston to Spain, Claire to Fleurières) and upon returning introduces the American to his family (the Proberts, the Bellegardes). The parents grudgingly accept the match until some aspect of the American forces them to withdraw their acceptance and block the marriage (Francie's blundering conversation with Flack, Newman's commercial heritage). Gaston has one sister favorable to the marriage (Susan de Brécourt) and Claire has one approving sister-in-law (Urbain's wife). Gaston's mother is dead and Claire's father is dead.

But in *The Reverberator* James changes the ending to allow Gaston and Francie to marry despite parental disapproval. The conclusion is the conventional question mark that appears at the ends of most comedies.

> The party left the Hotel de l'Univers et de Cheltenham on the morrow, but it appeared to the German waiter, as he accepted another five-franc piece from the happy and now reckless Gaston, that they were even yet not at all clear as to where they were going. (XIII, 210–11)

*The Awkward Age* represents a variation on the typical comic pattern. If we read the novel as pragmatists we see Mrs. Brook as a success and Nanda and Longdon as failures. If we are idealists, as James expects us to be, we see Nanda and Longdon as triumphant. Tragedy is averted at the end when Nanda takes the plot into her own hands. In her last interview with Van, Nanda lets the young man off easily, for to expose him would be to destroy him and the society.

Mitchy, who follows Van in the final scene, affirms:

> "The generations will come and go, and the *personnel* as the newspapers say, of the saloon will shift and change, but the institution itself, as resting on a deep human need, has a long course yet to run and a good work yet to do." (IX, 523)

Nanda assures the continuity of the salon, and in her surrogate union with Mr. Longdon, "modern" and traditional values are fused into a new moral consciousness. The humorous society is transformed and a new standard of value created.

*The Spoils of Poynton,* a parody of the usual romance comedy similarly closes on a heroine who can affirm her happiness, who remains "free," and who is able to create a beautiful marriage in her vivid imagination out of Mona and Owen's union.

A final kind of plot pattern in James is one which moves "out of the world of experience into the ideal world of innocence and romance."[43] Although James did not often write this kind of comedy, *The Europeans* is a close approximation. As I suggested earlier, *The Europeans* ends with a scene typical of light comedy in which the characters stumble upon the right combination of attitudes proper to a happy ending, without really changing. Four marriages are celebrated at the close, and Eugenia's self-expulsion is typical of the expulsion of the blocking figure of romance comedy. Peter Buitenhuis recognizes the novel's movement toward an ideal world when he calls it "a comic pastoral version of the international theme."[44] And in *The Golden Bowl* this struggle to assert an appropriate social arrangement takes on an almost religious cast and represents James's closest approximation of an ideal possibility that is neither Europe nor America.

James's characteristic plots, then, are those of comedy. The majority of his major novels are examples of the international comedy of manners, parodicomedy, social satire, or some subtle combination of kinds. The conclusions of the novels do not emphasize tragic renunciation or repudiation but reveal instead a creative affirmation of human potential and limitation and a birth of moral consciousness and personal freedom which seem indestructible. The sense of potential tragedy and destruction in James is controlled by the affirmative comic movement of the plots.

# V

# Notes on Style

In his 1967 preface to *The Comic Sense of Henry James* Richard Poirier insists that

> we should not read the early James as if he were already the later one. The James of the late novels has developed an air of muffled majesty toward which he makes us anxiously solicitous. . . . Before the emergence of this later style . . . James depended on a pointedly melodramatic and comic extravagance.[1]

Although Mr. Poirier's warning may be partially justified, it is certainly misleading. Such a sharp distinction between the early and late styles prevents Poirier from appreciating the comic elements in the late novels, elements which he finds only in the early works.

F. O. Matthiessen, however, long ago pointed out that "James's humor has often been lost sight of in discussion of the solemnities of his mandarin style. But he didn't lose it himself."[2] If the early style displays melodrama and comic extragance, the late style controls those elements with increased sophistication while introducing new possibilities for high comedy.

Many of James's most perceptive critics allude in passing to his witty style. Peter Buitenhuis notes that while the style is "indirect, complicated, polysyllabic, and stately . . . a closer look reveals that it is often being used for wonderful comic purposes."[3] And Richard Chase refers to James's "humor, which none of the critics has been able to describe very well." Chase concludes that "an incapacity to follow James's elaborate joking is more often than not the reason why some readers fail to

penetrate the famous difficult style."⁴ As a master of "significant
levity," and of the "elaborately serious joke," Chase notes, James
shares in the tradition of American humor.⁵

George Meredith's description of comic style applies to
James.

> A most subtle delicacy . . . must be a natal gift in the comic
> poet. . . . People are ready to surrender themselves to witty
> thumps on the back, breast, and sides; all except the head—
> and it is there that he aims.
> . . . . . . . . . . . . . . . . . . . . . . . . . . . . . . . . . . . . . . . . . . . . . . . . . . . . . . . . .
> If, instead of falling foul of the ridiculous person with a
> satiric rod, to make him writhe and shriek aloud, you prefer
> to sting him under a semi-caress, by which he shall in his
> anguish be rendered dubious whether indeed anything has
> hurt him, you are an engine of Irony.⁶

L. J. Potts suggests that irony is "the exact stylistic equivalent
of the comic mode of thought."⁷ Henry James's style functions
on a comic irony, a delicate sense of the incongruous which notes
both subtle and obvious discrepancies. James often uses the
comic potential of his style to define his characters, reflect on
the movement of the plot, and allow him to intrude his attitudes
into an otherwise objective story.

In his unpublished dissertation, Leo T. Hendrick notes that
one prominent stylistic feature in James, often used for comic
effect, is the repetition of a word or phrase, an "obtrusive and
emphatic repetition. Where another author might avoid repetition
by synonyms or paraphrase, James insists on it."⁸ In *What Maisie
Knew*, for example, James describes Maisie's encounter with her
father and the Countess: "There was an extraordinary mute
passage between her vision of this vision of his, his vision of
her vision, and her vision of his vision of her vision," (XI, 182)
an incremental repetition rendering the vision comic.

In *The Ambassadors* James uses repetition to emphasize and
ridicule Strether's shock at seeing Chad and Madame de Vionnet
in his Lambinet painting. Strether observes that the countryside
hotel is

> a quiet retreat enough, no doubt—*at which* they had been

spending the twenty-four hours, *to which* they had fully meant to return that evening, *from which* they had so remarkably swum into Strether's ken, and *the tacit repudiation of which* had been thus the essence of her comedy. (XXII, 265) [Italics mine]

Two related features of James's ironic comic style are exaggeration and deflation. By describing an essentially trivial event in solemnly precise terminology, or an important event in trivial language, James provides the linguistic incongruity necessary to evoke laughter. In *The American*, for instance, when Newman learns that Valentin will duel over Noémie James explains, "Newman uttered an imprecation which, though brief—it consisted simply of the interjection 'Oh!' followed by a geographical, or more correctly, perhaps a theological noun in four letters —had better not be transferred to these pages." (211)

But James often employs this technique as more than a mere narrative joke. In *The Golden Bowl* James reveals the Prince's predicament and criticizes English social life when he describes the Prince's daily activities in terms of battle imagery and ritual.

His body, very constantly, was engaged at the front—in shooting, in riding, in golfing, in walking, over the fine diagonals of meadow-paths or round the pocketed corners of billiard-tables; it sufficiently, on the whole, in fact, bore the brunt of bridge-playing, of breakfasting, lunching, tea-drinking, dining, and of the nightly climax over the *bottigliera*, as he called it, of the bristling tray; it met, finally, to the extent of the limited tax on lip, on gesture, on wit, most of the current demands of conversation and expression. (XXIII, 327–28)

The exaggerated catalogue reveals the absurdity of the society that treats the Prince as an "it," a body to fill the ranks of social triviality.

The reverse of this technique consists in demeaning, through the language itself, what should be a significant event or serious observation. Strether, in *The Ambassadors*, views the marvelous change which has been wrought in Chad, but somehow his description of it sounds more like the cry of a carnival barker promising wondrous results from his cure-all elixir. According to Strether, Europe had

> retouched his features, drawn them with a cleaner line.
> It had cleared his eyes and settled his colour and polished
> his fine square teeth. . . . It had toned his voice, established
> his accent, encouraged his smile. (XXI, 152)

The reader who perceives the comedy of the language has early proof that Chad is not all that Strether imagines.

Repetition, exaggeration, and deflation are prominent features of James's comic style. As Richard Chase notes, James's metaphors, too, "are likely to be given a tone of elevated levity which at once enjoys what is being said and takes note of its extravagance."[9] The extravagant extension of metaphor types characters and provides wit. In *The Europeans*, for example, James wittily types Charlotte. Her imagination "took no journeys whatever; she kept it, as it were, in her pocket, with the other furniture of this receptacle—a thimble, a little box of peppermint, and a morsel of court-plaster." (74)

James fully exploits the possibilities of extended metaphor, a favorite device of Molière and Congreve, in his own version of the comedy of manners genre, *The Awkward Age*. The conversation at Tishy Grendon's party, for instance, bristles with wit. Longdon comments:

> "Very horrid of two sisters to be both, in their marriages,
> so wretched."
> "Ah but Tishy, I maintain," Mrs. Brook returned, "*isn't*
> wretched at all. If I were satisfied that she's really so I'd
> never let Nanda come to her."
> "That's the most extraordinary doctrine, love," the
> Duchess interposed. "When you're satisfied a woman's 'really' poor you never give her a crust?"
> "Do you call Nanda a crust, Duchess?" Vanderbank
> amusedly asked.
> "She's all at any rate, apparently, just now, that poor
> Tishy has to live on."
> "You're severe, then," the young man said, "on our
> dinner of tonight." (IX, 412)

Another device which James borrows from the comedy of manners tradition is that of emblematic names for his characters. James's interest in names can be inferred from the long list of possible choices which he regularly kept in his notebooks. Names like Christopher Newman, Felix Young, Caspar Goodwood, and Fanny Assingham are all obvious comments on the characters. In *The American,* James is careful to point out the comedy inherent in Urbain de Bellegarde's name. At one point Urbain turns to Newman "with sustained urbanity," (121) and later he is "apparently determined to be even more urbane than usual." (243)

In addition to names, James uses a variety of the Dickensian "signature" to type characters. The Countess in *What Maisie Knew* "had a nose that was far too big and eyes that were far too small and a mustache that was, well, not so happy a feature as Sir Claude's." (XI, 193) Edward Brookenham of *The Awkward Age* "seemed to bend for sitting down more hinges than most men." (IX, 66) And in *The Spoils of Poynton* Mona Brigstock's "expression would probably have been beautiful if she had had one." (X, 9) In the later novels Waymarsh is a railway passenger and an Indian chief, and Maggie Verver is a performer in pink tights.

A final and highly elusive device which James employs for comic effect is that of self-parody. James was well aware of the potential for parody in his style and he exploited that potential. Although it is sometimes difficult to distinguish comic from serious intent in some of the later sentences, the difficulty is often resolved when the passage is read aloud. James requested that his works be read aloud and the practice often clearly reveals a deliberately inflated verbosity. James is never more explicit in his self-parody than in the following passage from *The Golden Bowl.* Mr. Verver sizes up the Prince:

> Nothing perhaps even could more have confirmed Mr. Verver's account of his surface than the manner in which these golden drops evenly flowed over it. They caught in no interstice, they gathered in no concavity; the uniform smoothness betrayed the dew but by showing for the moment a richer tone. The young man, in other words, unconfusedly smiled. (XXIII, 138)

The elaborate hyperbolic description of the smile is Verver's, and the undercutting comment is James's.

The devices of repetition, exaggeration and deflation, extended metaphor and conceit, and emblematic names and epigrams characterize Henry James's comic style and serve to reveal character. James uses imagery in a similar manner to clarify character and to comment obliquely on the plot. If James's characters, plots, and stylistic devices are often those of comedy, his imagery is also typical of the form.

Northrop Frye contrasts the imagery of comedy with that of tragedy:

> In the comic vision the *human* world is a community, or a hero who represents the wish-fulfillment of the reader. The archetype of images of symposium, communion, order, friendship and love. In the tragic vision the human world is a tyranny or anarchy, or an individual or isolated man. . . . Marriage or some equivalent consummation belongs to the comic vision; the harlot, witch and other varieties of Jung's 'terrible mother' belongs to the tragic one.
>
> In the comic vision the *animal* world is a community of domesticated animals, usually a flock of sheep, or a lamb, or one of the gentler birds, usually a dove. . . . In the tragic vision the animal world is seen in terms of beasts and birds of prey, wolves, vultures, serpents, dragons. . . .
>
> In the comic vision the *vegetable* world is a garden, grove or park. . . . In the tragic vision it is a sinister forest. . . .
>
> In the comic vision the *mineral* world is a city. . . .
>
> In the tragic vision the mineral world is seen in terms of deserts, rocks and ruins.[10]

It is obvious that Henry James took most of his imagery from the stock of comedy. Images of symposium, order, friendship, communion, love, marriage, domestic animals, gardens, groves, parks, and cities fill his novels. Images of isolation, harlots, wolves, serpents, vultures, dragons, sinister forests, deserts, rocks, and ruins are significantly rare.

In his tabular account of Jamesian imagery Robert L. Gale suggests that it is "often comic" and "habitually paints setting, characterizes, foreshadows, implements plot, and reinforces theme."[11] A summary of Gale's findings demonstrates James's preferences for the traditional images of comedy.

According to Gale, the animals named in the novels in order of frequency are "horse, sheep, dog, and cat . . . lion . . . rabbit, cow, donkey, tiger, deer, bear, wolf, monkey, and mouse."[12] The dove is the most frequently mentioned bird, and the animals are capped off by "half a dozen vague Thurberesque dragons, and two insignificant worms."[13]

In the human sphere James's most prominent images are, according to Gale, war, art, and religion. War is the only category atypical of comedy, but James often uses his war images comically as in the mock epic pattern in *The Spoils of Poynton.*

The writers most frequently mentioned in James's fiction are predominantly comic writers. In order of most frequency they are "Thackeray, Balzac, Dickens, and Cervantes."[14]

Gale relegates "death, deserts, and diseases" to virtual insignificance by leaving them unexamined. And F. W. Dupee concurs that "if the stories are full of the stress of penury and constraint, they are far richer in the related imagery of abundance: the summer season, the garden, the holiday, the party, the museum, the great house."[15]

Gardens and houses are among the most prevalent images in the novels. Gardens are a haven for Maisie Farrange, representing lovely regions with defined limits and fixed centers of security. All of the great climaxes of Isabel Archer's career, from her refusal of Warburton to her flight from Goodwood, occur in gardens. It is in Gloriani's garden that Strether makes his celebrated speech to Little Bilham.

Dale Underwood suggests that the park or garden in Restoration drama provides a value standard of art and nature, order and pleasure, for the world of the plays. Further, "the formal character of the park, which bespeaks its state of art, contributes its own irony to the state of nature for which it is the setting—the amoral appetitiveness, warfare, and general self-seeking."[16] The garden in James reflects the same ironic norm for his novels.

As garden imagery represents a physical reflection of the moral and aesthetic norm of the novels, season imagery parallels and comments on the plot and character. As is usual in comedy most of James's novels take place in spring and summer. Winter

is usually passed over in summary, and when winter is referred
to it usually condemns some character.

*The American*, for example, begins in May of one year and
ends in spring of the next, leaving Newman to face the season
of renewal and rebirth. *The Europeans* begins in May with a
snowfall, and the unseasonably wintry weather is always linked
to Eugenia. Eugenia's expulsion at the end is thus linked mythi-
cally to the triumph of spring over winter, life over death, and
joy over gloom. *The Tragic Muse* begins in summer and ends
in March as the characters marry or prepare to marry. *The Awkward Age* takes place in spring and ends with Nanda's renewal of
the salon in June. *The Portrait of a Lady* begins in "the perfect
middle of a splendid summer afternoon," (III, 1) winter passes
quickly in sunny Italy, and Isabel meets Osmond in May.
Whereas the first volume of the novel takes place predominantly
in spring and summer, the second volume is predominantly
winter. But Ralph dies in May, and at the end of the book Isabel
faces a new spring.

All of these novels follow the conventional mythic pattern
of comedy, beginning with spring and youth, passing through
winter and experience, and ending in a new spring and rebirth.
Further, the season imagery provides James with a means of
intruding obliquely to comment on character and plot. *The
Bostonians* represents a good example of the importance of such
imagery in the novels.

As I suggested earlier, *The Bostonians* is a novel dominated
by two humorous protagonists, and the conclusion merely trades
one humorous society for another. But James's sympathies are
clear, and he asserts his preferences through his use of season
imagery. The first section of the novel takes place from October
to December 187–, the place is Boston, and the focus is Olive.
The second section of the novel takes place two years later in
March 187– in New York, where the focus is Basil, and at
Cambridge, where the focus is Verena. During this month Basil
and Verena meet in Central Park. The third section takes place
in August of the same year at Marmion and Boston where the
focus is the whole group of characters.

Thus James presents the Olive-Verena relationship in the
context of images of winter, death, and frigidity. At one point

Matthias Pardon warns the two friends to come out of the cold before they "freeze together," (136) emphasizing the cold sexual undertones in their relationship. The Basil-Verena relationship is formed in early spring, emphasizing rebirth, love, and growth. The novel ends in summer, suggesting the ambiguity of a marriage that could look forward to either winter or Indian summer.

James's season imagery is functional in the later novels also, *The Ambassadors* ending ambiguously in summer, and *The Golden Bowl* pervaded by the "sunny gusty lusty English April." (XXIII, 332)

The pervasive functional imagery and the linguistic devices of comedy enable James to intrude obliquely to comment on the characters and plots while maintaining his "detached" pose. The critical emphasis on point of view has sometimes obscured the obvious intrusions which James is able to make through the style and imagery with which he describes the thoughts and actions of his "centers of consciousness." If he does not obviously "go behind" to explain, he subtly and wittily "goes behind" at almost every turn.

Ian Watt demonstrates the truth of this observation in his brilliant "explication" of the first paragraph of *The Ambassadors.* Watt shows how James, in adopting an ironic narrative tone, is able to be both inside and outside Strether's mind. Thus both reader and narrator know more about Strether than he knows himself. James's description of Strether's thoughts is sufficiently couched in witty circumlocution to reveal what only an omniscient outside observer could know: "Strether's delicate critical intelligence is often blinkered by a highly vulnerable mixture of moral generosity towards others combined with an obsessive sense of personal inadequacy."[17] Watt suggests that the best description of James's mature technique is not "irony," but "humor" because that term allows for the deeper emotional involvement and sympathetic treatment that James displays.

James used the same technique earlier in *The Spoils of Poynton.* While seeming to center only in Mrs. Gereth's consciousness at the outset, as if merely factually cataloguing her thoughts, James exposes and criticizes her at the same time. The epigrammatic style, the verbal ironies, and the exaggerated description of Mrs. Gereth's "suffering" both elevate and undercut her. It is James's witty voice we hear when we learn that Mrs. Gereth sees "imbecilities of decoration," is the "heroine of Poynton," and has been kept awake all night by the wallpaper in her bedroom. Through elevating her morning vigil to heroic proportions James "intrudes" to comment.

A similar stylistic feat enables James to stand behind Maisie and reveal things that she could never see, or at least never explain or describe. Indeed, much of the comedy of *What Maisie Knew* arises from the discrepancy between what Maisie sees as normal and what the reader, from James's omniscient perspective, sees as abnormal. The technique is, of course, much like that employed by Flaubert in *Madame Bovary* in which the narrator stands behind the uneducated heroine providing her with words she couldn't have understood and sentences she couldn't have constructed.

The comic elements of repetition, exaggeration, and deflation in James's style, and the functional comic imagery, suffuse and inform both the early and late novels. Poirier is wrong to claim "muffled majesty" as an excuse for not examining the rich comic possibilities of the major phase. The precision and wit of the language in the late novels makes possible a kind of comedy that was not evident in the earlier and more melodramatic works. Far from producing the vagueness, abstraction, and boredom claimed by some readers, the late style moves toward clarity, concretion, and amusement.

# VI

# The Major Phase

*The Ambassadors*

More has been written on *The Ambassadors*, perhaps, than on
any other Jamesian novel. James himself left three extended
"commentaries" on the book: the notebook "germ,"[1] the "project" for the novel which he sent to *Harper's*,[2] and the preface.
James considered the book "frankly, quite the best, 'all round,'
of my productions,"[3] but he is characteristically ambiguous
about its particular generic form. In the notebook entry he refers
to the novel as "the whole comedy, or tragedy, the drama,
whatever we call it."[4]

Criticism has since called *The Ambassadors* many things,
but few critics have called it predominantly comic, and only two
essays have been devoted to the comedy of the novel.[5] Flounder-
ing in generic uncertainty, critics have been unable to agree on
the quality of Lambert Strether's education or the meaning of
the conclusion of the novel. Does Strether learn everything or
nothing, and if he learns anything, exactly what is it? Is the
conclusion Strether's renunciation of all happiness and his return
to the pathetic dominance of Mrs. Newsome, or is it positive
affirmation, and if so, what does it affirm?

Such questions have interested critics since the novel was
published, and the answers have been various. An early review
in *The Nation* suggests that when Sarah Pocock arrives in Paris
to replace Strether as ambassador she "sweeps the cobwebs from
Strether's brain. . . . he was inevitably and by the nature of things
committed to Woollett."[6] E. M. Forster observes that the "rigid
pattern" of the novel "shuts the door on life and leaves the
novelist doing exercises, generally in the drawing-room."[7] Even
F. O. Matthiessen in his perceptive study of "the major phase"

complains that although Strether has awakened to a new sense
of life by the end "he does nothing at all to fulfill that sense. . . .
we cannot help feeling his relative emptiness."[8] And more re-
cently Robert E. Garis has argued that Strether's vision in the
French countryside "produces . . . a sickening sequence of acts
and attitudes devoid of imaginative energy but at the same time
depressingly agile in both romantic and moralistic self-deception—produces, in brief, final evidence of Strether's incapacity
for either education or life."[9]

Strether's education, his capacity for life, and his self-
awareness present the most important questions in the book, and
no answers which ignore the genre of the novel can approach
validity. The remarkable organic concision and the dramatic and
scenic unity make an understanding of the form of the novel
indispensable to a clear understanding of Strether's final vision.
Leon Edel suggests the proper approach when he describes *The
Ambassadors* as a "trans-Atlantic comedy of manners." "And like
all great comedies, it treated of matters grave as well as gay."[10]
The form of the novel is that of comedy, and Strether's final
vision is the highest comic vision available to the form.

*The Ambassadors* is the late novel which owes most to the
comedy of manners form. Chad, upon inheriting his money, has
gone to the bad; that is, to Paris. Mrs. Newsome, sitting on the
remainder of the family fortune, is divided between the dread
that Chad will marry the Parisian strumpet with whom he lives,
which will be awful, and the fear that he will merely continue
to live with her, which will be worse. In pursuit of the decadent
son, Strether is like the typical country visitor who comes to the
city and is seduced by its ways into exchanging a morally staid
life for a more sensuous and intellectually rich one. In his role
as Mrs. Newsome's emissary, Strether is also the typical blocking
figure, exerting paternal power to separate two lovers. As in
James's earlier parody romance, *The Spoils of Poynton, The
Ambassadors* is told from the blocking figure's point of view.
But in this novel the blocking figure is converted.

The other characters also are reminiscent of the conventional
social types from the comedy of manners: the man of the world,
the *jeune fille*, the *femme du monde*, the great artist, the young
rake, and the deceived husband. By contrast to Strether the other

players are, as Richard Chase observes, "the fools, gulls, and fops of the stage comedies."[11]

As in James's earlier comedies of manners, the opposing societies or conflicting sensibilities which produce the drama are America and Europe, here symbolized by Woollett and Paris. The conflict is not, however, as simple as Stephen Spender implies when he concludes that "Paris is life. Woollett is death."[12] Woollett does seem rigid, inflexible, and parochial while Paris seems relaxed, flexible, and cosmopolitan. But, as in the earlier novels, both societies represent potential for both good and evil. Strether's character reflects the America James loved, and Madame de Vionnet's suffering reflects the dangers of European manner and sensibility.

Nevertheless, the novel is structured partly on the polarity of Woollett and Paris, and Woollett is obviously the negative pole. In Woollett, individual identity is determined by names on the covers of green reviews or by marriage to prominent persons. When Maria Gostrey asks Strether who Jim Pocock is, Strether replies, "Why Sally's husband. That's the only way we distinguish people at Woollett." (XXI, 72) Strether himself has led the life of a nonentity.

In Woollett, productivity is another form of identity and there is something positively unpleasant or embarrassing about leisure. As Strether tells Maria, "Woollett isn't sure it ought to enjoy." (XXI, 16) Woollett's moral strictures and Puritan frame of mind prevent it from finding "amusement," a quality upon which James repeatedly insisted. Strether reveals that although "there were opinions at Woollett," they are on "only three or four" subjects, and people are ashamed of them. (XXI, 173) In Paris, however, Strether discovers that opinions are a prime aspect of enjoyment and are actually cultivated and made the basis of personal relationship.

Finally, despite its moral intensity and concern with the future, Woollett has no positive conception of the end toward which it so strenuously moves. The little unnamed article which symbolizes all of Chad's future and all of the Newsomes' dreams is "a small, trivial, rather ridiculous object of commonest domestic use." (XXI, 60) It is even too vulgar fro Strether to hazard naming it. And yet Strether, speaking as Mrs. Newsome's emissary, mechanically affirms that it is "a big brave bouncing business. A roaring trade . . . a great production, a great industry." (XXI, 59) All of Woollett's moral energy is centered on this object, and it becomes the real reason for Strether's mission to retrieve Chad who will become advertising manager.

Paris, on the other hand, is "a jewel brilliant and hard," (XXI, 89) and James chooses it as an antithesis to Woollett from among the cities of Europe because "There was the dreadful little old tradition, one of the platitudes of the human comedy, that people's moral scheme *does* break down in Paris."[13] Although Paris lacks the creative moral possibility of Woollett, it also lacks the repressive moral vigor. And Parisian society cultivates leisure and amusement, delighting in the ambiguities of human behavior.

Both cities, therefore, represent for Strether and for James attitudes which are valuable and dangerous. If Woollett is narrow and unimaginative it also represents a beautiful devotion to principle and morality. If Paris is the capacity to enjoy and expand awareness, it also represents appearance and cynicism. But, as Leon Edel observes, Europe is "the very touchstone of the novel"[14] and the comic action arises largely from the conflict between characters who see life from the narrow perspective of Woollett or from the larger perspective of Paris.

As the title suggests, James presents the movement from Woollett to Paris in the humorous terms of the mock-heroic, just as he had previously imaged the conflict over the "spoils" of Poynton. Throughout the novel Strether's affair is treated as a diplomatic mission, and the language and strategy of diplomacy are constantly evident. Strether's first private meeting with Madame de Vionnet reads like the transcript of an initial meeting between two representatives of opposing governments negotiating a peace. Marie begins:

> "I don't think you seriously believe in what you're doing," she said; "but all the same, you know, I'm going to treat you quite as if I did."
>
> "By which you mean," Strether directly replied, "quite as if you didn't! I assure you it won't make the least difference with me how you treat me."

"Well," she said, taking that menace bravely and philosophically enough, "the only thing that really matters is that you shall get on with me."

"Ah but I don't!" he immediately returned.

It gave her another pause; which, however, she happily enough shook off. "Will you consent to go on with me a little—provisionally—as if you did?" (XXI, 247–48)

The polite verbal battle, the initial diplomatic amenities, the jockeying for position, and final establishment of a compromise base for relations all suggest conscious parody of the ambassadorial role which Strether has assumed.

James adds to the mock-heroic tone by doubling the American ambassadors in Paris, sending a new deputation led by Sarah Pocock. Whereas Strether had originally come to Paris to rescue Chad, now the Pococks come to Paris to rescue Chad and Strether. As spokesman for "the deputation from Woollett" (XXII, 62) Sarah Pocock uses the ambassadorial "we." She tells Strether, "You're right, we haven't quite known what you mean, Mother and I, but now we see Chad's magnificent." (XXII, 80) Strether feels "like the outgoing ambassador . . . doing honor to his appointed successor." (XXII, 65)

The Pococks, in their moral rigidity and lack of response to "Europe," are a comic parody of Strether's earlier response to his new surroundings. Having himself been "effectively bribed," (XXII, 69) he wonders whether Sarah is likewise bribable, and in his shifted position he regards her as "the enemy." His strategy for revealing to the Pococks his questionable relationship with Maria Gostrey is "a conception of carrying the war into the enemy's country by showing surprise at the enemy's ignorance." (XXI, 163) Strether ironically becomes Chad's and his own ambassador, negotiating with the enemy Pococks.

But if the Pococks parody Strether's mission, they also force him to review his understanding of his situation. Upon their arrival he wonders:

Was he, on this question of Chad's improvement, fantastic and away from the truth? Did he live in a false world. . . . Was this contribution of the real possibly the mission of the Pococks?—had they come to make the work of observation,

as *he* had practised observation, crack and crumble. . . . Had
they come in short to be sane where Strether was destined
to feel that he himself had only been silly? (XXII, 80–81)

James had examined the possibilities of the ultimate insanity of
the creative mind in *The Sacred Fount*. But, unlike the narrator
of that novel, Strether shares a community of love and relationship with his new European allies, and his approach to life is
positive and compassionate. Strether survives the test of seeing
his own earlier self parodied in the Pococks, and wonders
whether it would not make "more for reality to be silly with
these persons [Chad, Marie, and Maria] than sane with Sarah
and Jim." (XXII, 81)

Finally, the Pococks serve the additional comic function of
providing the occasion for doubling and tripling both ambassa-
dors and "virtuous attachments." In his notebook outline James
recognizes the rich comic possibilities of the Pococks' arrival.
He catalogues the potential relationships: "The Vionnets and the
Pococks, Chad and his sister, Pocock and his brother-in-law,
Chad and Pocock's sister, Strether and Pocock, Pocock and
Strether, Strether and everyone and everything, but Strether and
Mrs. Pocock in especial."[15]

When Strether first arrives in Paris as Mrs. Newsome's ambassador, Maria Gostrey observes that Little Bilham is Chad's
ambassador, getting daily communiqués from Cannes. She perceives that the seemingly accidental meeting of Little Bilham
and Strether at Chad's apartment has been carefully and artfully
planned. After meeting Chad and Madame de Vionnet, Strether
thinks that Madame de Vionnet will be Chad's new ambassador,
but he soon learns that Chad is ambassador for Madame de
Vionnet. Again Maria Gostrey interprets the situation correctly.
"I dare say you're right . . . about Mr. Newsome's little plan.
He *has* been trying you—has been reporting on you to these
friends." (XXI, 187–88) If the American ambassadors are comically doubled, the European ambassadors are tripled.

The "virtuous attachments" also receive the same treatment.
Upon meeting the Vionnets, Strether assumes that little Jeanne
is Chad's virtuous attachment, but later learns that Madame de
Vionnet herself fills the role. Strether has already formed his own

"virtuous attachment" with Maria Gostrey, and the advent of
the Pococks forces him self-consciously to justify his friendship
with her. When Marie mentions Maria to Sarah, Strether abruptly
and somewhat nervously counters:

> "Oh yes indeed . . . Mrs. Pocock knows about Miss Gostrey.
> Your mother, Sarah, must have told you about her; your
> mother knows everything," he sturdily pursued. "And I
> cordially admit," he added with his conscious gaiety of
> courage, "that she's as wonderful a woman as you like."
> (XXII, 101)

Suspicious Sarah Pocock replies dryly that she knows nothing
about Maria Gostrey.

Thus Strether, who goes to Paris to rescue Chad from a
"virtuous attachment," forms one of his own. And when Sarah
comes to rescue Chad and Strether, she herself forms a "virtuous
attachment" with Waymarsh and goes off on a trip to Switzerland.
Again Maria Gostrey perceives the situation. Strether asks her
about Sarah, "You mean she has fallen in love?" and Maria
replies, "I mean she wonders if she hasn't—and it serves all her
purpose." (XXII, 135)

Finally, Jim Pocock, Waymarsh, and Chad all reflect aspects
of Strether and partially serve, like Sarah Pocock, as parodic
copies of him. In his notebook James suggests that Jim Pocock
"is an example, in characteristically vulgar form, and with all
due humorous effect, of the same 'fatal' effect of European
opportunities on characters giving way too freely, which Strether
more subtly embodies."[16] Jim's enthusiastic response to Europe
and the magnificent "varieties" is the "type" response of a tourist
in Paris who immediately wants to see all the girlie shows. And
Strether perceives his own potential similarity to Pocock. "Might
it even become the same should he marry in a few months?"
(XXII, 82) Pocock represents a picture of what would be in store
for Strether as Mrs. Newsome's husband.

Waymarsh is another aspect of Strether. As the "conscience
of Milrose" he represents Strether's American morality and sus-
picion of amusement and leisure. But Strether refuses to allow
the "humor" aspect of his own character to prevail, and Waymarsh is partially converted in the end.

Strether's relationship to Chad, however, provides the situation for the most obvious comic "turn" in the novel. Just when
Chad is ready to agree to return to Woollett, Strether decides
that he must stay. Chad is incredulous and Strether asks (as Chad
had earlier) that the young man have patience with him and give
him time. Chad asks, "You want me now to 'stay?'" (XXII, 31)
and James comments:

> The change of position and of relation, for each, was so oddly
> betrayed in the question that Chad laughed out as soon as
> he had uttered it—which made Strether also laugh. (XXII,
> 34)

James emphasizes this comic reversal of roles when he reveals
Strether's fear that Chad will misinterpret Strether's "virtuous
attachment" to Maria Gostrey and write home to Mrs. Newsome
about it. Although Strether is supposed to judge Chad's misbe-
havior, he worries that Chad will judge his. The juxtaposition
of a youthful but sophisticated Chad with the mature but innocent and gullible Strether is itself comic.

The structure of the novel, then, with its opposition of
conflicting societies, its mock-heroic tone, and its doublings and
triplings is that of the comedy of manners. Within this framework
Lambert Strether progresses slowly toward a great comic ironic
vision. Indeed, his final vision is the central focus of the novel,
and the steps in his education are important in fully understanding the nature of his ultimate insight.

F. W. Dupee suggests that at the beginning of the novel
Strether displays the "kind [of innocence] usually reserved for
the fools or dupes of comedy."[17] The American innocent, faced
with more things than Woollett has ever dreamed of in its
philosophy, will, nevertheless, be educated by his European
experience toward full, mature wisdom. By the end of the novel
Strether has gained a perspective on himself and his situation,
on morality and beauty, which places him above any other
Jamesian protagonist. James had expressed doubt about making
any fictional character too finely aware. But Strether's awareness
at the close, an awareness based on an understanding of his
previous ignorance, approaches omniscience.

Ian Watt observes that James's attitude toward Strether at the outset is "humorous."[18] Strether arrives at Liverpool sporting his "perpetual pair of glasses" (XXI, 8) and is rather too pleased in his discovery that Waymarsh has not yet arrived. In the first paragraph Strether reveals his concern for Waymarsh, his love of Waymarsh, and his relief that he doesn't have to see Waymarsh just yet. Strether is a conscientious friend who would feel guilty if anyone, including himself, knew that he was less than anxious to meet an old friend immediately. James couches Strether's thoughts in negative hyperbole, exposing Strether's desire to fool himself. Strether is "not wholly disconcerted" by Waymarsh's absence but he does "not absolutely . . . desire" his presence, and he happily laments the fact that he will have to "postpone for a few hours the enjoyment of" Waymarsh's company. He bravely tells himself that he can "wait without disappointment." (XXI, 3) Strether's pleasure is revealed through the language of disappointment, and his efforts to fool himself relate him unmistakably to the gull of traditional comedy.

But if Strether's self-deception is slightly comic at the outset, he appreciates the human necessity of forms. He considers it his duty to make Waymarsh believe that he is anxious to see him, and when he does meet Waymarsh he feigns absolute delight. At the beginning of the novel Strether already knows what it takes Maggie Verver so long to learn: the value of manners in personal relationships. The important knowledge Strether must gain is wholly different.

Part of Strether's problem from the beginning is his rigid adherence to Woollett morality, symbolized by his desire to formulate and categorize his experience in Europe. Like the humors of traditional comedy, Strether wants formulation rather than freedom. James suggests in the preface that "the false position for him, I say, was obviously to have presented himself at the gate of that boundless menagerie primed with a moral scheme of the most approved pattern which was yet framed to break down on any approach to vivid facts."[19]

Strether admits that "what he wanted was some idea that would simplify" (XXI, 82) and he grasps at any formula which might help him to understand Chad. On first meeting Chad, Strether quickly types him as "a man of the world—a formula that indeed seemed to come now in some degree to his relief."

(XXI, 152) But Strether's initial formula is abruptly overturned and Strether substitutes another equally erroneous label: "he asked himself if he weren't perhaps really dealing with an irreducible young Pagan." (XXI, 156–57) Since a pagan is "the thing most wanted at Woollett" (XXI, 157) Strether jumps at this idea. If Chad is indeed a pagan, he has been made so by a malign influence and is in need of rescue. As the problem begins to reveal its complexity Strether continues to search for an easy and moralistic way out. Late in volume 1 "He failed quite to see how his situation could clear up at all logically except by some turn of events that would give him the pretext of disgust." (XXI, 256–57)

Strether's initial education is a moral education. All his Woollett categories are destined to failure because they distort reality. Strether's first great moment of awareness comes, of course, in Gloriani's garden where he realizes that Woollett's morality at its worst is narrow and restrictive, and ultimately destructive to any creative living. At this point in his education Strether has given up his moral sense altogether, or so he thinks, and his famous advice to Little Bilham is a great amoral tribute to life.

James affirms in the preface that Strether's speech to Little Bilham is the "essence" of the novel. "Live all you can; it's a mistake not to." (XXI, 217) And later in the novel when Little Bilham reverts to the advice, "Didn't you adjure me . . . to see?" (XXI, 278) Strether fails to correct him. Living and seeing, consciousness and awareness, are the thematic heart of the novel. But if at this moment in Gloriani's garden Strether can affirm the necessity of living and seeing, he does not yet himself possess the full comic vision. Two subsequent painful experiences are required to impress upon Strether the consequences of his advice to Little Bilham.

Strether, weary of his ambassadorial responsibilities, journeys alone into the French countryside and comes upon a scene which recalls a Lambinet painting he had once thought of buying. As he steps into the Lambinet frame he sees "exactly the right thing" to complete the picture: "two very happy persons" floating down the river in a boat. But when he perceives that the couple in the boat is actually Marie and Chad, he experiences the ritual death typical of comedy and becomes sick to "his spiritual stomach." (XXII, 265) But James does not emphasize his disillusionment so much as he does Strether's struggle to make it right, to incorporate a broader vision of "life" into the Lambinet. Realizing that he is not "in Madame de Vionnet's boat," Strether quickly regains his balance and hails the couple loudly. What he learns through this experience is that "intimacy, at such a point, was *like* that—and what in the world else would one have wished it to be like?" He finds himself "supposing innumerable and wonderful things," (XXII, 266) for the intimacy is such a "vivid illustration of his famous knowing how to live." (XXII, 264)

But Strether does not fully appreciate the difference his new knowledge makes for himself until later. It is in the telegraph office on the following day that Strether attains a full comic vision which reconciles human ideality with human limitation, human morality with human passion. Glancing around at the bustling life in the *Postes et Télégraphes*, Strether realizes that "He was mixed up with the typical tale of Paris, and so were they, poor things—how could they all together help being? They were no worse than he, in short, and he no worse than they—if, queerly enough, no better." (XXII, 271)

Meredith writes that comedy "enfolds characters with the wretched host of the world, huddles them with us all in an ignoble assimilation,"[20] and Louis Kronenberger defines the comic vision as "the evidence that we are no better than other people, and ... the knowledge that most other people are no better than we are. It makes us more critical but it leaves us more tolerant."[21] Wylie Sypher observes that the comic recognition that one is a fool is the "moral perception that competes with tragic recognition."[22] Throughout the novel Strether had hesitantly and uncertainly moved toward this moral perception. Early in the book he wondered "Were there then sides on which his predicament threatened to look rather droll to him?" (XXI, 89) and he suspected that he "carried himself like a fool." (XXI, 138) In his adjuration to Little Bilham in Gloriani's garden he had expounded on the limitations inherent in freedom. Life is, he affirmed, "at the best a tin mould . . . into which, a helpless jelly, one's consciousness is poured. . . . Still, one has the illusion of freedom." (XXI, 218) What Strether experiences in the telegraph office is the illusory quality of his superiority and his freedom. Like everyone else he is imperfect and limited.

And yet, despite the sobering knowledge, Strether resiliently rebounds to affirm the beauty of the whole situation and his precious fallibility. Unlike Christopher Newman, *The Sacred Fount* narrator, or Isabel Archer before him, Strether completely accepts the awareness of his innate comicality while asserting the ever present possibilities of life. Earlier "he had seemed to wince at the amount of comedy involved; whereas in his present posture he could only ask himself how he should enjoy any attempt from her [Marie] to take the comedy back. He shouldn't enjoy it at all." (XXII, 277) And he sees himself as "the droll mixture . . . of his braveries and fears, the general spectacle of his art and his innocence." (XXII, 278)

Strether achieves what Hegel calls "the happy frame of mind, a hale condition of soul, which, fully aware of itself, can suffer the dissolution of its aims and realization."[23] Or in Meredith's terms he has been "able to detect the ridicule of them you love without loving them less; and . . . able to see yourself somewhat ridiculous in dear eyes, and accepting the correction their image of you proposes."[24] Strether discovers his own lack of moral superiority as well as the inadequacy of the moral views of either Woollett or Paris. His illusions and pretensions are squared with reality and he sees the beauty of his situation. "The work, however admirable, was nevertheless of the strict human order, and in short it was marvelous that the companion of mere earthly joys, of comforts, aberrations (however one classed them) within the common experience, should be so transcendently prized." (XXII, 285) At the height of vision Strether is able to see Madame de Vionnet as both "the finest and subtlest creature" and as "a maidservant crying for her young man." (XXII, 286)

The final dialogue with Maria Gostrey is probably the most misinterpreted passage in all of James. Richard Chase, who has written on the comedy in the novel, complains that the rejection of Miss Gostrey is "another one of those all too gratuitous renunciations that James prizes so highly."[25] F. O. Matthiessen feels that Strether "leaves Paris and Maria to go back to no

prospect of life at all."[26] And Yvor Winters claims it is a "sacrifice
of morality to appearances."[27]

But to see the end of the novel as tragic renunciation is to
misread both Strether's vision and the form of the book. Within
the comic structure Maria Gostrey is merely the comic confidante
described in chapter 3. James insists in the preface that Maria
is "the reader's friend much rather" than Strether's "and she acts
in that capacity, and *really* in that capacity alone."[28] She "has
nothing to do with the matter . . . but has everything to do with
the manner"[29] of the novel. To feel sorry for Miss Gostrey is
to forget that she is not really part of the "matter" of the book.

Strether's final dialogue with Maria is far from renunciation,
unless it be the renunciation of a return to narrower vision. Maria
asks,

> "To what do you go home?"
> "I don't know. There will always be something."
> "To a great difference," she said as she kept his hand.
> "A great difference—no doubt. Yet I shall see what I
> can make of it."
> . . . . . . . . . . . . . . . . . . . . . . . . . . . . . . . . . . . . . . . . . . . . . . . . . . . . . .
> She sighed it at last all comically, all tragically, away.
> (XXII, 325, 327)

The tragedy is Miss Gostrey's, the comedy is Strether's. With
the voice of the true high comic hero he vows to "see what I
can make of it." James interprets the conclusion clearly in his
preface:

> He *can't* accept or assent. He won't. . . . He has come so far
> through his total little experience that he has come out on
> the other side—on the other side even, of a union with Miss
> Gostrey. He must go back as he came—or rather, really, so
> quite other that, in comparison, marrying Miss Gostrey
> would be almost of the old order. Yes, he goes back other—
> and to other things.[30]

In his brilliant essay on comedy Wylie Sypher describes the
comic vision in terms that summarize Strether's awareness and
recall the final sentence of *The Ambassadors.*

At its most triumphant moments comic art frees us from peril without destroying our ideals. . . . Comedy can be a means of mastering our disillusions when we are caught in a dishonest or stupid society. . . . We see the flaws in things, but we do not always need to concede the victory. . . . Unflinching and undaunted we see *where we are.*[31]

It is no accident that Strether's final words in the novel affirm his vision: "Then there we are." (XXII, 327)

If Strether's ultimate recognition seems too sophisticated and profound for a comedy of manners, that is because *The Ambassadors* is not a typical comedy of manners. Beneath the conventional frame lies a deeper kind of comedy which floats the whole into the realm of mythic experience.

Austin Warren suggests the mythic shape of *The Ambassadors* when he remarks that "In poetic drama—*The Tempest* . . . James came nearest to finding precedents for his later novels."[32] A number of striking similarities between the two masterpieces reveal them to be of a similar archetypal structure and meaning.

In many ways Strether is the Prospero of *The Ambassadors*, creating the entire action of the plot out of his own mind. At the outset he seems more like the inverted Prospero of *The Sacred Fount*, comically ignorant but desiring to control the action. Strether uses his magic innocence and creativity to create the illusions he sees. Madame de Vionnet's apartment, for example, "was doubtless half the projection of his mind." (XXII, 125) In the Lambinet frame he feels that he is able "sufficiently [to] command the scene" (XXII, 247) and he "quite recalled . . . conjuring away everything but the pleasant." (XXII, 250) Part of what Strether must ultimately learn is that his conjurings have created visions of baseless fabric. Strether finally discovers that he has been a fool all along, and, at the close, he perceives that the real is no less wonderful than the imaginary.

Landing on his island, Strether encounters a Caliban in Waymarsh. As lovable as Waymarsh may be, Strether is not overly excited to see him, for Waymarsh has not been able to adjust to Europe. He complains, "It ain't my kind of a country." (XXI, 29) Like Caliban, he is humorless and unmannered, and he exerts a depressing influence on Strether.

As Waymarsh is superficially a Caliban, Maria Gostrey is an Ariel, an imaginative and creative spirit, who pulls Strether up whereas Waymarsh drags him down. Maria's magic is revealed in her incredible clairvoyance. When Strether meets her "She knew even intimate things about him that he hadn't yet told her." (XXI, 11) And when Strether asks her to teach him to "enjoy," she asks, "Is it really an 'order' from you?—that I shall take the job?" (XXI, 20) Maria is responsible for much of Strether's power of awareness and even for his mobility in Europe. At one point he finds himself "by Miss Gostrey's side at one of the theatres to which he had found himself transported, without his own hand raised, or the mere expression of a conscientious wonder." (XXI, 49) Indisputably magical, Miss Gostrey provides Strether with knowledge and perception.

Like Waymarsh, Chad seems to be a Caliban at the outset, a creature "under a spell, a blight, a dark and baffling influence,"[33] and Strether expects to find him a "brute." But this Caliban's nature has been improved by the nurture of a Miranda, and Strether immediately succumbs to Chad's charm, now mistaking him for a Ferdinand. At the close, however, when Chad expresses interest in "Advertising scientifically worked," (XXII, 315) it appears that he is reverting to his Caliban role, and Strether repeats to Chad that if he leaves Marie he is a "beast." (XXII, 313)

The conflicting societies of *The Ambassadors* also resemble those of *The Tempest.* Like Prospero, Strether is exiled from one society to another. Like Milan, Woollett is the world of crass, petty, and selfish affairs, and, like the island, Paris is a land of magic, freedom, and beauty. But Prospero's island is in many ways inferior to Milan, just as Paris is to Woollett. There are fens and marshes as well as beautiful music on the island, and human possibility is limited. The only love available to Miranda is that of her father. Strether finds Europe a land of enchantment but learns that enchantment can veil evil and suffering.

Finally, Strether and several of the other characters are, like the characters in *The Tempest*, shipwrecked. At the outset James refers to "poor Lambert Strether washed up on the sunny strand." (XXI, 81) Soon thereafter Strether notes that Little Bilham "hadn't saved from his shipwreck a scrap of anything but his beautiful intelligence." (XXI, 126) Both Prospero and Strether cause their relatives to shipwreck on their magic island, and when Strether sees Mamie Pocock on Chad's balcony he "fancied himself stranded with her on a far shore, during an ominous calm, in a quaint community of shipwreck." (XXII, 152)

*The Ambassadors*, then, resembles *The Tempest*. Banished to a magic island, Strether encounters a Caliban, an Ariel, and a pair of lovers, and forces the arrival of his relatives from the humorous society that sent him off originally. The parallels are, of course, somewhat superficial, for as James himself wrote in his essay on *The Tempest*, "any story will provide a remote island, a shipwreck and a coincidence."[34] But the underlying archetypal structure of the stories is, perhaps, more significant.

Both the novel and the play are, in shape, displacement stories. In a displacement story the action often begins in a normal world, moves into the green world where a metamorphosis and a comic resolution is achieved, and returns to the normal world. The hero is thus displaced from his ordinary sense of reality into an illusory dreamland, but his very displacement gives him a perspective on himself that enables him to return to the normal world renewed.

Strether is physically, intellectually, emotionally, and morally displaced before attaining the self-knowledge and renewed affirmation of life with which he returns to Woollett. His journey is much more than that from Woollett to Paris. At the outset he has the "sense of himself as at that moment launched in something of which the sense would be quite disconnected from the sense of his past." (XXI, 9) And later he suffers "the queer displacement of his point of view." (XXII, 124) In his disarranging adventure the hero is removed from the familiar real world into a strange and hostile, if beautiful, universe in which ordinary names don't fit and easy categories break down.

Europe disarranges Strether's intellectual and emotional balance, and the journey into the Lambinet painting disarranges Strether's moral balance. Back in the real world of the telegraph office, among other merely human people, Strether is able to reconcile the ideality of his vision with the reality of its collapse. But his experience implies no resignation; he has had his vision, and the life he returns to, as James tells us, will be "other"; he will "make something of it."

At the end of *The Tempest* Prospero acknowledges "this thing of darkness," Caliban, to be his, forgives his enemies, drowns his book, and returns to human responsibility in Milan where he had previously dedicated himself to the study of magic rather than to his people. He frees Ariel and returns to a world transformed only by love.

Strether's knowledge follows a similar pattern. Having been displaced in the enchanted world of Europe, Strether recognizes the reality and illusion of both worlds, acknowledges his responsibility in the Chad-Marie affair, and returns to new life in Woollett where he had been previously without identity. Strether's recognition of his common humanity in the telegraph office is Prospero's recognition of Caliban. And Strether's farewell to Maria is Prospero's freeing of Ariel. Strether sees Maria as "the offer of exquisite service, of lightened care, for the rest of his days." (XXII, 325–26) Yet "to be right" he leaves without her. He no longer needs her magic, and indeed to accept it would be to deny his vision. By importuning Chad to remain with Marie, and by leaving Europe himself, Strether gives up all claim to perpetual care from either Mrs. Newsome or Maria Gostrey. To give up magic is to take a chance on human failure, but the reward of the chance is "life."

James had prepared himself for the creation of Strether in his creation of Christopher Newman, the narrator of *The Sacred Fount*, and Longdon; but the form of *The Ambassadors* and the depth of Strether's vision surpass the form and vision of any of the earlier novels. A subtle combination of international comedy of manners and archetypal displacement myth, *The Ambassadors* is James's masterpiece as *The Tempest* was Shakespeare's. James wrote to Hugh Walpole in humorous terms:

> I remember sitting on it, when I wrote it, with that intending weight and presence with which you probably often sit in these days on your trunk to make the lid close and *all* your trousers and boots go in.[35]

Like *The Tempest*, *The Ambassadors* seems a composite of its author's productions, pulsing with all his sense of the tragedy and comedy of life. James's comedy of manners was to appear

again in E. M. Forster's first novel, *Where Angels Fear to Tread,*
a novel which closely parallels the plot and structure of *The
Ambassadors,* and James's mythic comedy was to appear again
in James Joyce's *Ulysses,* a novel in which another father
searches for his son. But no novelist was again to produce the
peculiar fusion of forms; it was James's alone.

### The Golden Bowl

As the shape of *The Tempest* underlies *The Ambassadors,* the
shape of *A Midsummer Night's Dream* underlies *The Golden
Bowl.* The plots of the play and the novel are remarkably similar.
Two pairs of lovers, subject to a cruel and irrational law, ex-
change places several times through no seeming fault of their
own, before attaining the proper harmonious relationship in
which a new society forms around the characters, symbolized
by multiple marriages celebrated at the close. Maggie's relationship to Adam and the Prince is like Demetrius's to Hermia and
Helena. Just as Demetrius first loves the wrong girl, Hermia, and
finally the right girl, Helena, so Maggie first loves Adam and
finally the Prince. The Prince's relationship to Maggie and Charlotte is like Lysander's to Hermia and Helena. Lysander switches
from Hermia to Helena and back to Hermia; the Prince marries
Maggie, takes Charlotte as mistress, and renews his marriage with
Maggie. Adam and Charlotte, like Hermia and Helena, remain
faithful to the same person throughout.

Further, Fanny Assingham is a kind of Bottom. Fanny is
low on the social scale, a pretender to status who is humorous
but nevertheless compassionate and lovable. Both characters are
eternal egoistic amateurs who want to play all the roles in their
respective dramas. Bottom falls in love with Queen Titania, and
Fanny falls in love with Prince Amerigo. And if Bottom is given
an ass's head, Fanny boasts a comically doubled ass's name.

The theme of both works is love-madness, and love is the
cause of all the confusion and reversal of roles. Maggie affirms
toward the end of the novel:

"I can bear anything."

"Oh, 'bear!'" Mrs. Assingham fluted.

"For love," said the Princess.

Fanny hesitated. "Of your father?"

"For love," Maggie repeated.

It kept her friend watching. "Of your husband?"

"For love," Maggie said again. (XXIV, 115–16)

Indeed, Maggie reveals more than she suspects in this famous speech to her confidante. "For love" Maggie arranges the marriage between Charlotte and Adam; "for love" she neglects the Prince and lavishes affection on her father; "for love" she devotes herself to the Prince at the end. Love without discrimination produces confusion and "madness." This is not at all to denigrate Maggie's final achievement, the creation of a new society. Rather it is to insist that Maggie is no Beatrice or goddess as some critics maintain, but a merely human girl facing merely human problems in a world that seems to partake of fairy tale magic. Like her counterparts in Shakespeare, Maggie finally awakens. And, like them, she never completely remembers her own foolishness. She never attains Strether's ironic perspective nor rises to his self-knowledge.

As in Shakespeare's play, a cruel, decadent, and festering evil seems to lurk beneath the comedy surface of *The Golden Bowl.* This is, of course, true of all great comedy. In *A Midsummer Night's Dream* Hermia would die by Athenian law if she persisted in choosing the wrong husband. Theseus, the lover of imagination, owns musical hounds which are used for hunting. The sleep of the magic flower resembles the sleep of death, and the spirits of the forest are capricious. But in both works the comic surface is maintained and transformed; evil never asserts its ultimately destructive power. Both stories are a profound revelation of human nature, of the paradox by which extreme fastidious refinement exists in us side by side with the most vulgar fleshly propensities.

If the similarities between the two works help to define the shape of the novel, the differences help to define the character of Maggie Verver. In the enchanted forest of *A Midsummer Night's Dream,* governed by a fairy king, error can be introduced into human affairs by the agency of a rascally Puck and a magical flower. Error can just as easily be removed by the juice of another herb. Things are not so simple in the social world of *The Golden Bowl.* Whereas Demetrius must merely fall asleep to regain his balance, Maggie must consciously work and struggle to create a final harmony. Human agency is required to remove the spell in *The Golden Bowl,* and human agency is responsible for the marital confusion in the first place. No flower unites Maggie to Adam, or the Prince to Charlotte, and the question of Maggie's responsibility for the error becomes significant.

In her artistic creativity and her self-deception, Maggie Verver represents a complex combination of qualities introduced by earlier Jamesian protagonists. Like Felix Young, Maisie Farrange, and Nanda Brookenham, Maggie takes the plot into her own hands and tries to create a new society; but like Christopher Newman, Isabel Archer, and Fleda Vetch, she remains somewhat humorous in her innocence and naiveté. James was so successful in uniting these seemingly conflicting characteristics that many critics have been unable to reconcile them, concluding that Maggie is either a goddess or a devil.

Joseph Firebaugh insists that James's attitude toward the Ververs is "unsympathetic" and "Maggie is an all but unmitigated tyrant."[36] Ferner Nuhn agrees that Maggie is "that crafty-innocent, smugly virtuous, cooly victorious little Princess."[37] Frederick Crews, on the other hand, sees Adam as God and Maggie as Christ.[38] And Quentin Anderson, arguing from the elder James's Swedenborgianism, concludes that Adam is "Divine Wisdom" and Maggie "Divine Love."[39] Dorothea Krook and Walter Wright recognize that Maggie shares all of these characteristics, but both critics feel that the novel is "predominantly tragic not comic. For the main intention of the ironic exposure is to show the price in human suffering that may have to be paid for this lack of candour."[40]

If Maggie were a superhuman character, and if the novel moved toward disintegration of the marriages, *The Golden Bowl* would be tragic. But the novel is structured on integration, and Maggie resembles James's earlier protagonists in her fallibility and final social artistry.

Like Felix, Maisie, and Nanda, Maggie is the artist criticizing a humorous society (here represented by Prince Amerigo and Charlotte Stant) and transforming that society in the direction of its full human potential. Having discovered the illicit relationship which seems to be thriving between her husband and her father's wife, Maggie artistically takes the plot into her own hands and plans to "bring about a difference, touch by touch, without letting either of the three, and least of all her father, so much as suspect her hand." (XXIV, 33) With the powers of evil seemingly set against her, Maggie heroically grows from innocence into an awareness of the possibilities of love and manners, the fusion of feeling and form. To assert her individuality, to scream out her wrong, would be the method of tragedy. But Maggie chooses to deprecate herself publicly, claiming to know nothing while revealing to the reader her nearly full knowledge of the affair. In this way she seeks to protect Charlotte and Adam and regain her own balance. Maggie establishes a new society founded on truth, but truth made possible through manners. By preserving appearances Maggie purges the relationships of their destructive evil and preserves the high civilization which all of the characters have rather crookedly constructed. Her redemption is not so much of individuals as of society, and is thus the redemption typical of high comedy.

The conclusion of the novel, in which the marriages are recelebrated, recalls *The Europeans.* In that novel Felix manages to work the plot toward four marriages which prefigure the more complete fusion of *The Golden Bowl.* The rejection of Eugenia prefigures that of Charlotte, but in the later novel the blocking figure is accommodated, and Charlotte goes off to American City with Adam. In both novels manipulation is directed toward a good social end, and in *The Golden Bowl* that end seems a grand combination of American moral energy and European sophistication, of conscience and tradition.

Those critics who see Maggie Verver as an artist courageously refusing to expose all the evil and hypocrisy of her society, and in so refusing, transforming moral ignorance and turpitude into moral knowledge and goodness by the power of love, are essentially correct. But if Maggie is a successful artist like Felix or Nanda, she is a fool as well. Her social triumph does not obscure her failure through much of the novel to gain full self-awareness. She fails to perceive that she herself is a major cause of the original evil situation.

James comically exposes Maggie as he exposed his earlier "bedimmed and befooled and bewildered" protagonists. Her acquisitiveness resembles that of Christopher Newman, her overly intense relationship with her father recalls Olive Chancellor's perverse affection for Verena, her self-knowledge remains truncated through much of the novel as does Isabel Archer's, and her final activity to straighten out the marriages partakes of the demonic as does the activity of the narrator of *The Sacred Fount.*

In treating people as things Maggie and her father, like Christopher Newman and Adela Gereth, endanger their own humanity. Adam views the Prince as an addition to his collection; he is one of the "pieces of the first order." (XXIII, 140) And Maggie accepts the denotation when she informs Amerigo, "You're at any rate a part of his collection . . . one of the things that can only be got over here." (XXIII, 12) James comments on this aspect of the Ververs: "Nothing perhaps might affect us as queerer, had we time to look into it, than this application of the same measure of value to such different pieces of property as old Persian carpets, say, and new human acquisitions." (XXIII, 196)

One thing that is, perhaps, "queerer" is Maggie's socially unnatural relationship with her father. Maggie's childish conception of marriage is reflected in her incredible innocence. Before her marriage to the Prince, Maggie considered herself "married" to Adam and she worries that her separation from her father will expose Adam to the wily traps of eligible fortune hunters. She tells him, "It was as if you couldn't be in the market when you were married to *me*. Or rather as if I kept people off, innocently, by being married to you." (XXIII, 172) Even after her real marriage to the Prince, Maggie keeps her clothes at Adam's house and treats him more like a husband than she treats Amerigo. (XXIII, 373)

Maggie's marriage makes little difference in her relationship with her father; if anything, it intensifies it. And Maggie blames Charlotte for disrupting the "beautiful" union she has managed to maintain with Adam despite her own marriage to the Prince.

Maggie laments

> the loss, more than anything else, of their old freedom, their never having had to think, where they were together concerned, of any one, of anything but each other. It hadn't been *her* marriage that did it; that had never, for three seconds, suggested to either of them that they must act diplomatically, must reckon with another presence—no, not even with her husband's. . . . nothing could have been more beautiful than the way in which, till Charlotte came so much more closely into their life, Amerigo hadn't interfered. (XXIV, 80–81)

At this point Maggie has been married to the Prince for two years and yet she maintains a naive view of marriage. Although she does have a child, even he is used as an excuse for Maggie and her father to be together. James points up the humorous fact: "It was of course an old story and a familiar idea that a beautiful baby could take its place as a new link between a wife and a husband, but Maggie and her father had, with every ingenuity, converted the precious creature into a link between a mama and a grandpapa." (XXIII, 156)

Maggie's affinity for her father provides the situation for Charlotte's and the Prince's adultery. But Charlotte and the Prince are, of course, responsible for taking advantage of the situation, and Charlotte is obviously more pleased with the possibilities than is the Prince. As I suggested earlier, Charlotte is the novel's "bad heroine." James describes her in terms of her "solid teeth" which are "well arrayed and flashingly white," and her "tawny" hair which "gave her at moments the sylvan head of a huntress." (XXIII, 46) Charlotte is after both money and the Prince, and, by careful manipulation of her circumstances, manages to acquire both. When Maggie so conveniently ignores the Prince, Charlotte challenges him, "What else can we do, what in all the world else?" (XXIII, 303)

Charlotte is the more aggressive member of the pair, thinking only of her personal pleasure and playing on her knowledge that the Prince's pride in being a "galantuomo" will triumph over any superficial moral scruples he might have adopted for Maggie.

Charlotte is the typical blocking figure of comedy who must ultimately be expelled or accommodated.

The Prince also manipulates his circumstances, if somewhat more reluctantly than does Charlotte. At the outset he warns Maggie of his long tradition of "crimes, . . . follies, . . . boundless *bêtises*," (XXIII, 9) but he privately and honestly vows to "*make* something different" (XXIII, 16) of his marriage. As he tells Maggie, "I'll go anywhere you want." (XXIII, 13) The Prince, ironically, follows Maggie's naive lead in reestablishing a relationship with a person outside their marriage.

James clarifies in his notebooks that "the son-in-law, with the sense of his wife's estrangement from him, finds himself at liberty, and finds it moreover only courteous to be agreeable to the other lady in the particular situation."[41] Despite his "courtesy," the Prince goes through the forms of keeping his relationship with Charlotte virtuous. He voices his opposition to the Bloomsbury excursion (XXIII, 61) and irritably objects to Charlotte's elaborate preparations for a deeper, more sexual relationship with him. (XXIII, 250–52) But the Prince finally capitalizes on his situation.

> Being thrust, systematically, with another woman and a woman one happened, by the same token, exceedingly to like, and being so thrust that the theory of it seemed to publish one as idiotic or incapable—this was a predicament of which the dignity depended all on one's own handling. What was supremely grotesque in fact was the essential opposition of theories—as if a galantuomo, as *he* at least constitutionally conceived galantuomini, could do anything *but* blush to "go about" at such a rate with such a person as Mrs. Verver in a state of childlike innocence. (XXIII, 335)

Faced with his predicament, reinforced by Maggie herself, the Prince finally justifies adultery with Charlotte. But whereas Charlotte justifies it in terms of her own pleasure, the Prince thinks more of protecting Maggie and her father. "They're extraordinarily happy," he concludes, "that's the great thing." (XXIII, 310)

The Prince is partially responsible for Maggie's deception, and Charlotte is highly culpable. But James emphasizes Maggie's .

guilt in creating the situation which leads to adultery.

> Nothing stranger surely had ever happened to a conscientious, a well-meaning, a perfectly passive pair: no more extraordinary decree had ever been launched against such victims than this of forcing them against their will into a relation of mutual close contact that they had done everything to avoid. (XXIII, 289)

John Clair has gone so far as to argue that the adultery is not real at all, but that Charlotte and the Prince have created a fictional adultery to jolt Maggie and Adam out of their complacent affection for each other.[42] Although that is exactly what the affair does, the adultery seems real enough. However, the fact of adultery is less interesting to James than Maggie's initial ignorance and slowly developing awareness of it. Midway in the novel James explains that Maggie and Adam "were in fact constitutionally inaccessible to [knowledge]." (XXIII, 334) In regard to her situation later, James tells us that "her grasp of appearances was thus out of proportion to her view of causes," (XXIV, 54) and toward the end of the novel, as Maggie stalks around Matcham eyeing Charlotte, James asserts, "Maggie's provision of irony, which we have taken for naturally small, had never been so scant as now." (XXIV, 284) Throughout much of the novel, the discrepancy between Maggie's limited understanding of the "lurid" affair and the homely reality of the actual situation is comic. In some ways Maggie resembles Fleda Vetch, who also constructs whole conversations and bases her initial action on an obviously naive view of her situation.

Maggie's initial strategies for dealing with her situation are somewhat humorous. Instead of merely dissociating herself from her father and devoting her attention and love to her husband when she suspects adultery, she plots to throw the Prince and Charlotte together even more. Maggie sends them off to a party together, and Fanny Assingham notes her perverse behavior. "But isn't it true that—after you had this time again, at the eleventh hour, said *you* wouldn't—they would certainly much rather not have gone?" Maggie replies, "Yes—they would certainly much rather not have gone. But I wanted them to go."

(XXIV, 113) Like Christopher Newman, Isabel Archer, and the narrator of *The Sacred Fount,* Maggie's machinations render her almost demonic. When she "infernally" promotes the adultery to give herself further proof of it "a certain queer wish . . . fitfully flickered up in her, a wish that usurped perversely the place of a much more natural one. If Charlotte . . . could only have been *worse!*—that idea Maggie fell to invoking instead of the idea that she might desirably have been better." (XXIV, 138) And she feels in her power "that fascination of the monstrous, that temptation of the horribly possible. . . . She might sound out their doom in a single sentence." (XXIV, 233)

The event which offers Maggie her final proof of a sustained and serious intimacy between the Prince and Charlotte is the discovery of the golden bowl at the little Bloomsbury shop. But Maggie immediately reads "facts" into the bowl which it doesn't necessarily represent, exaggerating its significance to Fanny Assingham. She insists that the bowl proves that the two were "intimate." "Before we were married—yes; but after we were engaged. . . . They were together all the while—up to the very eve of our marriage." (XXIV, 161) The facts, however, do not bear out this "discovery"; the real intimacy didn't begin until two years after Maggie's marriage to the Prince. The relationship before the marriage was not intimate enough to overcome the problem of money, and the incident of the bowl was really intimate only on Charlotte's part. James finally makes Maggie undercut her own discovery. She insists, "They spent hours together—spent at least a morning." (XXIV, 163) The facts and Maggie's exaggerated interpretation of them are comically discrepant.

When Maggie tells Fanny that the bowl has a crack, Fanny correctly surmises, "Then your whole idea has a crack." (XXIV, 178) And James underlines Fanny's perception. "The breakage stood not for any wrought discomposure among the triumphant three—it stood merely for the dire deformity of her [Maggie's] attitude toward them." (XXIV, 240) The "dire deformity of her attitude" toward the couples is an important element of the marital confusion; it is the magic flower that mixes up the lovers, and the breakage of the bowl is an initial application of the antidote. As the bowl hurtles to the floor, the Prince magically appears, and Maggie renounces vengeance, vowing to save her marriage.

James thus deflates Maggie in her role as a self-deceived protagonist. At the same time he elevates Maggie in her role as a creative artist. If she has been her own blocking figure, ignorantly disrupting her own marriage to the Prince, she also attains the level of artist, creating a new harmonious relationship.

James's final brilliant fusion of Maggie's self-knowledge and self-deception is Maggie's last conversation with Charlotte. Charlotte confronts Maggie and accuses Maggie of having "worked against" her:

> "You haven't worked against me?"
>
> Maggie took it and for a moment kept it; held it, with closed eyes, as if it had been some captured fluttering bird pressed by both hands to her breast. Then she opened her eyes to speak. "What does it matter—if I've failed?"
>
> "You recognize then that you've failed?" asked Charlotte from the threshold.
>
> . . . . . . . . . . . . . . . . . . . . . . . . . . . . . . . . . . . . . . . . . . . . . .
>
> "I've failed!" (XXIV, 317–18)

In this scene Charlotte accuses Maggie of trying to keep Adam from her. Maggie does not perceive that she has unconsciously been doing just that in her relationship with him. Lacking this self-knowledge, Maggie believes that she is lying to Charlotte to protect her. Maggie "pretends" to have "worked against" Charlotte when she knows that Charlotte has worked against her. Like Felix, Maisie, and Nanda, Maggie deprecates herself, pretending ignorance although she thinks she knows all. But like Newman, Isabel, and the narrator of *The Sacred Fount,* she is also fooling herself. What she knows is that Charlotte and the Prince have had an adulterous relationship; what she doesn't know is that she herself has been largely responsible for it. Thus when she thinks she is lying to Charlotte, she is actually merely being truthful. She *has* tried to keep Adam for herself, she *has* "worked against" Charlotte in a way her small provision of irony will not allow her to suspect, and she has "failed." The double irony of the conversation turns back on Maggie.

To the end Maggie denies any responsibility. She sadly

insists to Fanny that she and Adam are "lost to each other really much more than Amerigo and Charlotte are; since for them it's just, it's right, it's deserved, while for us it's only sad and strange and not caused by our fault." (XXIV, 333) James had earlier aptly described Maggie's growing awareness of the adultery as a shift in the position of her telescope. (XXIV, 207) Maggie's vision of external social reality increases profoundly; her inward vision remains relatively small.

As in *A Midsummer Night's Dream*, the participants' awareness in *The Golden Bowl* is never raised to the level of the audience's. When Maggie awakes from her period of love-madness and applies the magic flower of social forms to the relationships she, like the characters in Shakespeare's play, has forgotten her earlier silliness. The reader, but not Maggie, perceives her previous participation in the humorous society which she transforms at the end.

In *The Ambassadors* Strether's level of awareness parallels that of the reader; indeed, Strether even seems to know things that the reader will never know. But if Maggie is less finely percipient than Strether, she is probably, in her pragmatic knowledge, more finely happy. Strether attains a new moral awareness, perceiving the foolishness of his desire to see only ideal perfection in the human relationship of Chad and Marie, and criticizing his own previous moral rigidity. But he is unable to form a new society around that awareness. Maggie retains her rigid sense of morality, believing the Prince and Charlotte to be the sole guilty parties to the end, but she does manage to create a harmonious society despite her lack of awareness. And her small Principino remains as a symbol of the continuity of the new life ahead.

*The Golden Bowl* is a fitting climax to the James canon. The plot and theme of the novel recall his earlier comedies of manners while elevating them to the realm of mythic experience. Maggie Verver is herself a perfect fusion of Jamesian types, combining the creative self-deprecation and potential social artistry of Felix Young and Nanda Brookenham with the boastful self-deception and potentially destructive obsessiveness of Christopher Newman and the narrator of *The Sacred Fount*. The ending is an almost religious affirmation of the purely human possibility of creative life through a union of manners and morals, of old world and new.

The materials of *The Golden Bowl* were to appear again in E. M. Forster's *Howard's End,* a novel in which two seemingly opposing worlds are united through a symbolic marriage, and in James Joyce's *A Portrait of the Artist as a Young Man* in which another protagonist criticizes a humorous society while comically exposing himself. In its fusion of comic themes and in its comic form, *The Golden Bowl* represents a final culmination of James's comic spirit.

# VII

# Conclusion

Despite the critical emphasis on tragedy, renunciation, and repudiation in the fiction of Henry James, the archetypal elements of comedy in the characters, plots, themes, and stylistic devices of his novels reveal his relation to a "comic tradition" comprised of serious high-comic artists like Shakespeare, Cervantes, and Molière. Jamesian comedy is not confined to any one of his recognized "phases"; it is his characteristic genre, and it informs the entire canon. In their fusion of comic elements *The Ambassadors* and *The Golden Bowl* are a culmination of James's earlier experiments with comic form.

James is not narrowly a comic artist. Although his form is predominantly comic, it includes the tragedy, irony, satire, lyricism, and parody that concern all great artists. But critics approaching James with a preliminary generic conception of tragedy have repeatedly misinterpreted the novels. Wylie Sypher defines the basic problem when he writes:

> If we now have trouble isolating comedy from tragedy this is not because comedy and tragedy are identical, but rather because comedy often intersects the orbit of tragic action without losing its autonomy. Instead, comedy in its own right, boldly and illogically, lays claim to some of the values that traditionally are assigned to tragedy alone. Think, for example, of Henry James's "Beast in the Jungle," which really is comedy of manners.[1]

James's combination of comic and tragic elements in an essentially comic form produces a new sublime incongruity of high comedy.

James's high comedies, pervaded by a Meredithian comic

spirit which sees life as precariously balanced upon the brink of a disaster which it transcends, are primarily based on a conception of character. Faulty vision is James's major comic theme, and his use of two traditional archetypal characters serves to emphasize the theme and create the plot conflict.

The majority of James's characters, from fool to finely aware, might be viewed as descendants of two archetypal comic figures, the *eiron* and the *alazon* of Old Comedy. According to Northrop Frye, the *eiron* is "the man who deprecates himself." He is "a predestined artist, just as the *alazon* is one of his predestined victims."[2] The *eiron* is the seeming simpleton who is, in reality, the wisest character in his fictional society.

Frye goes on to describe three types of *eiron*—the benevolent withdrawing and returning figure, the tricky slave, and the hero and heroine. These three types appear throughout the James canon. The heroes and heroines who most obviously display *eiron* characteristics are Felix Young, Maisie Farrange, Nanda Brookenham, and Lambert Strether by the end of *The Ambassadors*. The tricky slave or dionysiac figure, "gifted with unusual vitality, an intense love of life and a wonderful capacity for enjoying it,"[3] is represented by Gabriel Nash, Ralph Touchett, Valentin de Bellegarde, and some of James's "bad heroines." The benevolent withdrawing and returning figure, a representative of goodness and wisdom, is evident in characters like Longdon and Mitchy in *The Awkward Age*.

The *eiron*, as recreated in James's' fiction, serves as the intelligent, self-aware, affirmative force which insists on living and seeing, and taunts the more narrow *alazon*. He is the artist who is endowed with the ability to take the plot into his hands or to live beyond its exigencies.

The *alazon*, according to Frye, is an impostor "who pretends or tries to be something more than he is."[4] He is often the boaster who acts as a block to the hero's or his own happiness. Because of the greater tendency of this type to be "bedimmed and befooled and bewildered," Henry James drew on it for many of his most important characters. The *alazon* figure generates protagonists like Christopher Newman, Isabel Archer, Basil Ransom, and the narrator of *The Sacred Fount*. Some confidantes and reflectors who also owe their origin to the *alazon* are Mrs. Wix,

Fanny Assingham, and Henrietta Stackpole. And numerous "villains" belong to this comic type; the Brigstocks, the Farranges, the Pococks, George Flack, and Gilbert Osmond are obvious examples.

Of course, James's major heroes and heroines, like Christopher Newman and Isabel Archer, are often a combination of *eiron* and *alazon* types. Rarely does James provide the pure type as he does in Gabriel Nash or the narrator of *The Sacred Fount.* But only Lambert Strether and Maggie Verver represent a complete fusion of the two, and most of the other protagonists in James owe more to one type than the other. One of James's favorite comic techniques is to depict the protagonist as an *alazon* unaware of his true nature, and pit an *eiron* against the protagonist to undercut him. In *The Portrait of a Lady*, for instance, Isabel Archer and Ralph Touchett are contrasted, and in *The American* Christopher Newman is set in relief by Valentin.

James's plots are usually an outgrowth of character, and his two basic plot patterns parallel the two basic character types. In the first pattern everything in the movement of the plot works against the character, causing his self-exposure. An *alazon* protagonist usually appears in such comedies, and Jamesian examples of this form are *The Sacred Fount, The American,* and *The Portrait of a Lady.* The second major plot pattern consists of the integration of the protagonist into an existent society or into one of his own making. A witty *eiron* usually appears as protagonist in such comedies, and this form structures James's *The Europeans* and *The Awkward Age.* The plot movements of *The Ambassadors* and *The Golden Bowl* combine the two types. Strether is essentially an *eiron* hero who is unable to create a new society for anyone but himself, and Maggie Verver is essentially an *alazon* heroine who is able to create a new, redeemed society.

Scenic presentation and balance of characters are James's fundamental methods of organizing a plot. James writes in the preface to *The Portrait of a Lady* that when he had found characters he had to "find for them the right relations, those that would most bring them out; to imagine, to invent and select and piece together the situations most useful and favorable to the sense of the creatures themselves."[5] "The novel is of its very nature an 'ado,' an ado about something, and the larger the form it takes the greater of course the ado. Therefore, consciously, that was what one was in for—for positively organizing an ado."[6]

James's plot ultimately becomes an "ado," a grouping of persons carefully designed to expose and set off the positive and negative aspects of the protagonist. He arranges the characters as in a director's diagram and we never lose sight of them on stage.

Meredith saw the stage of comedy as the drawing room "where we have no dust of the struggling outer world, no mire, no violent crashes."[7] As in other comedies of manners, James's scene is usually the drawing room or the garden, and the social occasions played out therein throw light on the central subject. As Francis Fergusson notes, James's situations are as much "reflectors" of the main character as are the minor characters.[8] The scene thus gives a sense of the character's belonging to society, as opposed to the relatively unpeopled tragic stage.

James's sense of scenic presentation provides the balance of character necessary for comedy. L. J. Potts affirms that "what is essential to a good comic plot is an exact balance and proportion between the characters, and a progressive revelation of their true nature by means of contrast, interplay, and mutual influence."[9] And Dale Underwood summarizes the kinds of scenic balance which characterize comedy:

> At every basic point of structure there exists a fundamental opposition: In character, man versus woman and hero and heroines versus dupes; in action, the "heroic" undertaking versus farcically false imitations; in setting, the opposition just described; in being, appearance versus reality; in values, orthodoxy. To an extent these polarities make certain unambiguous assertions concerning the nature of man.[10]

Henry James's plots reveal exactly the balance and proportion of characters that Potts describes, and the polarities that Underwood summarizes. Symmetrical recurrences of character and event, for example, proliferate. Maria Gostrey opens and closes *The Ambassadors* as Caspar Goodwood does *The Portrait of a*

*Lady.* In *The Golden Bowl* the successive "love" scenes between father-daughter and daughter-Prince virtually become farcical mirror sequences. And *What Maisie Knew* provides extreme examples of the incredibly balanced structure James favored.

The technique of balance, repetition, and symmetry, a staple of comedy, is a favorite Jamesian method of adding multiple dimensions of meaning. In *The Spoils of Poynton* the balance and parallelism of the plot forces the reader to revise continually his formulations of character, and in *The Ambassadors* the parodic arrival of the Pococks forces a reevaluation of Strether's own mission. James Joyce was to see the potential of this method in his *A Portrait of the Artist as a Young Man*, where each chapter dialectically adds a new dimension to the plot and character, forcing a revision of categories on the part of both Stephen and the reader.

The balance and symmetry of the plot is comic in itself, but, as Dale Underwood notes, it also suggests a comic outlook on life. To mold social intercourse and individual human beings into a symmetrical arrangement is to make of life a drama, and if the drama is beautiful, controlled, and amusing it is high comedy. Further, as Bergson defines the basis of the comic, "*any arrangement of acts and events is comic which gives us, in a single combination, the illusion of life and the distinct impression of a mechanical arrangement.*"[11] The rigidity of pattern imposed on life is just the "mechanical encrusted on the living" that Bergson emphasizes. When E. M. Forster complained that *The Ambassadors* suffers from a too rigid pattern which closes out life, what he really discovered was just the plot arrangement that makes the novel a great serious international comedy of manners.[12]

Scenic balance usually results in complication, and as Northrop Frye and other theorists note, complication is indispensable to comedy for there is something inherently absurd about complications. Whereas the tragic writer simplifies his action, the comic writer presents a richer action and a greater variety of characters. James recognizes the importance of complication, and in *The Golden Bowl* even provides a character, Fanny Assingham, whose main function is to complicate the plot and confuse the reader and herself. In the preface to *What Maisie Knew* James affirms:

No themes are so human as those that reflect for us, out of
the confusion of life, the close connexion of bliss and bale.
. . . To live with all intensity and perplexity and felicity in
its terribly mixed little world. . . .

. . . . . . . . . . . . . . . . . . . . . . . . . . . . . . . . . . . . . . . . . . . . . . . . . . . . .

The great thing is indeed that the muddled state too is one
of the very sharpest of the realities, that it also has colour
and form and character, has often in fact a broad and rich
comicality.[13]

The "rich comicality" of the Jamesian plot, then, is an
outgrowth of character, based broadly upon James's theory of
national types. The plot provides a framework on which to hang
scenes that are made up of a grouping of characters who reflect
aspects of the protagonist. The minor reflectors are arranged
symmetrically, and the plot itself reveals a balance of structure
which suggests a formal equivalent of James's desire for balance
and an ideal fusion in life. The hero, in pursuit of happiness
and expanded consciousness, must oppose the blocks to his
quest, blocks represented by other characters, the society itself,
or negative aspects of the hero's own mind. The movement of
a Jamesian hero is typically toward an escape from tyranny or
conventionality into freedom and self-expression. The endings
of the novels are a complex variation on the traditional comic
ending in which the hero is integrated into his society or forms
a new society around himself.

Plots which focus on integration and self-exposure as opposed to isolation and self-discovery necessarily emphasize society. Comedy is the social art, and Henry James's sense of scenic
presentation serves to unite his characters inseparably with the
social world surrounding them.

If there is one fact upon which all theories of comedy agree
it is that comedy depends on a definite strong orientation toward
society.[14] T. S. Eliot observes that James's "general scheme is
not one character, nor a group of characters in a plot or merely
in a crowd. The focus is a situation, a relation, an atmosphere. . . .
The real hero, in any of James's stories, is a social entity of which
men and women are constituents."[15] And James himself emphasizes the importance of the social world in his novels. As he

writes to William Dean Howells, "It is on manners, customs, usages, habits, forms, upon all these things matured and established, that a novelist lives—they are the very stuff his work is made of."[16] Later, in the preface to *The Princess Casamassima*, he continues, "Experience, as I see it, is our apprehension and our measure of what happens to us as social creatures."[17] And in an article on Emerson he concludes, "We know a man imperfectly until we know his society."[18]

An overriding concern with society and men as social creatures led James naturally into the writing of comedy. And for James, as for all comic artists, society represents possibilities of ugliness and manipulative self-interest as well as ideal relationship and beauty.

The real antagonist in many James novels is the world, and the enemy of society is a spirit within that society. The fathomless depths of equivocation to which a sophisticated society is by nature committed can easily produce ugliness. Even the most seemingly beautiful forms and manners can enclose a vicious and corrupt morality. Society as depicted in *The Sacred Fount*, for example, could conceal vampiristic depletion within an elegant, formal surrounding, and in *The Portrait of a Lady* the tendency of social forms to turn people into portraits is a force of immorality. The social world of *What Maisie Knew* is presented as a kind of Dickensian chaos.

But if James is well aware of the destructive aspects of society he also appreciates its potential for good. While criticizing the society of his time James also uses it as an arena in which individual human values are invested with meaning. As Frederick Crews notes, "Society as an ideal of concern for one's fellow man appeals to the same moral insight that condemns society as an instrument of self-interest. There is no reason why social forms cannot be worked for good ends as well as evil ones."[19] Through a creative use of manners a Jamesian protagonist such as Nanda or Maggie is often able to invest the whole process with a beauty which results in corporate self-preservation.

Joseph Warren Beach observes these triumphs of social creativity in James and suggests that his "ethical system of values is essentially an esthetic system. What he is concerned with, from the beginning to the end of his writing, is *the fine art of living*."[20]

This observation both relates James's conception of plot and character to and distinguishes it from Jane Austen's. In Jane Austen, the ideal standard is usually the existent society of the novel. In *Emma,* for example, Knightly represents the highest possibility of Highbury society. The comic curve of Jane Austen's plots moves from the ignorance of the heroine to a final recognition of and adherence to the preexistent standard. In James, the norm of moral conduct is rarely present in the society of the novel, waiting only to be discovered by the protagonist. James's wise fools, as we have seen, often reflect Jamesian values. Unlike Knightly, these *eiron* figures espouse values which are often regarded as deviant by the other characters in the novel. James's comic curve is one that moves toward a *creation* of value, toward the adoption of a standard of conduct which did not exist within the original society. Strether, for instance, cannot base his action on either Woollett morality or Parisian sophistication; he must create his own moral value.

James's plots move from fixity to freedom, reflecting Northrop Frye's description of the typical comic pattern:

> The society emerging at the conclusion of comedy represents . . . a kind of moral norm, or pragmatically free society. Its ideals are seldom defined or formulated: definition and formulation belong to the humors who want predictable activity.[21]

In aspiring toward the pragmatically free society, however, the Jamesian hero must perceive the potential of manners and the possibilities of coherence and cooperation implicit in social and aesthetic forms.

Although unique in many ways, James's comedy reveals, as I have pointed out, a strong affinity with other comic art. *The Europeans, The American,* and *The Reverberator* are typical comedies of manners in which an innocent character is placed in a sophisticated society, falls in love, is opposed by a blocking figure, and ultimately triumphs. *The Spoils of Poynton* is a parody of this convention, which resembles the parodies of Cervantes and Fielding. *The Sacred Fount* is Swiftean and Hawthornian in its wild ironic and satiric unmasking of a self-deluded narrator, and *The Portrait of a Lady* resembles Molière, Jane Austen, and George Eliot in its portrayal of Isabel Archer's faulty vision. *What Maisie Knew* is Dickensian in its criticism of the London social world, and society in *The Awkward Age* recalls the society of Restoration comedy and Congreve in particular. *The Ambassadors* and *The Golden Bowl* are James's closest approximations of the breadth, scope, and profundity of Shakespearean comedy. Much work remains to be done on the subject of James's relationship to Shakespeare and the other comic writers mentioned above.

Comedy is at the base of James's intrinsic genre, linking his novels to a comic tradition. An awareness of James's novel form should lead to a more accurate interpretation of character and scene and should resolve some of the antithetical conclusions drawn by critics. For instance, when the reader perceives that *The Ambassadors* and *The Golden Bowl* are basically comic in form, he perceives that neither Strether nor Maggie can be wholly praised or condemned. And the reader who clearly perceives the intrinsic genre of the novels will more correctly interpret the general thematic focus. James's emphasis is on consciousness, awareness, moral fluidity, freedom, and social triumph which typifies most high comedy. Although renunciation and repudiation may be implied in some of the endings, James never affirms negativity or defeatism. Comedy is both his and his characters' major weapon against pessimism, cynicism, and failure. James's comic spirit consistently celebrates life and social continuity.

A misunderstanding of James's intrinsic genre has further led several critics into a misinterpretation of the "Christian" archetypes that pervade the novels. With the erroneous conviction that the Christian philosophy is basically tragic, some critics have demonstrated the "tragedy" inherent in James's forms by analyzing the Christian elements. Maggie Verver is, for example, both a tragic heroine and a sacrificial redeemer for critics like Quentin Anderson and Frederick Crews.[22] But as Wylie Sypher points out, "the drama of the struggle, death, and rising—Gethsemane, Calvary, and Easter—actually belongs in the comic rather than the tragic domain. The figure of Christ as godman is surely the archetypal hero-victim."[23] Christianity, with its emphasis on ritual death and redemption, and its refusal to admit spiritual annihilation, is basically a comic philosophy. Chaucer and the writers of the miracle and mystery plays recognized this fact as did James. Comedy, like Christianity, moves from innocence through experience and ritual death, to a higher innocence.

But James's novels are triumphantly secular, celebrating the creativity of merely human beings in a merely human society in which there is no recourse to any divine justice or omnipotent god. Indeed, James was well aware of the shift from a basically religious society to one in which traditions were crumbling and values seemed to be disappearing. He looked back with fondness at the stable traditional norms which were failing, and forward with anticipation toward a new system of values. What is most important, he looked inward, placing a great burden upon the individual consciousness and moral sense of his major characters. With no spiritual representation of the moral norm and with no acceptable public philosophy to turn to, the Jamesian protagonist must personally create his own values and norms.

James's view of the human situation in which man must create his own values therefore prefigures the existentialist view of the twentieth century. As Naomi Lebowitz remarks, the metaphysical assumptions of existentialist literature would probably have alienated James. But the existentialist vision of man poised precariously on the brink of the absurd, heroically refusing to admit the ultimate triumph of death and destruction, and learning to laugh at the discrepancy between his capacity for consciousness and the infinite vastness of the universe, is really an extreme version of Jamesian comedy.

Faced with a world in which the preposterous, the trivial, and the monstrous seem to rule, James, like our contemporary existential novelists, marshals comedy as a weapon against chaos and absurdity. If contemporary comedy is more radically wild and bizarre, and if a standard of value is much more clearly represented in James's works, the basic philosophical assumptions are similar. Both James and the contemporary novelists affirm the inviolable integrity of the creative spirit and insist upon the importance of the rare and strange and beautiful in even the smallest and most seemingly trivial gestures. James's

Strether and Saul Bellow's Herzog, for instance, perceive their common humanity, suffer the slings and arrows of outrageous limitation, and retreat at the ends of their respective novels with a new awareness and a moral power which opens up a creative future. Naomi Lebowitz concludes that "the same enemies have been defeated. . . . Bellow, as forcefully as Camus, has asserted that to be a man, neither more nor less, is far more difficult than to be more or less."[24]

Although the Jamesian hero, like the contemporary hero, often receives no material reward at the close of a novel, his spiritual reward is almost transcendent. The spirit of James's novels is not one of escape or evasion or repudiation of human behavior; it is one that delights in discovering the limitations of human life on earth, and, instead of being overwhelmed by this knowledge, uses it as a means of power. James's final comic vision is that of the potential consciousness and freedom of man coupled with an awareness of his innate limitations. The personal triumph of the individual Jamesian hero is capped by James's, if not always the hero's, recognition that he is superbly and ridiculously human. In the struggle between the forces that bring disintegration to the universe and those that hold it together, between what diminishes life and what expands and enhances it, James affirms the latter. Arnold H. Chadderdon concludes:

> The result of the comic impasse is inevitably for James, if not for his heroes, the broadening of vision until some transcendence is attained—transcendence over his own view as well as that which is opposed to it—so that ultimately his view is broad enough to cope with all of reality, of which the absurd is undeniably a part.[25]

James's comic forms reflect this affirmation. The heroes of the novels must preserve or create a society while the world seems to be collapsing around them. The protagonist originates in and is oriented toward society, and the insistence upon this fact is what ultimately gives James's comic view the edge over his tragic sense. The comic sense of life is one that constantly tries to expose life's imperfections and ugliness, not with the object of condemning life, but with the object of expressing it and making it acceptable. James's vision is of the possible fusion of life and art, of freedom and form, of the limitation and potential of man. Manners, form, art, and the novel itself are weapons *against* destruction and absurdity, and implements *for* preservation and creativity.

> What it all came back to was, no doubt, something like *this* wisdom—that if you haven't, for fiction, the root of the matter in you, haven't the sense of life and the penetrating imagination, you are a fool in the very presence of the revealed and assured; but that if you *are* so armed you are not really helpless, not without your resource, even before mysteries abysmal.[26]

Then there we are.

# Appendix

# Comedy in the Artist Tales

*"the usual twaddle"*

In the 1890s Henry James wrote a series of tales about the literary life. As critics have noted, these tales are obviously autobiographical, reflecting James's own difficulties as an artist. The poor reception of *The Tragic Muse* and *The Princess Casamassima,* the embarrassing debacle of *Guy Domville* and the general failure of the theater venture, the inability to write letters vulgar enough for Whitelaw Reid, all served as impetus for James's stories of artists faced with an unresponsive reading public. James himself confessed that the tales collected in volume 15 of the New York Edition "deal all with the literary life, gathering their motive, in each case, from some noted adventure, some felt embarrassment, some extreme predicament, of the artist enamoured of perfection, ridden by his idea or paying for his sincerity."[1]

The biographical approach, taken by most critics, is therefore valid and revealing. Stories like "The Death of the Lion," "The Next Time," and "The Figure in the Carpet," are, in a sense, fables which clarify James's frustrations as a writer, and offer a nice parallel to the theory of art and the role of the artist he described in his prefaces. But in focusing attention on biography, most critics have neglected the *method* of the tales. While noting the curious combination of comedy, irony, and tragedy, few critics have analyzed its effect. In his preface to volume 15, James mused that although the tales testified "to no general intention," they did "minister . . . to an emphasised effect." (*viii*) It seems obvious that the form of the tales produces this "effect," and an examination of the form will clarify their focus.

Critics remain divided as to the generic form of the stories.

R. P. Blackmur, for example, refers to the "coarse melodrama" and "high tragedy" of the tales,[2] while Leon Edel suggests that although "they partake of that 'tragic vision' which so many critics have found in James" they are really "artificial comedies."[3] James himself is characteristically ambiguous about the particular generic form of the stories, labelling them "the states represented, the embarrassments and predicaments studied, the tragedies and comedies recorded." (*ix*) If the major focus in the tales is the artist, as many critics would suggest, then the stories are ultimately tragic in form, despite the obvious comic brilliance of their tone and style. Neil Paraday, Ralph Limbert, and Hugh Vereker all die, and the humorous society which symbolically kills them remains grotesquely powerful in the end. The novelist in each of these stories therefore resembles the typical tragic character, an elevated figure approximating a god, whose potential for good is ultimately destroyed. The plots move toward death and loss, reflecting the typical tragic curve.

But if the tales seem tragic in shape, they are also obviously comic in style and tone. Leon Edel's observation that the subject of "The Lesson of the Master" is "treated largely as a joke" could be applied to most of the artist tales.[4] Indeed, "The Death of the Lion," "The Next Time," and "The Figure in the Carpet," are all structured around a central extended "joke." In "The Death of the Lion" an author is literally loved to death by a public eager to lionize him but unwilling to do anything so mundane as read his books; in "The Next Time" a mediocre author strives to write a masterpiece but merely turns out best sellers, while a great novelist strives to write a best seller but merely turns out masterpieces; in "The Figure in the Carpet" a critic who prides himself on his acuity and cleverness learns that he can't even perceive the "general intention" in his favorite author's novels. These "jokes," underlying the tales, are developed in James's wittiest style through scenes that sometimes approach burlesque and slapstick. If we read the stories from the artist's point of view, the combination of tragedy and comedy provides the "coarse melodrama" which Blackmur perceives. But the comic irony of the tales, and James's savage humor, suggest that the focus is elsewhere.

If one of James's "effects" in writing tales of the literary life is to evoke the essentially tragic expulsion of the artist (and excellence in general) from modern society in favor of merely modish popular fashion, another, and more important "effect," is to ridicule the habits of mind which make the tragedies possible. The artists in the tales are themselves rather flat characters, a fact which has led several critics to conclude that they are merely poseurs or frauds.[5] But James referred to the authors as "givens," indicating that the real focus was the stupidity, blindness, and self-deception of the public. (*xiii*) In his notebooks James recognized that "The Figure in the Carpet," for example, presented a "lovely chance for fine irony on the subject of that fraternity [of critics],"[6] and in the preface he refers to the "chattering unperceiving world" surrounding Vereker. (*xvi*) He insists that "The Next Time" "is in essence a 'story about the public,'" (*xiv*) and clarifies, "Hadn't one again and again caught 'society' in the very fact of not caring in the least what might become of the subject, . . . so long as the social game might be played a little more intensely." (*xiii*) He relates that "The Death of the Lion" "should be admirably satiric, ironic," and he thinks of "The Next Time" (in the planning stages) as perhaps "a mate to 'The Death of the Lion.'"[7] In the preface to *The Tragic Muse* James most clearly suggests the form and general focus of the tales. Writing of his experience in the theater James recalls:

> There had hovered before me some possible picture (but all comic and ironic) of one of the most salient London "social" passions, the unappeasable curiosity for the things of the theatre; for every one of them, that is, except the drama itself, and for the "personality" of the performer (almost any performer quite sufficiently serving) in particular. This latter, verily, had struck me as an aspect appealing mainly to satiric treatment; the only adequate or effective treatment, I had again and again felt, for most of the distinctively social aspects of London.[8]

This statement on the theater applies equally well to art in general, clarifying James's attitude toward the London social world which valued "personalities" over the work of art itself. And "satiric treatment," James insists, is "the only adequate or effective treatment" for such a situation.

Northrop Frye's description of satire closely defines James's method:

> satire is irony which is structurally close to the comic: the comic struggle of two societies, one normal and the other absurd, is reflected in its double focus of morality and fantasy.... Two things, then, are essential to satire; one is wit or humor founded on fantasy or a sense of the grotesque or absurd, the other is an object of attack.[9]

The moral norm of James's comic ironic tales is, of course, the artist—Paraday, Limbert, and Vereker. The object of attack is the blindly stupid public. And the conflict of artist and society provides the grotesque or absurd situation. The almost bitterly ironic plots, combined with the high comedy of the style, results formally in satire.

Neil Paraday's situation in "The Death of the Lion" is really the reverse of James's own. Whereas James had enjoyed early success but was suddenly unpopular, Paraday gains sudden fame after years of relative obscurity. The movement of the plot is ironic, for the effect of *The Empire*'s having "fired . . . a salute of a whole column" at Paraday is, the narrator notes, that "the poor man was to be squeezed into his horrible age." (110, 111) Meanwhile, Paraday's admirers begin to celebrate their "discovery" of him, not by reading his books, but by courting his personality. "His book sold but moderately . . . but he circulated in person to a measure that the libraries might well have envied." (122) Like Hugh Vereker in "The Figure in the Carpet," Paraday laments that "No one has the faintest conception of what I'm trying for." (122) The narrator of the story perceives Paraday's probable fate and devotes himself to protecting the doomed lion. But in the end, Paraday dies, his priceless plan for an exquisite new novel irrevocably lost, and his place as literary lion usurped by two modish novelists. Only the narrator and the devoted Fanny Hurter remain to keep his memory alive.

Despite the tragic movement of the plot, however, the story is for the most part highly comic, focusing not so much on Paraday's plight as on the humorous society that ignorantly lionizes him. Paraday's "admirers" consist of a whole gaggle of comic caricatures: Mr. Morrow who writes for *The Tattler* in a department called "Smatter and Chatter," (113) Mrs. Weeks Wimbush, "wife of the boundless brewer and proprietress of the universal menagerie," (123) Guy Walsingham, the delicate lady author of *Obsessions,* and Dora Forbes, the mustached gentleman author of *The Other Way Round.*

James, of course, indulges his fondness for Dickensian caricature in the handling of these figures, exploiting his witty epigrammatic style, and his ability comically to dramatize an absurd situation. When Mr. Morrow appears on the scene (almost as if conjured up by *The Empire* article) his eyes "suggested the electric headlights of some monstrous modern ship," and his gloves, like his tastes, are "violently new." (112, 113) Mr. Morrow's main interest is in Paraday's surroundings, "His study, his literary sanctum, the little things he has about, or other domestic objects and features." (118) And he is horrified when the narrator suggests that he should examine anything so irrelevant to his purpose as Paraday's works. Although the narrator insists "My dear sir, the best interviewer's the best reader," (119) Morrow finally publishes "a charming chatty familiar account of Mr. Paraday's 'Home-life,' and on the wings of the thirty-seven influential journals it went, to use Mr. Morrow's own expression, right round the globe." (121)

Mr. Morrow, silly as he is, remains merely bumptious, and his article doesn't seem to do Paraday much harm. Mrs. Weeks Wimbush is more destructive in her lionizing. Mrs. Wimbush is "a blind violent force" "constructed of steel and leather" who nevertheless "all the world agreed, was tremendous fun." She views Paraday as "a prime attraction, a creature of almost heraldic oddity." (123) And, like the narrator, she vows to "protect" the author. James points up her humorous activity: "No one took such an interest as herself in his doing only what was good for him, and she was always on the spot to see that he did it. She made appointments with him to discuss the best means of economising his time and protecting his privacy." (125) And yet, when Paraday falls ill at her country house, she becomes somewhat disillusioned with him. "This was not the kind of performance for which she had invited him to Prestidge." (152, 153)

Although everyone in the tale seems very anxious to "protect" Paraday, ostensibly so that he may continue to write, no

one thinks of reading his old books or of guarding his plan for
a new book, a plan which is, in itself, "a mine of gold." (106)
At Prestidge, the highly praised novel goes from piece of furniture to piece of furniture and becomes "rather smudgy about
the twentieth page," while the exquisite plan circulates into
oblivion. (141) Mrs. Wimbush gives the plan to Lady Augusta
Minch who gives it to her maid to give to Lord Dorimont's man
who leaves it on a train. And the narrator realizes his own folly
in originally keeping the plan from Mr. Morrow. "Fool that I
had been: the thirty-seven influential journals wouldn't have
destroyed it, they'd only have printed it." (150)

Indeed, much of the comedy in the story is a result of the
narrator's own unconscious participation in the humorous society
which he himself ridicules. Both Mr. Morrow and Mrs. Wimbush, for example, are comic doubles of the narrator, exposing
the absurdity of his actions. At the outset the narrator reveals
his community with Mr. Morrow when he proposes to his own
editor, Mr. Pinhorn, that he "should lay my lean hands on Neil
Paraday." (99–100) Upon meeting Paraday and Mr. Morrow, and
being shocked at Morrow's motives, the narrator suddenly
"winced as I remembered that this was exactly what I myself
had wanted." (112) And he decides that "having come, like Mr.
Morrow, to betray, I must remain as long as possible to save."
(114) He even ultimately recognizes the comic element in his
decision. "Getting newspapermen out of the house was odd
business for an emissary of Mr. Pinhorn." (117) But despite his
good resolve, the narrator dismally fails in his attempt to educate
Morrow and prevent his "chatty" account of Paraday's home-life
from appearing, a failure which prefigures his later and more
serious lapses.

Mrs. Wimbush also wants to protect Paraday. But both her
and the narrator's means of protection are ultimately absurd. Mrs.
Wimbush protects Paraday from other people by taking up all
his time herself; the narrator protects Paraday from a true ad-
mirer, Fanny Hurter, thus leaving him vulnerable to Mrs. Wimbush. The narrator's ability to keep the devoted Fanny away is
an ironic contrast to his inability to keep away the more formi-
dable Mrs. Wimbush. James complicates the situation by having
the narrator fall in love with Fanny, thus raising an ambiguity

which he had raised earlier in "The Lesson of The Master." In that story, Henry St. George "protects" the young novelist, Paul Overt, from Miss Fancourt, the girl Overt loves, by marrying her himself, with the explanation that marriage would interfere with Overt's work. Here the narrator becomes so involved with Fanny that he fails to protect Paraday at all, even allowing the novelist's precious plan to get lost. As in "The Lesson of the Master," we are left wondering whether the admiration of a truly concerned young woman, "one of the right sort," (129) wouldn't have been better for the artist than this strange form of protection. The discrepancy throughout between the narrator's good intentions and his actual achievements adds a comic irony.

If Mr. Morrow and Mrs. Wimbush provide comic doubles of the narrator, Guy Walsingham and Dora Forbes provide comic doubles of Paraday. Although Paraday himself is never comic, representing the moral norm of the satire, his two doubles humorously point up the superficial taste of the absurd society around him. In addition, the reversal of the sexes of these authors provides James with a running joke which gives rise to numerous comic misunderstandings. The scene in which Mr. Morrow first mentions the two authors to the narrator is too long to quote in full, but excerpts will serve to reveal its tone. Mr. Morrow reflects that he has written an article on Guy Walsingham for *The Tattler.* Morrow continues,

> "She pronounced herself thoroughly pleased with my sketch of her method; she went so far as to say that I had made her genius more comprehensible even to herself."
>
> . . . . . . . . . . . . . . . . . . . . . . . . . . . . . . . . . . . . . . . . . . . . . . . . . . .
>
> I presently enquired with gloomy irrelevance if Guy Walsingham were a woman.
>
> "Oh yes, a mere pseudonym—rather pretty, isn't it—and convenient, you know, for a lady who goes in for the larger latitude. 'Obsessions, by Miss So-and-so,' would look a little odd, but men are more naturally indelicate. Have you peeped into 'Obsessions'?"
>
> . . . . . . . . . . . . . . . . . . . . . . . . . . . . . . . . . . . . . . . . . . . . . . . . . . .
>
> "Dora Forbes, I gather, takes the ground, the same as Guy Walsingham's that the larger latitude has simply got to come.

He holds that it has got to be squarely faced. Of course his sex makes him a less prejudiced witness. But an authoritative word from Mr. Paraday—from the point of view of *his* sex, you know—would go right round the globe. He takes the line that we *haven't* got to face it?"

I was bewildered: it sounded somehow as if there were three sexes. My interlocutor's pencil was poised, my private responsibility great. I simply sat staring, none the less, and only found presence of mind to say: "Is this Miss Forbes a gentleman?"

Mr. Morrow had a subtle smile. "It wouldn't be 'Miss'—there's a wife!"

"I mean is she a man?"

"The wife?" (113–16)

Jokes based on similar misunderstandings suffuse the tale, revealing that while these popular authors preach the "larger latitude" (meaning more freedom of expression for women), they hide behind pseudonyms that reverse their sex, and thus really affirm the narrower latitude.

"The Death of the Lion," while seemingly tragic in shape, is clearly comic in character and tone. The comic doublings, the profusion of caricatures, and the witty epigrammatic style finally prevail, and the combination of irony and comedy produces the satire of a public which creates such absurd situations.

If Neil Paraday's situation in "The Death of the Lion" is the reverse of James's, Ralph Limbert's situation in "The Next Time" seems a direct reflection of it. Twenty years before writing "The Next Time" James had lost a position writing letters for *The New York Tribune.* The episode, James suggests in his notebooks, provided the "germ" for "The Next Time": "The idea of the poor man, the artist, the man of letters, who all his life is trying—if only to get a living—to do something *vulgar,* to take the measure of the huge, flat foot of the public." James recalls Whitelaw Reid's ultimatum to make his own letters "baser and paltrier, to make them as vulgar as he could, to make them, as he called it, more 'personal.'"[10] The memory, stimulated by the embarrassing failure of *Guy Domville,* resulted in James's creation of Ralph Limbert. Limbert, like James, ultimately "fails" because he cannot overcome his literary genius. No matter how hard he tries to write down to the public, he just keeps turning out economically disastrous masterpieces.

Mrs. Highmore, Limbert's sister-in-law, provides a comic parallel to Limbert's dilemma. Like Dora Forbes and Guy Walsingham in "The Death of the Lion," Mrs. Highmore is a popular success and a prolific author. Mrs. Highmore is the "spoiled child of the booksellers," (161) and her novels are "a little family, in sets of triplets, which properly handled would be the support of his [Mr. Highmore's] declining years." (164) Mrs. Highmore, however, is somewhat more sympathetic than her predecessors in the earlier tale because she, at least, recognizes literary excellence and strives to approximate it in her own writing. The narrator relates that she "yearned to be, like Limbert, but of course only once, an exquisite failure." (158) Her problem is the reverse of his. No matter how hard she tries, she is unable to turn out anything more than a financial success. The narrator humorously observes that "The harmony between his companions rested on the fact that . . . each would have liked so much to be the other." (176)

The contrast between Mrs. Highmore and Ralph Limbert provides the situation for the central comic reversal of the story. James employs the inversion of the terms "success" and "failure" in "The Next Time" as he did the reversal of the sexes in "The Death of the Lion." Logic is turned topsy-turvy as the characters constantly lament the fact that Limbert has written another masterpiece and Mrs. Highmore another best seller. When Limbert tries to write a popular success the narrator wonders whether it was "a monstrous joke." "Popular?—how on earth could it be popular? The thing was charming with all his charm and powerful with all his power: it was an unscrupulous, an unsparing, a shameless merciless masterpiece. It was, no doubt . . . the worst he could do; but the perversity of the effort, even though heroic, had been frustrated by the purity of the gift." (194) The narrator is disappointed that the novel is so good, and he confesses his embarrassment to Jane Highmore:

"His experiment's nothing worse than a failure."
"Then Bousefield *is* right—his circulation won't budge?"

"It won't move one, as they say in Fleet Street. The book has extraordinary beauty."

"Poor duck—after trying so hard!" (202)

The situation itself is doubled by the presence of the narrator. At the outset the narrator reveals that his critical praise of a book invariably condemns it to economic failure, while his condemnation of a book virtually assures its economic success. Mrs. Highmore and Ralph Limbert are painfully aware of this curious law, both having suffered under its effects. Mrs. Highmore, therefore, pleads with the narrator to write a review praising one of her books so that it will be an "exquisite failure" and not sell. James clarifies in his notebooks, "She wants me to praise her, so that THAT may help her not to sell. But I *can't*—so sell she does."[11] In the tale the narrator is able only to write her "an embarrassed note." (162) Meanwhile, Limbert begs the narrator to pan one of his books, or at least ignore it, so that it may have a chance of success. The narrator recalls "how, toward the end, when his case was worst, Limbert would absolutely come to me with an odd shy pathos in his eyes and say: 'My dear fellow, I think I've done it this time, if you'll only keep quiet.'" (161)

Throughout the story Limbert struggles to find a formula which will make his writing popular. Mrs. Stannance, "pretty pink Maud's" ailing mother, makes a steady job the price of her daughter's hand, and the narrator manages to get Limbert a post with the *Blackport Beacon*. As Limbert begins to write for the journal the narrator worries that perhaps Ralph has gotten *too* vulgar. "I was just a trifle disconcerted at the way he had caught the tone. The tone was of course to be caught, but need it have been caught so in the act?" (169) Ironically, Limbert loses the job, not because he had caught too much of the tone, but because he had caught too little. Limbert is depressed, insisting that "such work as he has done is the very worst he can do for the money," (171) but he places great hope in his new book, *The Major Key*. When that novel is "at last served cold" "like a little dish of three custards" (179) it, too, is disappointingly good, and therefore loses money.

Three babies, an ailing wife, and a sick mother-in-law later, Ralph Limbert is still a "'failure." The situation seems to improve with the appearance of Mr. Bousefield, an editor who wants his journal to be "a protest against the chatty." "He wanted literature, he saw the great reaction coming, the way the cat was going to jump." (186) Limbert takes over the editorship with a new secret remedy for his frustrating situation. His plan is to have everything in the magazine be literary except his own contributions. The narrator puzzles it out: "He'd be vulgar, he'd be vile, he'd be abject: he'd be elaborately what he hadn't been before." (190) While keeping the journal highly literary, Ralph hopes to cultivate in his own serial novels "the mediocrity that attaches, that endears." (191) But once again he fails. The new novel is brilliant.

The narrator again provides a comic double, this time for Limbert. As in "The Lesson of the Master," James has both writers love the same girl. But by the opening of "The Next Time," the narrator has given Maud Stannance up to Limbert. "Our odd situation, that of the three of us, became perfectly possible from the moment I recognized how much more patience he had with her than I should have had. I was happy at not having to supply this quantity, and she, on her side, found pleasure in being able to be impertinent to me without incurring the reproach of the bad wife." (166)

A more important aspect of James's comic doubling of Limbert is, of course, the narrator's own inability to be anything other than an "exquisite failure." James explores the narrative possibilities in his notebooks. After rejecting the idea of using Mrs. Highmore as narrator, James focuses on a new idea. "I am a critic who doesn't sell, i.e., whose writing is too good—attracts no attention whatever. *My* distinguished writing fairly damages *his* distinguished—by the good it tries to do for [him]."[12] In the finished tale the narrator points up the parallel. "If it took a failure to catch a failure I was by my own admission well qualified to place the laurel." (159) And when the narrator writes a critical study of Limbert a rumor circulates that Limbert had written it himself "because, you know, it's just the way he *would* have written!" (180)

The most comic doubling occurs when Limbert adopts his special "remedy" of secretly publishing vulgar popular prose in Mr. Bousefield's magazine. While Limbert goes quietly about his plan, the narrator secretly implements his own "project for a bigger reverberation." (192) Like Limbert, the narrator vows to write with "a monstrous levity, only praying heaven that my editor might now not tell me, as he had so often told me, that my result was awfully good. I knew what that would signify—it would signify, sketchily speaking, disaster." (192) The earlier situation and roles are reversed. Now the narrator wants Limbert to pan *his* writing, thus ensuring its popular success. Limbert tries to fool Bousefield by "writing down" to the public, and the narrator tries to fool Limbert by "writing down." The secret plans parallel each other while reversing the roles of the characters.

Like the narrator in "The Death of the Lion," the narrator of "The Next Time" unconsciously contributes to the artist's disaster. When Limbert loses his position with Mr. Bousefield, Jane Highmore tells the narrator that it was largely over him that Limbert and Bousefield had quarreled. "Your 'Remarks' are called 'Occasional,' but nothing could be more deadly regular; you're there month after month and you're never anywhere else. And you supply no public want." (199) Like Limbert, the narrator is a failure. In trying to save Limbert by secretly supplying him with vulgar popular material, the narrator ironically condemns him.

Limbert, like Paraday, is not really a comic figure; indeed, when we find him alone at the end in "the country of the blue," (216) we cannot help feeling the sad irony of his situation. The comedy of the story is instead directed at what James termed the "broad-backed public." According to James the story was a "story about the public" (*xiv*) and the real focus is the artless wag of its "great collective tail." (160) As the narrator learns toward the end, the public wants and will get "a series of screaming sketches" by Minnie Meadows for "even twaddle cunningly calculated was far above people's heads." (174) The doubling and tripling of character and event, the inversion of normal emotional response and of the terms "success" and "failure," and the witty style all serve to satirize the public and to give James a detached and humorous view of his own frustrating situation.

In "The Death of the Lion" and "The Next Time" James

focuses on a novelist as a means of satirizing a public which either fails to appreciate genius or appreciates it in the wrong way. The main emphasis is on the *effect* of stupid critics and lionizing hostesses rather than on the critics and hostesses themselves. Mrs. Highmore, Minnie Meadows, Mr. Morrow, and Mrs. Wimbush all represent the public, but all remain essentially minor characters. In "The Figure in the Carpet" James again focuses his satiric attack on the public. But in this elusive tale the narrator, who is practically a direct personification of the humorous society, is the major character.

Critics have perhaps been more befuddled by "The Figure in the Carpet" than by any of James's other tales of the literary life. R. P. Blackmur complains that the story "represents . . . no more than at most can be made out of obsessed gossip. James may have meant more for it—his preface suggests that he did— but it would seem actually, as written, to mean no more than that there is a figure in the carpet if you can imagine it for yourself; it is not there to discover."[13] F.O. Matthiessen insists that the tale was "designed as a plea for . . . mature criticism," but feels that James was "forced . . . to his own extremes, to . . . overly ingenious effects."[14] Pelham Edgar suggests that "one is tempted to say that an artist of Vereker's competence had no business to leave his intention so obscure."[15] And Percy D.Westbrook goes so far as to assert that "Both on the surface and in its implications the fable is a warning to the critics not to take a self-important author too seriously. . . . The critics in the story are mere dupes; the novelist is a poseur, a fraud."[16]

What these critics fail to appreciate in the story, I think, is its comedy, a comedy based on the very "extremes" and "obsessions" to which they object. James himself seems to emphasize the comic focus of his tale. In the preface James draws attention to "this odd numbness of the general sensibility, which seemed ever to condemn it, in presence of a work of art, to view scarce of half the intentions embodied . . . ." *(xv)* And he suggests that the theme might be "whether the very secret of perception hasn't been lost." *(xvi)* In the notebooks he even more specifically concludes that the tale would represent a "lovely chance for fine irony on the subject of that fraternity [of critics]," implying that through Hugh Vereker he will catalogue his "amusement at all our densities and imbecilities."[17]

Although critics are divided, most would agree that the narrator, himself a critic, is, to some extent at least, a satiric figure. At the outset the narrator reveals an obvious parallel to the narrator of "The Death of the Lion." Like his predecessor, the narrator initially hopes to use his article on Hugh Vereker as a stepping stone in his own career. He remarks, "This was his new novel, an advance copy, and whatever much or little it should do for his reputation I was clear on the spot as to what it should do for mine." (219, 220) But whereas the earlier narrator quickly renounces such intentions, preferring to focus on Paraday's works, the narrator of "The Figure in the Carpet" rather egotistically concludes that Vereker "shouldn't remain in ignorance of the peculiar justice I had done him." (223) Gloating over his own self-importance, the narrator continues, "We had found out at last how clever he was, and he had had to make the best of the loss of his mystery. I was strongly tempted, as I walked beside him, to let him know how much of that unveiling was my act." (224) At this point in the story, of course, the narrator doesn't realize the irony of his statement, being ignorant of the fact that *no one* yet understands the "general intention" of the great author's works. To prevent the reader from missing the narrator's humorous self-deception, James immediately introduces a comic double, Lady Jane, whose ignorance obviously reflects the narrator's. Lady Jane flaunts the narrator's article at Vereker, insisting "The man has actually got *at* you, at what *I* always feel, you know." (225) When the narrator boasts to Lady Jane that *he* is the author of the article, she decides that "If the author was 'only me' the thing didn't seem quite so remarkable," (225) foreshadowing the narrator's own inability later to divorce the writer's work from his personality. At dinner the narrator waits in vain for Lady Jane publicly to announce his brilliant article, but finally Miss Poyle, "a robust unmodulated person," does refer to it. As the narrator strains his ears for Vereker's reply he is shocked to hear the great man "call back gaily, his mouth full of bread: 'Oh it's all right—the usual twaddle!' " (226) Rather than questioning his own critical acuity, the narrator self-righteously concludes that Vereker is "cruelly conceited." "The usual twaddle," he snorts, "my acute little study!" (227)

Later that night, realizing his social blunder, Vereker takes the narrator into his confidence. According to Vereker, the narrator is not alone in his blindness; no one has seen "the particular thing I've written my books most *for*." (230) With comical eagerness and wrongheadedness, the narrator begins a guessing game, asking all the wrong questions and exposing his interest in tricks of style and esoteric messages rather than in the depth of the work itself. Vereker tiredly but patiently listens to the narrator's "cheap journalese" (233) repeating again and again that the "particular thing" resides in "The order, the form, the texture of my books." (231) Author and critic finally agree that the general intention might be imaged as a figure in a carpet, and the rest of the story catalogues the narrator's search for the figure.

As in the earlier tales, James multiplies the comedy by multiplying the characters. When the narrator begins to despair of discovering Vereker's "intention," he relates the problem to his friend George Corvick, another critic, and Corvick, in turn, relates the story to his fiancée Gwendolyn Erme, who is also a writer. All three characters pace Vereker's carpet in search of its figure. But James emphasizes the differences between the narrator and the other two characters. Corvick, for example, is a more experienced critic. The narrator notes, "He had done more things than I, and earned more pence." (219) And Corvick early reveals his superiority to the narrator through his dissatisfaction with the narrator's review of Vereker. Corvick at least suspects a "general intention" whereas the narrator has to be told that there even *is* such an intention. Like the admirable, if excessive, Fanny Hurter of "The Death of the Lion," Corvick "really avoided the chances London life might have given him of meeting the distinguished novelist." (246) Unlike the narrator who constantly tries to provoke Vereker into flatly stating the "secret" (an impossible task, since, as Vereker insists, the "secret" is his entire canon) Corvick and Miss Erme "would take him page by page, as they would take one of the classics, inhale him in slow draughts and let him sink all the way in." (243) Although the narrator realizes that "They appeared to have caught instinctively at Vereker's high idea of enjoyment," (242) he admits that "I had taken to the man still more than I had ever taken to the books." (247) This admission relates the narrator directly to Mrs.

Weeks Wimbush and the other lion hunters of "The Death of the Lion" who celebrate their author but neglect to read him.

Corvick's method of close analysis appears to pay off, for he telegrams from India, "Eureka. Immense," indicating that he has discovered the figure. (251) Although the narrator, and critics like Percy Westbrook, reject the validity of Corvick's claim, suggesting that he is lying to win Miss Erme's hand since she has made the discovery of the figure a condition of marriage, James indicates in his notebooks that he intended Corvick's discovery to be valid. James writes of "the importance of *his* [Corvick's] having been sure he had got hold of the right thing. The only way for this would be to have made him submit his idea to the Author himself."[18] In the finished tale Corvick does submit his idea to Vereker, and Vereker confirms it.

Finally, Corvick and Miss Erme are in love, and Vereker admits that their love "may help them." (240) Their love for each other perhaps substitutes for the urge to love the author, thus enabling them to concentrate on his works.

It seems obvious, then, that the multiplication of critics here serves to emphasize the narrator's own lovelessness and wrong-headedness. Whereas Corvick and Miss Erme pursue the correct method of analyzing Vereker's work to discover his general intention, the narrator pursues the author, and becomes almost demonically obsessive in his pursuit. Throughout the tale James emphasizes the narrator's egotism and obsessiveness, qualities which prevent him from responding humanly to either literature or life. From the beginning he feels smugly superior to everyone around him. When a fellow guest at the country house begins a conversation with Vereker, the narrator complains "one of the ladies of our party, snatching a place at his other elbow, just then appealed to him in a spirit comparatively selfish. It was very discouraging: I almost felt the liberty had been taken with myself." (224) And when Vereker unconsciously wounds the narrator by dismissing his review, the narrator's response is petty. "I was really ruffled, and the only comfort was that if nobody saw anything George Corvick was quite as much out of it as I." (227) Later, the narrator shifts the responsibility for his own stupidity to Vereker. The novels, he explains, "bored me, and I accounted for my confusion—perversely, I allow—by the idea that Vereker had made a fool of me. The buried treasure was a bad joke, the general intention a monstrous *pose*." (236) After all his own reversals of mood and resolve, the narrator ironically concludes that Vereker "was most good-natured, but I couldn't help pronouncing him a man of unstable moods." (240) The narrator's own mood shifts when Corvick announces his discovery. Although the narrator dismisses the telegram, he is secretly disturbed that Corvick might have information which he himself lacks.

The narrator ultimately becomes almost inhuman in his obsession. When Corvick is killed in a riding accident, the narrator is only disappointed that one source of possible knowledge has disappeared. "I pass rapidly over the question of this unmitigated tragedy, of what the loss of my best friend meant for me." (262) The loss of his "best friend" seems to affect him little. Indelicately, the narrator begins to badger Mrs. Corvick, and only wonders in passing whether his "appeal" to her "the week after the catastrophe" "might strike her as mistimed." (264) Despite his momentary self-awareness the narrator solemnly considers the possibility that "I should have to marry Mrs. Corvick to get what I wanted." (265) Gwendolyn finally dismisses the narrator, vowing to keep the secret to herself, and marries another critic, Drayton Deane. When Vereker himself dies the narrator laments, "I was shut up in my obsession for ever." (270)

The conclusion of the tale is James's final comic twist on his obsessive and misdirected critic. Gwendolyn dies, and the narrator "seemed to see another ghost of a chance." (274) He accosts Drayton Deane at his club and demands that Deane reveal the secret, which, he assumes, Gwendolyn would have told him. Deane is immediately embarrassed at his lack of knowledge, and "like a dim phrenological bust" "he began to flush—the numbers on his bumps to come out." (274, 275) His curiosity aroused, Deane becomes another comic double of the narrator, foolishly devoting himself to the narrator's search.

The narrator remains to the end, as James notes in the preface, "in the presence but of the limp curiosity." (xvi) James's satiric emphasis is on the reading public, and the narrator of "The Figure in the Carpet" symbolizes what is wrong with the critics of the age. F. O. Matthiessen and Kenneth B. Murdock are correct to assume that the tale is an effort to reinstate "analytic appreciation"[19] but it is also an effort to reinstate human response in general. James's method of developing this theme is to portray a critic whose approach to literature and to life is so obsessive that it renders him ridiculous and whose unconscious exposure of his own shortcomings results in the comic irony of the tale. His delusions of superiority, his satisfaction in other people's suffering, his inability to read a work of art, all make him the butt of satire. As in "The Death of the Lion" and "The Next Time," the theme of "The Figure in the Carpet" is finally the negative statement of a positive theme. In comically exposing the public's misdirected eagerness, stupidity, and lovelessness, James argues the necessity of their opposites.

Henry James's tales of the literary life, while seemingly tragic in form are finally comic in effect, for the emphasis is not so much on the waste of the artist's creative talent as on the stupidity and blindness of a superficial society. The combination of irony and comedy in the tone of the stories provides a witty satire of that society.

Indeed, the tales seem closely to reflect the usual descriptions of comedy. "The Death of the Lion" documents Susanne Langer's observation that "society is continuous through its members . . . and even while each individual fulfills the tragic pattern it participates also in the comic continuity."[20] Paraday dies, but his works live on in the narrator and his new wife. Bergson's definition of the comic as "the mechanical encrusted on the living" seems a good description of "The Next Time."[21] The mechanical "laws" which keep Ralph Limbert from writing a popular novel and the narrator from writing a chatty review lead to a comic reversal of values, and the plot of the story is so mechanically symmetrical as to be absurd. In "The Figure in the Carpet" James's witty exposure of the narrator's self-deception reflects Meredith's view that in high comedy "irony tips the wit, and satire is a naked sword."[22] And L. J. Potts might be summing up the effect of the comedy in these tales when he notes that "comedy is our . . . weapon against the forces of disintegration within human society."[23]

The tales, curiously enough, seem even to imply a kind of

"happy ending." Although the artists die, their work lives on, ultimately undamaged by the squabbling public. Even Ralph Limbert, despite all his efforts to renounce his genius, at the end commits himself to his true vocation, writing a novel which may be his best. The endings are, of course, more sad than happy, but they remain affirmative.

In a sense, the tales represent a simplification of comic elements more subtly present in the novels. James structures his international novels on a juxtaposition of two opposing societies. Christopher Newman, for example, is humorous from the Belle-gardes' perspective, and they are humorous from his. In novels of the middle period such as *What Maisie Knew* and *The Awkward Age,* James evokes the comic by opposing a wise protagonist with fools in his own society. And James often satirizes the situations created by the juxtapositions in his novels.

In the tales, James structures the plot on a similar opposition of character and society; Paraday, Limbert, and Vereker are opposed by Mrs. Weeks Wimbush, Mrs. Highmore, and the general reading public. Moreover, James's sense of irony in the tales, as in *The American* and *The Sacred Fount,* enables him to internalize the conflict within the narrators, who remain ignorant of their own participation in the humorous society. And the artists of the tales seem simplified versions of the more complex "artists of life" in the novels: Felix Young and Nanda Brookenham are obvious examples. The opposition of wisdom and foolishness, the balance and symmetry of the plots, and the witty epigrammatic style, are common to both the novels and the tales.

It is not difficult to see why James wrote these potentially tragic tales in a comic mode. Matthiessen and Murdock observe that

> [James's] notebooks show him realizing the ironic fact that at the very time he was growing into fuller mastery of his resources, he was beginning to be rejected by magazines that had previously accepted him. He foresaw lucidly the widening gap between the slick popular magazines and the serious reader, and fought vigorously against each new sign of vulgarization of taste. His chief weapons in this fight were such stories as "The Next Time," "The Death of the Lion,"

and "The Figure in the Carpet," which were designed as
fables for critics."[24]

The stories are autobiographical, but the comedy enables James
to distance them from his personal experience, avoiding self-in-
dulgence and pathos. One effect of the comic irony is to shift
the emphasis from the ar..,< to the critics, or to the general social
situation which initiates the "tragedy."

Thus the comedy and irony of the tales finally result in
satire, a satire with the artist as its norm. Society is measured
against the artist and ultimately exorcised through ridicule. And
the ridicule implies affirmation. James concludes in his preface:

> When it's not a campaign, of a sort, on behalf of the some-
> thing better (better than the obnoxious, the provoking object)
> that blessedly, as is assumed, *might* be, it's not worth speak-
> ing of. But this is exactly what we mean by operative irony.
> It implies and projects the possible other case, the case rich
> and edifying where the actuality is pretentious and vain. So
> it plays its lamp; so, essentially, it carries that smokeless
> flame, which makes clear, with all the rest, the good cause
> that guides it. *(ix–x)*

# Notes

## CHAPTER I

1. Leon Edel, ed., *Henry James: A Collection of Critical Essays*, p. 3.
2. R. P. Blackmur, Introduction to *The Golden Bowl*, by Henry James, p. 7.
3. Sallie Sears, *The Negative Imagination: Form and Perspective in the Novels of Henry James*, p. xii.
4. Quoted in Ferner Nuhn, *The Wind Blew From the East: A Study in the Orientation of American Culture*, p. 159.
5. Quoted in Leon Edel, *Henry James: The Conquest of London, 1870–1881*, p. 256.
6. *Ibid.*, pp. 256–57.
7. Lionel Trilling, *E. M. Forster*, p. 8.
8. Henry James, *The Art of the Novel: Critical Prefaces by Henry James*, ed. with an intro. by R. P. Blackmur, p. 324.
9. *Ibid.*, p. 52.
10. *Ibid.*, pp. 59, 63.
11. Henry James, *The Notebooks of Henry James*, ed. by F. O. Matthiessen and Kenneth B. Murdock, p. 151.
12. *Ibid.*, p. 155.
13. *Ibid.*, p. 157.
14. *Ibid.*, pp. 127–28.
15. Henry James, *The Scenic Art: Notes on Acting and the Drama*, ed. by Alan Wade, p. 84.
16. Constance Rourke, *American Humor: A Study of the National Character*, p. 257.
17. Leon Edel, review of *The Comic Sense of Henry James: A Study of the Early Novels*, by Richard Poirier, in *American Literature* 33 (March, 1961): 87.
18. Henry James, *Partial Portraits*, p. 29.
19. James, *Art of the Novel*, p. 111.
20. *Ibid.*, p. 229.
21. Northrop Frye, *Anatomy of Criticism*, pp. 3–29.
22. E. D. Hirsch, Jr., *Validity in Interpretation*, p. 74.

23.  *Ibid.*, p. 90.
24.  Henry James, *The Complete Tales of Henry James*, ed, by Leon Edel, vol. 9, p. 282.
25.  Bonamy Dobree, *Restoration Comedy: 1660–1720*, pp. 10–16.
26.  *Ibid.*, p. 15.
27.  Susanne K. Langer, *Feeling and Form: A Theory of Art*, p. 363.
28.  Henry James, *The Novels and Tales of Henry James*, The New York Edition, vol. 4, p. 413; subsequent references are in the text.
29.  L. J. Potts, *Comedy*, p. 44.
30.  George Meredith, "An Essay on Comedy," in *Comedy: "An Essay on Comedy" by George Meredith, "Laughter" by Henri Bergson*, ed. with an intro. and appendix: "The Meanings of Comedy," by Wylie Sypher, p. 47.
31.  Henri Bergson, "Laughter," in *Comedy*, ed. by Wylie Sypher, p. 64.
32.  Meredith, "Essay on Comedy," p. 39.
33.  *Ibid.*, p. 37.
34.  Henry James, "London," *Harper's Weekly*, March 27, 1897, p. 315.
35.  George Meredith, *The Egoist*, p. 11.
36.  See Oscar Cargill, *The Novels of Henry James*, pp. 183–202, for a summary of criticism. See also Lyall H. Powers, "Mr. James's Aesthetic Mr. Nash—Again," *Nineteenth Century Fiction* 13 (March, 1959): 341–49.
37.  Meredith, *Egoist*, p. 9.
38.  James, *Novels and Tales*, vol. 8, p. 34; subsequent references are in the text.
39.  Meredith, "Essay on Comedy," p. 48.
40.  *Ibid.*, p. 47.
41.  Bergson, "Laughter," p. 64.
42.  *Ibid.*, p. 89.
43.  Leon Edel, Introduction to the Torchbook Edition of *The Tragic Muse*, by Henry James, p. *xv*.
44.  T. S. Eliot, "A Prediction," in *Henry James: A Collection*, ed. by Leon Edel, p. 55.
45.  Wylie Sypher, "The Meanings of Comedy," in *Comedy*, ed. by Wylie Sypher, p. 212. Some other critics who recognize James's comedy are Peter Buitenhuis, Richard Chase, and Leon Edel.

## CHAPTER II

1.  Bergson, "Laughter," p. 62.
2.  Potts, *Comedy*, p. 115.
3.  James, *Art of the Novel*, p. 42.
4.  *Ibid.*

5. Bergson, "Laughter," p. 166.
6. James, *Partial Portraits*, p. 318.
7. James, *Art of the Novel*, p. 16.
8. *Ibid.*, p. 63.
9. Louis Kronenberger, *The Thread of Laughter: Chapters on English Stage Comedy from Jonson to Maugham*, p. 5.
10. Elizabeth Luther Cary, *The Novels of Henry James: A Study*, p. 60.
11. Richard Poirier, *The Comic Sense of Henry James: A Study of the Early Novels*, p. 46.
12. Meredith, "Essay on Comedy," p. 42.
13. Rourke, *American Humor*, p. 238.
14. Edel, *Conquest of London*, p. 249.
15. *Ibid.*, p. 250.
16. Henry James, *The Letters of Henry James*, vol. 1, p. 22.
17. *Ibid.*
18. James, *Art of the Novel*, p. 187.
19. *Ibid.*, p. 188.
20. *Ibid.*
21. *Ibid.*, p. 189.
22. Henry James, *The American*, with Afterword by Leon Edel, p. 5; subsequent references are in the text. I have adopted Edel's suggestion in using the 1879 text over the later revision. See his Afterword, p. 333.
23. Edel, *Conquest of London*, p. 252.
24. Frederick C. Crews, *The Tragedy of Manners: Moral Drama in the Later Novels of Henry James*, p. 17.
25. Edel, *Conquest of London*, p. 421.
26. Northrop Frye, "The Argument of Comedy," in *Comedy: Plays, Theory, and Criticism*, ed. by Marvin Felheim, pp. 237–38.
27. Cargill, *Novels of Henry James*, p. 37.
28. See James, *Art of the Novel*, p. 49.
29. Lionel Gossman, "The Comic Hero and His Idols," in *Molière: A Collection of Critical Essays*, ed. by Jacques Guicharnaud, pp. 72–73.
30. *Ibid.*, p. 73.
31. See pp. 101–2.
32. Quoted in Leon Edel, Introduction to *The Sacred Fount*, by Henry James, pp. xxx–xxxi.
33. Dorothea Krook, *The Ordeal of Consciousness in Henry James*, p. 183.
34. Cynthia Ozick, "The Jamesian Parable," *Bucknell Review* 11 (May, 1963): 57.
35. Joseph Warren Beach, *The Method of Henry James*, Enlarged Edition, p. 250.
36. F. W. Dupee, *Henry James*, p. 164.

37.  Edmund Wilson, "The Ambiguity of Henry James," in *The Question of Henry James,* ed. by F. W. Dupee, p. 171.

38.  Cargill, *Novels of Henry James,* p. 292.

39.  Wilson Follet, "Henry James's Portrait of Henry James," review of *The Sacred Fount,* by Henry James, in *New York Times Book Review,* Aug. 23, 1936, p. 2.

40.  Walter F. Wright, *The Madness of Art: A Study of Henry James,* p. 185.

41.  Henry James, *The Sacred Fount,* p. 2; subsequent references are in the text.

42.  Henry James, review of *Honest John Vane,* by J. W. De Forest, in *The Nation,* Dec. 31, 1874, p. 441.

43.  Jonathan Swift, "A Tale of a Tub," in *Johnathan Swift: Selected Prose and Poetry,* ed. by Edward Rosenheim, Jr., p. 44.

44.  *Ibid.,* p. 104.

45.  *Ibid.,* pp. 120–21.

46.  Nathaniel Hawthorne, *The Blithedale Romance,* pp. 167–68.

47.  *Ibid.,* p. 182.

48.  Henry James, *The Bostonians,* ed. with an intro. by Irving Howe, p. 18; subsequent references are in the text.

49.  William Faulkner, *The Sound and the Fury,* p. 237.

50.  Lionel Trilling, Introduction to *The Bostonians,* by Henry James (London: J. Lehmann, 1953), p. *xii.*

51.  James, *Art of the Novel,* p. 129.

52.  *Ibid.,* p. 67.

53.  James, *Novels and Tales,* vol. 11, p. 7; subsequent references are in the text.

54.  James, *Novels and Tales,* vol. 13, p. 96; subsequent references are in the text.

55.  James, *Art of the Novel,* p. 131.

56.  James, *Novels and Tales,* vol. 10, p. 4; subsequent references are in the text.

57.  Henry James, *The Europeans: A Sketch,* p. 217; subsequent references are in the text.

58.  James, *Novels and Tales,* vol. 21, p. 21; subsequent references are in the text.

59.  Edel, *Conquest of London,* p. 426.

60.  Leo B. Levy, *Versions of Melodrama: A Study of the Fiction and Drama of Henry James, 1865–1897,* p. 46.

61.  *Ibid.,* p. 2.

62.  Sypher, "Meanings of Comedy," p. 254.

63.  Bergson, "Laughter," p. 166.

64.  James, *Art of the Novel,* pp. 54–55.

65.  R. P. Blackmur, "The Loose and Baggy Monsters of Henry James: Notes on the Underlying Classic Form in the Novel," *Accent* 11 (Summer, 1951): 141–42.

66. James, *Novels and Tales*, vol. 23, p. 34; subsequent references are in the text.

## CHAPTER III

1. James, *Art of the Novel*, p. 67.
2. F. O. Matthiessen, *Henry James: The Major Phase*, p. 39.
3. James, *Art of the Novel*, p. 147.
4. Frye, *Anatomy*, p. 48.
5. James, *Novels and Tales*, vol. 9, p. 508; subsequent references are in the text.
6. *Ibid.*, vol. 2, p. 126.
7. James, *Art of the Novel*, p. 290.
8. William Congreve, *The Way of the World*, ed. by Kathleen M. Lynch (Lincoln: University of Nebraska Press, 1965), act 1, sc. 1, pp. 144–45.
9. Leon Edel, *Henry James: The Treacherous Years, 1895–1901*, p. 257.
10. See, for example, Jean Kimball, "Henry James's Last Portrait of a Lady: Charlotte Stant in *The Golden Bowl*," *American Literature* 28 (Jan., 1957): 449–68.

## CHAPTER IV

1. James, *Art of the Novel*, p. 187.
2. *Ibid.*, p. 188.
3. *Ibid.*, p. 189.
4. Leon Edel, Afterword to *The American*, p. 327.
5. Frye, *Anatomy*, p. 178.
6. See Peter Buitenhuis, "Comic Pastoral: Henry James's *The Europeans*," *University of Toronto Quarterly* 31 (Jan., 1962): 153. See also Joseph A. Ward, *The Search for Form: Studies in the Structure of James's Fiction*, p. 95.
7. Buitenhuis, "Comic Pastoral," p. 157.
8. Lyall H. Powers, *Henry James: An Introduction and Interpretation*, p. 57.
9. Buitenhuis, "Comic Pastoral," p. 162.
10. Hirsch, *Validity in Interpretation*, p. 74.
11. James, *Art of the Novel*, pp. 45–46.
12. Dorothy Van Ghent, *The English Novel: Form and Function*, pp. 23–24.
13. Yvor Winters, *In Defense of Reason*, p. 319.
14. Ward, *Search for Form*, p. 162.
15. Powers, *Henry James*, p. 123.

16.    James, *Art of the Novel*, p. 82.
17.    James, *Notebooks*, p. 263.
18.    *Ibid.*
19.    Winters, *In Defense of Reason*, p. 321.
20.    F. R. Leavis, *The Great Tradition: George Eliot, Henry James, Joseph Conrad*, p. 170.
21.    Krook, *Ordeal of Consciousness*, p. 138.
22.    James, *Letters*, vol. 1, p. 333.
23.    James, *Art of the Novel*, p. 78.
24.    James, *Letters*, vol. 1, p. 333.
25.    James, *Art of the Novel*, p. 107.
26.    Krook, *Ordeal of Consciousness*, p. 151.
27.    James, *Scenic Art*, p. 18.
28.    Wilson, "Ambiguity of Henry James," pp. 180–81.
29.    Potts, *Comedy*, p. 11.
30.    James, *Art of the Novel*, pp. 289–90.
31.    Sypher, "Meanings of Comedy," p. 254.
32.    Rourke, *American Humor*, p. 258.
33.    James, *Art of the Novel*, pp. 129–30.
34.    See Frye, *Anatomy*, pp. 177–85, for a generic description of comic endings.
35.    James, *Notebooks*, p. 18.
36.    Frye, *Anatomy*, pp. 177–78.
37.    *Ibid.*, p. 180.
38.    James, *Art of the Novel*, p. 149.
39.    *Ibid.*, p. 25.
40.    *Ibid.*, p. 35.
41.    Frye, *Anatomy*, p. 180.
42.    *Ibid.*
43.    *Ibid.*, pp. 181–82.
44.    Buitenhuis, "Comic Pastoral," p. 154.

## CHAPTER V

1.    Poirier, *Comic Sense*, pp. 5–6.
2.    Matthiessen, *Major Phase*, p. 157.
3.    Peter Buitenhuis, Introduction to *Twentieth Century Interpretation of "The Portrait of a Lady": A Collection of Critical Essays*, ed. by Peter Buitenhuis, p. 10.
4.    Richard Chase, "James's *The Ambassadors*," in *Twelve Original Essays on Great American Novels*, ed. by Charles Shapiro, p. 131.
5.    *Ibid.*, p. 133.
6.    Meredith, "Essay on Comedy," pp. 3, 42.
7.    Potts, *Comedy*, p. 78.
8.    Leo T. Hendrick, "Henry James: The Late and Early Styles (A Stylistics Study)," p. 28.

9. Chase, "James's *The Ambassadors*," p. 131.
10. Northrop Frye, *Fables of Identity*, pp. 19–20.
11. Robert L. Gale, *The Caught Image: Figurative Language in the Fiction of Henry James*, pp. 19–20.
12. *Ibid.*, pp. 58–59.
13. *Ibid.*, p. 59.
14. *Ibid.*, p. 102.
15. Dupee, *Henry James*, pp. 109–10.
16. Underwood, *Etherege*, p. 68.
17. Ian Watt, "The First Paragraph of *The Ambassadors:* An Explication" in *Henry James: Modern Judgments*, ed. by Tony Tanner, p. 297.

## CHAPTER VI

1. James, *Notebooks*, pp. 225–28.
2. *Ibid.*, pp. 370–415.
3. James, *Art of the Novel*, p. 309.
4. James, *Notebooks*, p. 401.
5. See Chase, "James's *The Ambassadors*," and Leon Edel, Introduction to *The Ambassadors*, by Henry James (Boston: Houghton Mifflin Co., 1960), pp. *v–xvi*.
6. "The Ambassadors," *The Nation*, Feb. 4, 1904, p. 95.
7. Forster, *Aspects of the Novel*, p. 163.
8. Matthiessen, *Major Phase*, p. 39.
9. Robert E. Garis, "The Two Lambert Strethers: A New Reading of *The Ambassadors*," *Modern Fiction Studies* 7 (Winter, 1961–62):307.
10. Edel, Introduction to *The Ambassadors*, p. *vi*.
11. Chase, "James's *The Ambassadors*," p. 131.
12. Stephen Spender, *The Destructive Element: A Study of Modern Writers and Beliefs*, p. 82.
13. James, *Art of the Novel*, p. 316.
14. Edel, Introduction to *The Ambassadors*, p. *xi*.
15. James, *Notebooks*, p. 401.
16. *Ibid.*, p. 400.
17. Dupee, *Henry James*, p. 214.
18. Watt, "The First Paragraph of *The Ambassadors*," p. 298.
19. James, *Art of the Novel*, p. 315.
20. Meredith, "Essay on Comedy," p. 14.
21. Kronenberger, *Thread of Laughter*, p. 6.
22. Sypher, "Meanings of Comedy," p. 253.
23. Amur, *Concept of Comedy*, p. 14.
24. Meredith, "Essay on Comedy," p. 42.
25. Chase, "James's *The Ambassadors*," p. 138.
26. Matthiessen, *Major Phase*, p. 39.

27.    Winters, *In Defense of Reason*, p. 335.
28.    James, *Art of the Novel*, p. 322.
29.    *Ibid.*, p. 324.
30.    James, *Notebooks*, p. 415.
31.    Sypher, "Meanings of Comedy," p. 245.
32.    Austin Warren, *Rage for Order: Essays in Criticism*, pp. 144–45.
33.    James, *Notebooks*, p. 380.
34.    Henry James, Introduction to *The Tempest*, vol. 8 of *The Complete Works of William Shakespeare*, with annotations and a general intro. by Sydney Lee, p. *xxii*.
35.    James, *Letters*, vol. 2, p. 245.
36.    Joseph J. Firebaugh, "The Ververs," *Essays in Criticism* 4, iv (1954): 401.
37.    Nuhn, *Wind Blew from the East*, p. 137.
38.    Crews, *Tragedy of Manners*, p. 107.
39.    Quentin Anderson, *The American Henry James*, pp. 281–346.
40.    Krook, *Ordeal of Consciousness*, p. 279.
41.    James, *Notebooks*, p. 131.
42.    John A. Clair, *The Ironic Dimension in the Fiction of Henry James*, pp. 79–102.

CHAPTER VII

1.    Sypher, "Meanings of Comedy," p. 213.
2.    Frye, *Anatomy*, p. 40.
3.    G. S. Amur, *The Concept of Comedy: A Re-statement*, Research Series, no. 4, pp. 88–89.
4.    Frye, *Anatomy*, p. 39.
5.    James, *Art of the Novel*, p. 43.
6.    *Ibid.*, p. 48.
7.    Quoted in Sypher, "Meanings of Comedy," p. 193.
8.    Francis Fergusson, "James's Idea of Dramatic Form," *Kenyon Review* 5 (Autumn, 1943): 501.
9.    Potts, *Comedy*, p. 140.
10.    Dale Underwood, *Etherege and the Seventeenth Century Comedy of Manners*, p. 67.
11.    Bergson, "Laughter," p. 105.
12.    E. M. Forster, *Aspects of the Novel*, p. 163.
13.    James, *Art of the Novel*, pp. 143, 149.
14.    See, for example, my Introduction, pp. 7–9, 12.
15.    T. S. Eliot, "In Memory," in *The Question of Henry James*, ed. by F. W. Dupee, p. 110.
16.    James, *Letters*, vol. 1, p. 72.

17.   James, *Art of the Novel*, pp. 64–65.
18.   James, *Partial Portraits*, p. 3.
19.   Crews, *Tragedy of Manners*, p. 83.
20.   Beach, *Method of Henry James*, p. *lxxxvi*.
21.   Frye, *Anatomy*, p. 169.
22.   See Crews, *Tragedy of Manners*, pp. 81–114, and Anderson, *American Henry James*, pp. 307, 330, 336.
23.   Sypher, "Meanings of Comedy," p. 220.
24.   Naomi Lebowitz, *The Imagination of Loving: Henry James's Legacy to the Novel*, p. 156.
25.   Arnold H. Chadderdon, "Comic Method in Henry James's Fiction," p. 69.
26.   James, *Art of the Novel*, p. 78.

## APPENDIX

1.   James, *Novels and Tales*, vol. 15, p. *viii*; subsequent references are in the text.
2.   R. P. Blackmur, "In the Country of the Blue," in *The Question of Henry James*, p. 196.
3.   Edel, "The Tales," in *Henry James: A Collection of Critical Essays*, pp. 177, 178.
4.   Edel, Introduction to *The Complete Tales of Henry James*, vol. 7, p. 9.
5.   See, for example, Percy Westbrook, "The Supersubtle Fry," *Nineteenth-Century Fiction* 8 (Sept., 1953): 134–40; or Robert Lynd, *Books and Writers* (London: J. M. Dent & Sons, 1952), pp. 114–16.
6.   James, *Notebooks*, p. 220.
7.   *Ibid.*, pp. 148, 180.
8.   James, *Art of the Novel*, pp. 81–82.
9.   Frye, *Anatomy of Criticism*, p. 224.
10.   James, *Notebooks*, p. 180.
11.   *Ibid.*, p. 203.
12.   *Ibid.*, p. 202.
13.   Blackmur, "In the Country of the Blue," p. 204.
14.   F. O. Matthiessen, "Henry James's Portrait of the Artist," in *Stories of Writers and Artists*, ed. by F. O. Matthiessen (New York: New Directions, n.d.), pp. 6, 16.
15.   Pelham Edgar, *Henry James: Man and Author* (Boston: Houghton Mifflin Company, 1927), pp. 167–68.
16.   Westbrook, "Supersubtle Fry," pp. 137–38.
17.   James, *Notebooks*, pp. 220–21.
18.   *Ibid.*, p. 223.

19.   *Ibid.*, p. 224.
20.   Langer, *Feeling and Form*, p. 363.
21.   Bergson, "Laughter," p. 105.
22.   Meredith, "Essay on Comedy," p. 39.
23.   Potts, *Comedy*, p. 44.
24.   Matthiessen and Murdock, *Notebooks*, p. *xvi*.

# Selected Bibliography

## GENERAL

"The Ambassadors." *The Nation*, February 4, 1904, p. 95.

Anderson, Quentin. *The American Henry James*. New Brunswick, N.J.: Rutgers University Press, 1957.

Andreach, Robert J. "Henry James's *The Sacred Fount:* The Existentialist Predicament." *Nineteenth-Century Fiction* 17 (Dec., 1962): 197–216.

Andreas, Robert J. *Henry James and the Expanding Horizon: A Study of the Meaning and Basic Themes of James's Fiction*. Seattle: University of Washington Press, 1948.

Bass, Eben. "Dramatic Scene and *The Awkward Age*." PMLA 79 (March, 1964): 148–57.

Baym, Nina. "Fleda Vetch and the Plot of *The Spoils of Poynton*." PMLA 74 (Jan., 1969): 102–11.

Beach, Joseph Warren. *The Method of Henry James*. Enlarged Edition. Philadelphia: Albert Saifer, 1954.

Beebe, Maurice, and Stafford, William T. "Criticism of Henry James: A Selected Checklist." *Modern Fiction Studies* 12 (Spring, 1966): 117–77.

Bewley, Marius. *The Complex Fate: Hawthorne, Henry James, and Some Other American Writers*. Introduction by F. R. Leavis. London: Chatto & Windus, 1952.

Blackall, Jean Frantz. *Jamesian Ambiguity and "The Sacred Fount."* Ithaca, N. Y.: Cornell University Press, 1965.

_____."The Sacred Fount as a Comedy of the Limited Observer." PMLA 78 (Sept., 1963): 384–93.

Blackmur, R. P. Introduction to *The Golden Bowl*, by Henry James. New York: Dell Publishing Co., 1963.

_____."The Loose and Baggy Monsters of Henry James: Notes on the Underlying Classic Form in the Novel." *Accent* 11 (Summer, 1951): 129–46.

Booth, Wayne C. *The Rhetoric of Fiction*. Chicago: University of Chicago Press, 1961.

Bowden, Edwin T. *The Themes of Henry James: A System of Observation Through the Visual Arts.* New Haven: Yale University Press, 1956.

Buitenhuis, Peter, "Comic Pastoral: Henry James's *The Europeans.*" *University of Toronto Quarterly* 31 (Jan., 1962): 152–63.

———, ed. *Twentieth-Century Interpretations of "The Portrait of a Lady": A Collection of Critical Essays.* Englewood Cliffs, N. J.: Prentice-Hall, 1968.

Canby, Henry Seidel. *Turn West, Turn East: Mark Twain and Henry James.* Boston: Houghton Mifflin Co., 1951.

Cargill, Oscar. *The Novels of Henry James.* New York: Macmillan Co., 1961. .

Cary, Elizabeth Luther. *The Novels of Henry James: A Study.* New York and London: G. P. Putnam's Sons, 1905.

Chadderdon, Arnold H. "Comic Method in Henry James's Fiction." Ph.D. dissertation, Yale University, 1965.

Chase, Richard. "James's *The Ambassadors.*" In *Twelve Original Essays on Great American Novels,* edited by Charles Shapiro. Detroit: Wayne State University Press, 1965.

Clair, John A. *The Ironic Dimension in the Fiction of Henry James.* Pittsburgh: Duquesne University Press, 1965.

Cooney, Seamus. "Awkward Ages in *The Awkward Age.*" *Modern Language Notes* 75 (March, 1960): 208–11.

Cox, C. B. *"The Golden Bowl." Essays in Criticism* 5 (April, 1955): 190–93.

Crews, Frederick C. *The Tragedy of Manners: Moral Drama in the Later Novels of Henry James.* New Haven: Yale University Press, 1957.

Dupee, F. W. *Henry James.* New York: Dell Publishing Co., 1965.

———, ed. *The Question of Henry James.* New York: Henry Holt & Co., 1945.

Durr, Robert A. "The Night Journey in *The Ambassadors.*" *Philological Quarterly* 35 (Jan., 1956): 24–38.

Edel, Leon. "Henry James: The Americano-European Legend." *University of Toronto Quarterly* 36 (July, 1967): 321–34.

———, ed. *Henry James: A Collection of Critical Essays.* Englewood Cliffs, N. J.: Prentice-Hall, 1963.

———. *Henry James: The Untried Years 1843–1870, The Conquest of London, 1870–1881, The Middle Years, 1882–1895, The Treacherous Years, 1895–1901, The Master, 1901–1916.* 5 vols. Philadelphia: J. B. Lippincott Co., 1953–72.

———. Introduction to *The Ambassadors,* by Henry James. Boston: Houghton Mifflin Co., 1960.

———. Introduction to *The Sacred Fount,* by Henry James. New York: Grove Press, 1953.

———. Introduction to *The Tragic Muse,* by Henry James. New York: Harper & Brothers, Torchbook Edition, 1960.

_____.Review of *The Comic Sense of Henry James: A Study of the Early Novels*, by Richard Poirier. *American Literature* 33 (March, 1961): 87–88.

Edel, Leon and Laurence, Dan H. *A Bibliography of Henry James*. 2d ed., rev. London: Rupert Hart-Davis, 1961.

Faulkner, William. *The Sound and the Fury*. New York: Random House, 1956.

Fergusson, Francis. *The Idea of a Theatre*. Princeton: Princeton University Press, 1949.

_____."James's Idea of Dramatic Form." *Kenyon Review* 5 (Autumn, 1943): 495–507.

Firebaugh, Joseph J. "The Ververs," *Essays in Criticism* 4, iv (1954): 400–10.

Foley, Richard N. *Criticism in American Periodicals of the Works of Henry James from 1866–1916*. Washington, D.C.: Catholic University of America Press, 1944.

Follett, Wilson. "Henry James's Portrait of Henry James." Review of *The Sacred Fount*, by Henry James. *New York Times Book Review*, Aug. 23, 1936, pp. 2, 16.

Forster, E. M. *Aspects of the Novel*. New York: Harcourt, Brace & World, 1954.

Gale, Robert L. *The Caught Image: Figurative Language in the Fiction of Henry James*. Chapel Hill: University of North Carolina Press, 1964.

Garis, Robert E. "The Two Lambert Strethers: A New Reading of *The Ambassadors*." *Modern Fiction Studies* 7 (Winter, 1961–62): 305–16.

Grigg, Womble Quay, Jr. "The Molds of Form: Comedy and Conscience in the Novels of Henry James, 1895–1901." Ph.D. dissertation, University of Pennsylvania, 1961.

Hall, William F. "Gabriel Nash: 'Famous Center' of *The Tragic Muse*." *Nineteenth-Century Fiction* 21 (Sept., 1966): 167–84.

_____."James's Conception of Society in *The Awkward Age*." *Nineteenth-Century Fiction* 23 (June, 1968): 28–48.

Hamblen, Abigail A. "Henry James and the Power of Eros: *What Maisie Knew*." *Midwest Quarterly*, 9 (July, 1968): 391–99.

Hartsock, Mildred E. "The Dizzying Crest: Strether as Moral Man." *Modern Language Quarterly* 26 (Sept., 1965): 414–25.

_____."The Exposed Mind: A View of *The Awkward Age*." *Critical Quarterly* 9 (Spring, 1967): 49–59.

_____."A Light Lamp: *The Spoils of Poynton* as Comedy." *English Studies, Anglo-American Supplenent, (1969): xxix–xxxviii*.

Hawthorne, Nathaniel. *The Blithedale Romance*. New York: W. W. Norton & Co., 1958.

Hays, H. R. "Henry James, the Satirist." *Hound and Horn* 7 (April–May, 1934): 515–22.

Hendrick, Leo T. "Henry James: The Late and Early Styles (A Stylistics Study)." Ph.D. dissertation, University of Michigan, 1953.

Hirsch, E. D., Jr. *Validity in Interpretation.* New Haven and London: Yale University Press, 1967.

Holder-Barell, Alexander. *The Development of Imagery and its Functional Significance in Henry James's Novels.* Cooper Monographs on English and American Language and Literature, no. 3. Bern: Francke Verlag, 1959.

Holland, Laurence Bedwell. *The Expense of Vision: Essays on the Craft of Henry James.* Princeton: Princeton University Press, 1964.

Hynes, Joseph A. "The Middle Way of Miss Farrange: A Study of James's *Maisie.*" *Journal of English Literary History* 32 (Dec., 1965): 528–53.

Isle, Walter. *Experiments in Form: Henry James's Novels, 1896-1901.* Cambridge: Harvard University Press, 1968.

James, Henry. *The American.* With Afterword by Leon Edel. New York: New American Library of World Literature, 1963.

———. *The Art of the Novel: Critical Prefaces by Henry James.* Edited and with an introduction by R.P. Blackmur. New York: Charles Scribner's Sons, 1962.

———. *The Bostonians.* Edited and with an introduction by Irving Howe. New York: Random House, 1956.

———. *The Complete Tales of Henry James.* Edited by Leon Edel. 12 vols. Philadelphia: J.B. Lippincott Co., 1962–65.

———. *The Europeans: A Sketch.* Boston and New York: Houghton Mifflin Co., 1878.

———. Introduction to *The Tempest. The Complete Works of William Shakespeare.* Vol. 3. With annotations and a general introduction by Sydney Lee. Boston and New York: The Jefferson Press, 1907.

———. *The Letters of Henry James.* Edited by Percy Lubbock, 2 vols. New York: Charles Scribner's Sons, 1920.

———. "London." *Harper's Weekly,* March 27, 1897, p. 315.

———. *The Notebooks of Henry James.* Edited by F.O. Matthiessen and Kenneth B. Murdock. New York: Oxford University Press. 1947.

———. *The Novels and Tales of Henry James.* The New York Edition. 24 vols. New York: Charles Scribner's Sons, 1907–9.

———. *Partial Portraits.* London: Macmillan & Co., 1911.

———. Review of *Honest John Vane,* by J. W. De Forest. *The Nation,* Dec. 31, 1874, p. 441–42.

———. *The Sacred Fount.* New York: Charles Scribner's Sons, 1901.

———. *The Scenic Art: Notes on Acting and the Drama.* Edited by Alan Wade. New Brunswick, N.J.: Rutgers University Press, 1948.

Kaufman, Marjorie Ruth. "Henry James's Comic Discipline: The Use of the Comic in the Structure of his Early Fiction." Ph.D. dissertation, University of Minnesota, 1954.

Kaye, Julian B. *"The Awkward Age, The Sacred Fount,* and *The Ambassadors:* Another Figure in the Carpet." *Nineteenth-Century Fiction* 17 (March, 1963): 339–51.

Kimball, Jean. "Henry James's Last Portrait of a Lady: Charlotte Stant in *The Golden Bowl." American Literature* 28 (Jan., 1957): 449-68.

Krause, Sydney J. "James's Revisions of the Style of *The Portrait of a Lady." American Literature* 30 *(March, 1958):* 67–88.

Krook, Dorothea. *The Ordeal of Consciousness in Henry James.* Cambridge: Cambridge University Press, 1962.

Langer, Susanne K. *Feeling and Form: A Theory of Art.* New York: Charles Scribner's Sons, 1953.

Leavis, F. R. *The Great Tradition: George Eliot, Henry James, Joseph Conrad.* London: Chatto & Windus, 1948.

———."James's *What Maisie Knew: A Disagreement." Scrutiny* 17 (Summer, 1950): 115–27.

———."The Novel as Dramatic Poem (III): *The Europeans." Scrutiny* 15 (Summer, 1948): 209–21.

Lebowitz, Naomi. *The Imagination of Loving: Henry James's Legacy to the Novel.* Detroit: Wayne State University Press, 1965.

Levy, Leo Ben. *Versions of Melodrama: A Study of the Fiction and Drama of Henry James, 1865–1897.* Berkeley and Los Angeles: University of California Press, 1957.

———."What Does *The Sacred Fount* Mean?" *College English* 23 (Feb., 1962: 381–84.

Leyburn, Ellen Douglass. *Strange Alloy: The Relation of Comedy to Tragedy in the Fiction of Henry James.* Chapel Hill: University of North Carolina Press, 1968.

Lubbock, Percy. *The Craft of Fiction.* New York: J. Cape & H. Smith, 1929.

Marks, Robert. *James's Later Novels: An Interpretation.* New York: William-Frederick Press, 1960.

Matthiessen, F. O. *Henry James: The Major Phase.* New York: Oxford University Press, 1963.

Nuhn, Ferner. *The Wind Blew From the East: A Study in the Orientation of American Culture.* New York and London: Harper & Brothers, 1942.

Oliver, Clinton. "Henry James as a Social Critic." *Antioch Review* 7 (Summer, 1947): 243–57.

Ozick, Cynthia. "The Jamesian Parable." *Bucknell Review* 11 (May, 1963): 55–70.

Poirier, Richard. *The Comic Sense of Henry James: A Study of the Early Novels.* New York: Oxford University Press, 1967.

Powers, Lyall H. *Henry James: An Introduction and Interpretation.* New York and others: Holt, Rinehart & Winston, 1970.

———."Henry James's Antinomies." *University of Toronto Quarterly* 31 (Jan., 1962): 125–35.

———."Mr. James's Aesthetic Mr. Nash–Again." *Nineteenth-Century Fiction* 13 (March, 1959): 341–49.

———."*The Portrait of a Lady:* 'The Eternal Mystery of Things.'" *Nineteenth-Century Fiction* 14 (Sept., 1959): 143–55.

Putt, S. Gorley. "James the First." *English* 14 (Autumn, 1962): 93–96.

Roper, Alan H. "The Moral and Metaphorical Meaning of *The Spoils of Poynton.*" *American Literature* 32 (May, 1960): 182–96.

Rose, Alan. "The Spatial Form of *The Golden Bowl.*" *Modern Fiction Studies* 12 (Spring, 1966): 103–16.

Rourke, Constance. *American Humor: A Study of the National Character.* New York: Harcourt, Brace & Co., 1931.

Rouse, H. Blair. "Charles Dickens and Henry James: Two Approaches to the Art of Fiction." *Nineteenth-Century Fiction* 5 (Sept., 1950): 151–57.

Schneider, Daniel J. "The Ironic Imagery and Symbolism of James's *The Ambassadors.*" *Criticism* 9 (Spring, 1967): 174–96.

Sears, Sallie. *The Negative Imagination: Form and Perspective in the Novels of Henry James.* Ithaca, N. Y.: Cornell University Press, 1968.

Sharp, Sister M. Corona. *The "Confidante" in Henry James: Evolution and Moral Value of a Fictive Character.* Notre Dame, Ind.: University of Notre Dame Press, 1963.

Shine, Muriel G. *The Fictional Children of Henry James.* Chapel Hill: University of North Carolina Press, 1969.

Simon, Irene. "Jane Austen and the Art of the Novel." *English Studies* 43 (June, 1962): 225–39.

Soderberg, R. G. "The Comic Element in Henry James." M. A. thesis, Leeds University, England, 1951.

Spender, Stephen. *The Destructive Element: A Study of Modern Writers and Beliefs.* Philadelphia: Albert Saifer, 1953.

Spiller, Robert E. "Henry James." in *Eight American Authors: A Review of Research and Criticism,* edited by Floyd Stoval. New York: Modern Language Association of America, 1956.

Stafford, William T. "The Ending of James's *The American:* A Defence of the Early Version." *Nineteenth-Century Fiction* 18 (June, 1963): 86–89.

Stein, William Bysshe. "The Method at the Heart of Madness: *The Spoils of Poynton.*" *Modern Fiction Studies* 14 (Summer, 1968): 187–202.

Stevenson, Elizabeth. *The Crooked Corridor: A Study of Henry James.* New York: Macmillan Co., 1949.

Stone, Albert E., ed. *Twentieth Century Interpretations of "The Ambassadors": A Collection of Critical Essays.* Englewood Cliffs, N. J.: Prentice-Hall, 1969.

Swift, Jonathan. "A Tale of a Tub." In *Jonathan Swift: Selected Prose and Poetry,* edited and with an introduction by Edward Rosenheim, Jr. New York and others: Holt, Rinehart & Winston, 1959.

Tanner, Tony. *Henry James: Modern Judgments.* London: Macmillan & Co., 1968.

Trilling, Lionel. *E. M. Forster.* Norfolk, Conn.: New Directions, 1943.

———. Introduction to *The Bostonians,* by Henry James. London: J. Lehmann, 1952.

Tyler, Parker. "*The Sacred Fount:* 'The Actuality Pretentious and Vain' vs. 'The Case Rich and Edifying.' " *Modern Fiction Studies* 9 (Summer, 1963): 127–38.

Van Ghent, Dorothy. *The English Novel: Form and Function.* New York: Harper & Row, 1953.

Ward, Joseph A. *The Imagination of Disaster: Evil in the Fiction of Henry James.* Lincoln: University of Nebraska Press, 1961.

———. *The Search for Form: Studies in the Structure of James's Fiction.* Chapel Hill: University of North Carolina Press, 1967.

Warren, Austin. *Rage for Order: Essays in Criticism.* Ann Arbor: University of Michigan Press, 1962.

Weisenfarth, Joseph. *Henry James and the Dramatic Analogy: A Study of the Major Novels of the Middle Period.* New York: Fordham University Press, 1963.

Willey, Frederick. "The Free Spirit and the Cleaver Agent in Henry James." *Southern Review* 2 (Spring, 1966): 315–28.

Winters, Yvor. *In Defense of Reason.* Denver: University of Denver Press, 1947.

Wright, Walter F. *The Madness of Art: A Study of Henry James.* Lincoln: University of Nebraska Press, 1962.

## COMIC THEORY

Amur, G. S. *The Concept of Comedy: A Re-statement.* Research Series, no. 4. Dharwar: Karnatak University, 1963.

Aristotle. "The Poetics." In *On Poetry and Style,* edited by G. M. A. Grube, Indianapolis and New York: Bobbs-Merrill Co., 1958.

Beach, Joseph Warren. *The Comic Spirit in George Meredith: An Interpretation.* New York: Longmans, Green, & Co., 1911.

Cook, Albert S. *The Dark Voyage and the Golden Mean: A Philosophy of Comedy.* Cambridge: Harvard University Press, 1949.

Cooper, Lane. *An Aristotelian Theory of Comedy.* Oxford: Basil Blackwell, 1924.

Dobree, Bonamy. *Restoration Comedy: 1660–1720.* Oxford: Clarendon Press, 1924.

Enck, John J.; Forter, Elizabeth T.; and Whitley, Alvin. *The Comic in Theory and Practice.* New York: Appleton-Century-Crofts, 1960.

Feibleman, James. *In Praise of Comedy.* New York: Russel & Russel, 1962.

Félheim, Marvin, ed. *Comedy: Plays, Theory, and Criticism.* New York: Harcourt, Brace & World, 1962.

Frye, Northrop. *Anatomy of Criticism.* New York: Atheneum, 1967.

———.*Fables of Identity.* New York: Harcourt, Brace & World, 1963.

Gossman, Lionel. "The Comic Hero and His Idols." In *Moliére: A Collection of Critical Essays,* edited by Jacques Guicharnaud. Englewood Cliffs, N. J.: Prentice-Hall, 1964.

Kaul, A. N. *The Action of English Comedy: Studies in the Encounter of Abstraction and Experience from Shakespeare to Shaw.* New Haven and London: Yale University Press, 1970.

Kerr, Walter. *Tragedy and Comedy.* New York: Simon & Schuster, 1967.

Knight, G. Wilson. "King Lear and the Comedy of the Grotesque." In *Shakespeare: The Tragedies,* edited by Alfred Harbage. Englewood Cliffs, N. J.: Prentice-Hall, 1964.

Kronenberger, Louis. *The Thread of Laughter: Chapters on English Stage Comedy from Jonson to Maugham.* New York: Alfred A. Knopf, 1952.

Krutch, Joseph Wood. *Comedy and Conscience after the Restoration.* New York: Columbia University Press, 1949.

Lauter, Paul, ed. *Theories of Comedy.* Garden City, N. Y.: Doubleday & Co., 1964.

Lewis, D. B. Wyndham. *Molière: The Comic Mask.* New York: Coward-McCann, 1959.

Meredith, George. *The Egoist.* New York: New American Library of World Literature, 1963.

Potts, L. J. *Comedy.* London: Hutchinson's University Library, 1948.

Schilling, Bernard N. *The Comic Spirit: Boccaccio to Thomas Mann.* Detroit: Wayne State University Press, 1965.

Styan, John L. *The Dark Comedy: The Development of Modern Comic Tragedy.* Cambridge: Cambridge University Press, 1962.

Sypher, Wylie, ed. *Comedy: "An Essay on Comedy" by George Meredith, "Laughter" by Henri Bergson.* Introduction and Appendix: "The Meanings of Comedy" by Wylie Sypher. Garden City, N. Y.: Doubleday & Co., 1956.

Thompson, Alan Reynolds. *The Dry Mock: A Study of Irony in Drama.* Berkeley: University of California Press, 1948.

Underwood, Dale. *Etherege and the Seventeenth Century Comedy of Manners.* New Haven: Yale University Press, 1957.

# Index